Postmodernism Across the Ages

Postmodernism Across the Ages

*Essays for a Postmodernity
That Wasn't Born Yesterday*

Edited by

BILL READINGS and BENNET SCHABER

SYRACUSE UNIVERSITY PRESS

The paper used in this publication meets the minimum requirements of American National Standard for Information Sciences—Permanence of Paper for Printed Library Materials, ANSI Z39.48-1984. ∞™

Library of Congress Cataloging-in-Publication Data

Postmodernism across the ages : essays for a postmodernity that wasn't born yesterday / edited by Bill Readings and Bennet Schaber.
    p. cm.
    Includes index.
    ISBN 0-8156-2577-4 (cl.).—ISBN 0-8156-2581-2 (pbk.)
    1. Postmodernism (Literature)   2. Literature—History and criticism.   I. Readings, Bill, 1960–   II. Schaber, Bennet.
PN98.P67P678   1993
809'.91—dc20   93-13747

Manufactured in the United States of America

"Fear and Whisky kept us going."
—The Mekons, *Original Sin*

Contents

PART SIX

Postscripts, Ripostes, Afterwords

Illustrations

xi

Preface

The number of critical collections being published on postmodernism demands some specification of our purposes. The difference that animates this collection is not a matter of bringing another discourse to the heights of its contemporary identity, under the rubric of "Postmodernism and. . . . " Nor does this collection affirm a classical or modern identity against the ravages and frivolities of a contemporary moment called "postmodern." Rather, this book tries to examine the way in which an event called postmodern has forced a rethinking of the intersection of temporality and textuality. Our consistent theme is that the postmodern is neither simply "where we are today" nor "where we will end up if we are not careful." Our argument is that the postmodern displaces the rigidly periodized temporality that has hitherto governed the institutional discourse of literary studies, that it does so in a way that doesn't render the past irrelevant or precious but makes it more pressing and less familiar. For this displacement to be legible the order of this book parodies a chronological arrangement. The essays perform a series of acts of reading whose difference lies in the relationship that they evoke between texts and a time that is no longer "theirs." That they have their differences is no surpise, since what they share is a sense of history as a debatable mode of representation.

These papers are largely drawn from presentations made to the 1989 New York College English Association fall conference at Syracuse University. Our thanks are due to all the participants, to John Mulryan of the New York College English Association and Dean Marshall Segall and Steven Mailloux of Syracuse University for their administrative support, to Eloise Knowlton and Karen Moore for their organizational endeavors, and to Gilles Dupuis for preparing the index.

Bill Readings
Bennet Schaber

Montreal and Syracuse
August 1992

Contributors

GREGORY W. BREDBECK teaches English at the University of California at Riverside. He is the author of *Sodomy and Interpretation: From Marlowe to Milton* (Cornell University Press).

JUDITH BUTLER teaches philosophy at the Johns Hopkins University. She is the author of *Subjects of Desire* (Columbia University Press), *Gender Trouble* (Routledge), and numerous essays on feminism and philosophy.

THOMAS DIPIERO teaches French and comparative literature at the University of Rochester. He has published articles on mythology, narrative realism and ideology, and psychoanalysis. He recently edited a special issue of *Diacritics* on money and representation, and he has just completed a book on seventeenth- and eighteenth-century French fiction.

DIANE ELAM teaches English at Indiana University, Bloomington. She is the author of *Romancing the Postmodern* (Routledge) and of several articles on Victorian fiction, literary theory, and feminism.

MARSHALL GROSSMAN teaches English at the University of Maryland at College Park and no longer gazes out over Brooklyn. He is the author of *Authors to Themselves: Milton and the Revelation of History* (Cambridge Univ. Press) and of several articles on Renaissance literature and literary theory.

GRANT I. HOLLY is professor of English and comparative literature at Hobart and William Smith Colleges. He has published on Swift, Pope, Austen, the novel, and literary theory. He is currently at work on manuscripts entitled *Theory as the Sublime: Essays on the Interrelationships Between Eighteenth-Century Culture and Contemporary Theory* and *Letters from the Eighteenth Century: Figuration, Politics, Sexual Difference.*

STACY CARSON HUBBARD is assistant professor of English at SUNY at Buffalo. She is the author of several articles on modern poetry and is at work on a series of essays on Gertrude Stein's autobiographies. She is also completing a book on twentieth-century American women's poetry.

VERONICA KELLY teaches English at De Paul University. She has published essays on Pope and Swift and is currently writing a book on the genres of truth in the English Enlightenment.

STEPHEN MELVILLE teaches art history at Ohio State University. He is the author of *Philosophy Beside Itself: On Deconstruction and Modernism* (Univ. of Minnesota Press), as well as numerous articles on art history, literary theory, and eighteenth-century literature.

BILL READINGS is associate professor of comparative literature at the University of Montreal. He is the author of *Introducing Lyotard: Art and Politics* (Routledge) and of several essays on literary theory and Renaissance studies. He is currently working on a book on Milton, and goes to the movies whenever he can.

BRUCE ROBBINS teaches English at Rutgers University. He is the author of *The Servant's Hand* (Harvard Univ. Press), along with a range of articles on the theory and politics of literary study. He is an editor of *Social Text,* and has just completed a book on the status of the intellectual, forthcoming from the University of Minnesota Press.

ROBERT M. ROBERTSON teaches English at Compton College. He is currently working on a book on Willa Cather and modernism.

JAMES ROMM teaches classics at Bard College. His book *The Edges of the Earth in Ancient Thought,* a topic related to his essay in this collection, is forthcoming from Princeton University Press.

NICHOLAS ROYLE is lecturer in English at the University of Stirling, Scotland. He is the author of *Telepathy and Literature* (Blackwell).

BENNET SCHABER teaches English at SUNY, Oswego. He has published articles on psychoanalysis and medieval literature.

Postmodernism Across the Ages

1

Introduction

The Question Mark in the Midst of Modernity

BILL READINGS AND BENNET SCHABER

In the future little boys with long beards will stand aside and applaud, while old men in short trousers play handball against the side of a house.

—James Joyce

Either this man is dead, or my watch has stopped.

—Groucho Marx

T he finding of an object," as Freud makes clear in one of the more famous statements of the *Three Essays on the Theory of Sexuality*, "is the refinding of it."[1] And this is the case with the topic of this book—postmodernism. Not because the writers of these essays, in tracing the contours of a "postmodernism across the ages," have simply rediscovered an age of postmodernity in the past, remembering themselves in the words and images of past ages. This book is not an exercise in pointing: "Look, over there, postmodernity." Nor is it simply an afterword to modernity. Even if we weren't sick and tired of modernity, at least in the various guises modernism has presented it to us, what more could we do except mourn the corpse with worn-out scholarship, methodology, criticism? Instead, the postmodern evoked in these pages signals a certain return *to* past

1

ages as a return *of* past ages, history's coming home to roost, so to speak, in the troubled house of modernity. This coming home to roost may be thought in terms of the popular imagination, at the price of changing our understanding of history. When Nicolai Ceaucescu's son turns out to be Dracula, the despotic Romanian aristocrat who preys on the daughters of the people, we recognize more than the recurrence of a stereotype in the press. The history of the popular imagination has always been that of the "return of the living dead," of Frankenstein and Dracula, of the scandalous presence of the past for which no rational history can account. This is much more radical than the New Historicism's revivification of literary history.[2] The limitation of the New Historicism has been to vitiate the intellectual liberation of Foucault's insistence that culture is constituted in and as representation by the concomitant admission that representations are themselves culturally constructed. This preserves a secure immediacy of "political relevance" at the cost of instituting a classical hermeneutic circle, revolving around a subject of history.

History, presented to us in newspapers, journals, books, and especially in the university, still bears an uncanny resemblance to the ages of man. Since at least Cicero (*De Senectute*), the course that runs from youth to old age via middle age has held the personal, the natural, the political, and the historical within an harmonious balance. The organic unity of the *cursus aetatis* has provided a series of analogies whose *ratio* has supported the name of man and the humanities in general. Hence, thinking in the humanities has enforced its claims to being fit, appropriate, timely, in season—*tempestivus*, as Cicero has it.[3] Against this, Freud's "re-found" object arrives as a disruption and dislocation of the schema, a thought that is out of season or "untimely" in its recognition of the infantile babbling within adult reason.[4]

This volume indulges, if in fragmentary form, several acts of untimely thinking. Even if they fall short of Foucault's dream of the disappearance of man, at least these types of untimeliness have the advantage of resubmitting man to his difference—gendered, historical, figural, political.[5] In short, if the various desires written across these pages find their support in a certain tradition of the ages invoked in our title, they also submit themselves to a constant, if not quite consistent, interpretation. The result is that the traditional no-tion of the ages, the linear analogy of human development, comes in for its own share of interpretation, of reading, and hence doubles back upon itself: Piranesi builds a shopping mall, Giotto supervises a training analysis, Milton directs a film. This is not done on the model of *Shakespeare Our Contemporary* [6] but so that postmodernism might signal the irresolvable struggle of the contemporary to name itself beyond its own differences and repetitions.

The essays in this book, far from unified and invoking the names of literary periods only to displace them, do not so much lend their ears to the past as borrow ears in order to hear the present—they hear the past speak in the present tense of writing.

> O problem! to be both old and young, both at once, to be a wise man, to be a child!
>
> I have pondered these thoughts all my life. They have been with me always, to my shame and despair. In them I have felt our wretchedness, the impotence of men of letters, of subtle-minded men. I have despised myself. I was born of the people, I have the people in my heart. . . . But the people's language, its language was inaccessible to me. I have not been able to make the people speak. [7]

These words are Michelet's, written in the nineteenth century. But they address a problem that continues to be our own: a problem of temporality, the ages of man displaced and revalued. This is also a problem of language, a hitherto inaccessible and impossible lan-guage beyond those our disciplines and culture enjoin us to hear, beyond the disciplinary voices we heed at the price of producing an ever-expanding zone of silence. [8] These essays attempt to do some-thing more than fill in the blanks in the great historical narratives that the left and the right, in the name of revolution or of enlighten-ment, continue to force upon us with their well-formed but too-well-worn reasons. The essays in this book attempt to think beyond these reasons, even if they appear to think in the same place, under the rubrics of literary periods.

The reader of the present volume is therefore rightly suspicious. It will appear, for example, that these essays, proceeding in an order given in advance through the traditional periodic organization of texts and works of art, leave the canons of literary or art history intact. But what is said above of the "great historical narratives" is true as well for canons and periods as they appear here. It is not a question, for example, of adding to or subtracting from an established canon, nor of doing away with it entirely (which usually means that another canon is at work silently). Rather, canons, like periods, are submitted to the dispersion that writing makes possible—at the simplest level, through the comparison of terms usually thought to be incomparable, or through the strategic use of tenses. The periods invoked by these essays become purloined, simulated periods, no less real because they are untimely.

Who are we, then, the writers of this book? Marxists like Robertson willing to lose the name of Marx in a struggle with history; Freudians willing to risk the name of Freud in an encounter with the unconscious; Foucauldians willing to wager the name of Foucault in confronting a past that did not just speak to itself but continues to speak in us; and so on down the line. These essays all have one thing in common: they are not afraid to let go of the names of authority in order to authorize themselves.

Self-authorization should not be understood here as a series of individualistic acts of will or assertion buttressed by the unimpeachable authority of a proper name (even one's own), a text, a theory, or a history. These are alibis, and we understand self-authorization as a reading and writing without alibis, without the security of a turn toward an always already established beyond or elsewhere. No doubt this marks our general proximity to and affinity with deconstruction, if deconstruction is understood as a mode of reading and writing that submits every textual structure to its temporality and every history to the traces of its own writing qua text. No history reveals the truth of a text, no text simply inhabits, represents, or obscures the truth of history. Rather than flee from history (and by extension from politics, as hearsay would have it), deconstruction engages the historical only to dispel the claim that history or politics might be the locus of a sole determinant meaning.[9] Hence Readings finds in *Paradise Lost* a textual work in excess of the political and theological meanings that would claim to exhaust the poem or limit it to a historical moment of its own. DiPiero and Hubbard, in a manner reminiscent of the Yale school, work over the double binds inherent in the conjunctions of truth and verisimilitude, or of books, debts, and anxiety. A similar proximity to deconstruction is apparent when Grossman finds in the blindness of Samson a *figura* for the displacement of a Brooklyn library by the Morgan Stanley Bank. It should be noted that here allegorical interpretation becomes once again a powerful mode of engagement with contemporary politics and its simulacra. Likewise Grant I. Holly, in a nondeconstructive essay, comes across the problem of the simulacrum in a manner somewhere between Foucault and the baroque.

What these essays, deconstructive or otherwise, have in common is the attempt to fissure the space and signifying orders of history and politics, to offer an other to history and politics, not merely another historical or political reading. Thus, for example, Schaber shows that Giotto's *tondo* may be read not only as the circular guarantee of a rational nature at the ground of representation but as the phobic hole disrupting the easy flow and circulation of representations in any political history of reason. Little Hans took Freud for a walk and stopped short in terror at various points on the map of Vienna. Likewise these essays traverse historicopolitical space only in order to loosen the hold of history and politics on the appearance and circulation of representations. Today the critic has to accompany Hans on his interrupted walk, to risk being a little frightened rather than reducing all she or he reads to another triumphant moment in the history of sociology.

In the midst of disciplines crumbling with a manifest acceleration (even apologists for "cultural literacy" reduce disciplines to lists of key works, to have something to hold onto), postmodernism presents itself not as an appeal to history, nor as the end of history, but as a chance for history, finally. This chance will demand of us a new literacy, one no longer assimilable under the heading of *The History of Western Culture*. A new literacy and a new authority that no longer simply transform disciplinary competence into the rhetoric of intellectual power and authority: this is the meaning, as vague (and polemical) as it may sound, of postmodernism across the ages. Let us explain ourselves here, then watch us work.

We all have heard the word postmodernism. It is in the news. And yet it cannot be just the news, what is new, what is modern. It must be in some sense after the new, *post,* and yet must *at the same time* not yet have arrived, must have got caught in the post.[10] We will come back to this problem of a postponed time of arrival later on. Postmodernism is not a new word, not now. For us, the postmodern marks a temporal aporia, a gap in the thinking of time that is constitutive of the modernist concept of time as succession or progress. This is something we feel strongly about. It commits us here to resisting a number of existing usages of the postmodern. We do not resist in the name of truth or purity, but in order to refuse that the postmodern be given a truth, circulated as current and legitimate coinage. It is an indication of the weakness of certain current accounts of postmodernism that their balance can form part of a historical recounting, that they can be banked on to fit neatly into a modernist, diachronic development of checks and progressions.

We do not think of the postmodern as the new "now" that came along after the Second World War or when the 1960s ended or began. This puts us at odds with *The New York Times* fashion section, where the postmodern is a look, the latest vogue. To say that the postmodern simply comes after the modern in diachronic succession is to say that it is the most recent modernism. Theorists of the postmodern share this refusal to disrupt modernist temporality, performing such exemplary containments of the postmodern within modernism as *The Postmodern Scene: Excremental Culture and Hyper-Aesthetics*—by Kroker and Cook, who think all contemporary culture is postmodern, or headed that way, becoming "panic philosophy...just for the fun of it."[11] And underneath the parody lies only more parody, just for the fun of it.

Linda Hutcheon thinks she doesn't agree, since "postmodernism cannot be simply used as a synonym for the contemporary."[12] According to Hutcheon, the postmodern is not just the look of the contemporary, it is the look of part of the contemporary. It is not everything, it is a style. Our view is that all such attempts to identify the postmodern as an attitude or style simply repeat the reduction of postmodernism to a new modernity, phrasing postmodernity as the negative moment of modernist self-consciousness. For example, if modernism is self-conscious artistic practice, postmodernism is merely artistic practice conscious of its limitation. Such accounts usually point to certain exemplary architectural practices—a distinctly modernist maneuver by which process becomes object.

Under these descriptions, postmodernism comes about when modernism loses confidence in itself, causing art to take on certain formal characteristics: assurance become irony (Hassan),[13] originality become parody (Hutcheon),[14] formal purity become bricolage (Jencks),[15] progress become the cynicism of infinite deferral (Baudrillard),[16] authorial voice become dialogue or polyphony ("Bakhtin").[17] We do not deny that the postmodern may have formal features, we merely insist that these features be tied to a temporal problematic, not to the attitude of a subject. That subject is not necessarily an individual, or even bourgeois, but may be authorial (Hassan), cultural (Jencks), historical (Kroker and Cook), or political (Hutcheon). As we argue below, postmodernism is an event, not a moment in the consciousness of things for the artist, for the people, for the spirit of an age; nor is it a realization of the political nature of art.

Hutcheon's *A Poetics of Postmodernism: History, Theory, Fiction*[18] is a masterly narrative of formal elements that might characterize cultural activities named postmodern. According to Hutcheon, postmodernism is thus a not-quite-new style that takes up the past in a way that neither simply reiterates it (classicism) nor rejects it (modernism). Postmodernism's rejection of these alternatives refuses the binary strait jacket of the modernist understanding of history as simple diachronic succession offered to a subject who is its point of synthesis.[19] The rejection of modernist temporal choices is thus not the break with modernism that Hutcheon claims if it remains only a matter of style, or an attitude toward history that appears as a style. For Hutcheon, however, style reveals the postmodern subject to be ironic, playful, irreverent, and contradictory or anachronistic. Her survey boils down the postmodern at every turn to an untramontane modernist attitude, a consciousness of the finitude of self-consciousness. Postmodernism is not a simple rupture, not a "new paradigm" (we agree), because "it is contradictory and works within the very systems it attempts to subvert."[20] According to Hutcheon, the irreverences of postmodernism are directed at history, and are found in the practices of anachronistic *bricolage*. This has two consequences. First, modernism's striving for the new and the original, Pound's "Make it New," is rejected. Second, incongruous citation of elements from various historical styles and practices lends the postmodern the appearance of historical self-contradiction. In each case, parodic practices undermine the understanding of history as progress.

What Hutcheon shares with Jencks's stylistic description of postmodernism as "the continuation of Modernism and its transcendence"[21] is an insistence that the "presence of the past" is understandable as an attitude of irony, critique, or playful dialogue, situating the postmodern as a combination of negation and negotiation. This attitude is then given meaning by an appeal to the "political." To put it another way, it is assumed that the ultimate meaning of all attitudes is political, so that postmodernism may be securely evaluated, even ultimately legitimated, in relation to the eventual success of its project of subversion (for Jencks, the sociopolitical meaning of the postmodern attitude is not a matter of subversion but a transcendence of modernist aesthetic purism, a shift from elitism into the social field of public communication[22]).

The desire to fix a politics of the postmodern, to pin down an inherent subversiveness, guides the animadversions of Fredric Jameson's "Postmodernism and Consumer Society" and Hal Foster's *Recodings*.[23] Foster convincingly identifies both a "neoconservative" and a "poststructuralist" "position" in postmodernism.[24] We do not think that any position, consciousness, or attitude can bring the postmodern to account, although we share Foster's interest in the postmodern as resistant. If resistant to anything, postmodernism resists the assurance of a conscious stance or position of knowledge, critique, or historical survey.[25] This seems to involve a questioning of the political (or the economic) as the "last instance" in which the truth of all things will be revealed.

Thus we contest the understanding of postmodernism as a style, a look, or an attitude on several counts. Our quarrel has to do with the containment of the postmodern within the modern as the negative moment of a pure self-consciousness. First, we do not think that postmodernism can offer the "new theoretical concepts"[26] required for critique (even from within) without being another modernism. We think the postmodern as other to modernism, not as a super- or hyper-modernism. To reduce postmodernism to an epistemological break is to think the chronology of "post-" in purely modernist terms.[27]

Second, we think postmodernism is bound up with the question of history, but this involvement is not simply a critical negation of the modernist idea of history (roughly, the idea of a diachronic succession of moments known from a position of transcendent subjectivity abstracted from that sequence). The blocking together of incommensurable historical elements should not be understood as a matter of self-contradiction, of conscious negation. Anachronism does not just cancel itself out; to disrupt historical succession is not to negate temporality. Those who claim to realize that postmodernism is not simply the negation of modernist history then tend to reduce it to the condition of "critique from within." Thus the postmoderns are distinguished from the critical modernist avant-garde only by their having the honesty not to step beyond negation into proclaiming a new synthesis. This king of caution is evident in Hutcheon's tendency to reserve the possibility that a new modernity may be just around the corner (though it would be dishonest to anticipate it): "there is not a break—or not yet, at any rate."[28] Finally, "we may find no answers, but the questions that will make any answering process even possible are at least starting to be asked."[29]

We find this a very religious thought. Religious because it replaces the modernist conception of the future as the site of rational calculation with a future as pure negation, infinite postponement. This deferral leads to the admonition that the modernist dream of universal emancipation will arrive only if we do not let on that we are thinking about it. The future is not so much problematized as preserved, postponed precisely in order that it may be kept pure. Like all true gods, the future is strictly impossible.

Above all, as has already been signaled, we do not think that the temporal aporia introduced by a postmodern insistence on the event can be reduced to a matter of attitude. We like to think of the temporality of postmodernity by analogy with Freud's *Nachträglichkeit*, or deferred action, by which the event occurs both too soon and too late. It occurs too soon to be understood, and is understood too late to be recovered. To follow Freud, it only enters consciousness as a re-transcription.[30] Although postmodernism is not the age or epoch of pscyhoanalysis, it is its temporality.[31] This displaced temporality characterizes for Lyotard the aesthetic and critical experimentation of the postmodern artist and writer.

> The artist and the writer, then, are working without rules in order to formulate the rules of what *will have been done*. Hence the fact that work and text have the characters of an *event*; hence also, they always come too late for their author, or, what amounts to the same thing, their being put into work, their realization (*mise en oeuvre*) always begin too soon. *Post modern* would have to be understood according to the paradox of the future (*post*) anterior (*modo*).[32]

Writing after Lyotard, we may now turn to the question that he, perhaps more than anyone, has posed to us: the question of thinking the postmodern.

We are sorry it has taken so long to get here. Yet it is only modernism that would suggest that the meaning of postmodernism had to be a matter of origin or finality, that it would be either the first question we asked, or the answer that came at the end. Modernism claims to be a new origin, a break with the past that is the opening of a project, the beginning of the movement that will end in the revealed finality of a universal idea, of truth, of freedom, of beauty. The origin of modernity is thus on a *tabula rasa*, an empty space from which the fragments of the past have been swept away. Knowledge demands a vacuum.

The extent to which postmodernism is unable to make a clean break with modernism no doubt influences our anxiety about what postmodernism is not. To claim that the postmodern came after modernity in any simple sense would be to produce another modernism. The work of the postmodern is rather to produce an other to modernism. Thus, postmodernism comes before modernism rather than after it, in the sense that it is the other that the modern forecloses at its inception, in order for modernity to begin.

We are going to draw on Lyotard, not to define postmodernity so much as to situate the way postmodernity restates the relationship between temporality and the disciplinarity of the humanities, once we have lost our assurance about history.[33] This means that we have to ask questions about the conditions of knowledge, about the writing of history, and about the status of the aesthetic object. In each case it is precisely the thought of time that disrupts historical assurance. For us, this disruption takes three exemplary forms: a) Narrative introduces a temporality to knowledge in excess of that permitted by the history of ideas. b) Deconstruction's insistence on the materiality of writing enforces the recognition that the possibility of history depends upon the effacement of the event of writing. c) The aesthetic object is detached from the temporality of creation and repetition, no longer to be a commodity circulating between artist and critic. In each case, postmodernism testifies to what Lyotard has called the time of the event.

To understand this, it is necessary to be aware of the particular force of the event in reading postmodernity. The event is the occurrence after which nothing will ever be the same. The event, that is, happens in excess of the referential frame within which it might be understood, disrupting or displacing that frame. History will never be the same after the French Revolution. The revolution can only be understood elsewhere, in another history, for which it is no longer an event. The event is the radically singular happening that cannot be represented within a general history without the loss of its singularity, its reduction to a moment. The time of the event is postmodern in that the event cannot be understood *at the time,* as it happens, because its singularity is alien to the language or structure of understanding to which it occurs. The pure singularity of its occurrence, the "it happens" that cannot be reduced to a representation, cannot be identified with "what happens." As Lyotard puts it, "In sum, there are events: something happens which is not tautological with what has happened."[34] To return to our three exemplary instances, the time of the event is that which is unaccountable in representation, appearing as the difference inscription makes to the temporality of linguistic phrases,[35] or the difference narrative makes to the temporality of knowledge, or the difference unrecognizability makes to the institutional commodification of art.[36]

Lyotard has defined the epistemological condition of postmodernism as "an incredulity towards metanarratives."[37] The grand or meta- narrative is the organization of the succession of historical moments in terms of the projected revelation of a meaning. This project works through a rupture with the past that will perform the emancipation of a universal subject of history. It is the story that organizes and legitimates knowledge, reason, and history. All modernist accounts rest upon such metanarratives. Thus the *Encyclopaedia* will free humanity from superstition through enlightenment leading to universal knowledge; the dialectic of history will reveal the Hegelian transhistorical Spirit; Marxism will free the proletariat from bondage by means of revolution; democracy will reveal human nature as the people become the subject of a universal history of humanity; or the creation of wealth will free mankind from poverty through the technological breakthroughs of free-market capitalism. Lyotard points out that these grand narratives have broken down in the face of events.[38]

The incredulity that accompanies the recognition of grand narratives as no more than grand, or as no more than narratives, does not give rise to a metaphysics of little narratives on the order of "small is beautiful" (though this did happen in the Foucauldian upholding of the local or marginal against the center). There is no inverted sovereignty of little narratives; as Lyotard points out, that is the Romantic illusion that sought a coherent legitimacy in popular narratives (be it folk wisdom, a more natural expressivity, or transgression), whereas in fact popular knowledge exibits the contradictory quality of diametrically opposed proverbs.[39]

All this suggests that incredulity towards metanarratives is not a position of critique, but a recognition of political narratives as constituted by a rhetorical figure (of narrative) for which they are unable to account. Politicians cannot account for the figural quality of their discourse because it claims to be organized by universal rational concepts, not by the figurations of specific acts of narration. Politics claims that either its ideals or its pragmatic compromises belong to the realm of reality, not of "mere rhetoric." An understanding of narrative as figure insists that the necessarily narrated quality of events marks them as radically singular happenings. No metanarrative is possible because there is no criterion for the legitimation of narratives that is not itself marked by the figure of narrative, disrupting that criterion's claim to universality. Narrative cannot be conceptualized, made the object of a rational nonnarrative discourse and, in this sense, narrative is a figure rather than a concept. Narrative as figure occurs in every story as the event of its performance, its singularity. The act of telling is singular in that it cannot be repeated in any retelling of the story (a different act of telling). This particularity disrupts the possibility of legitimation by any universal narrative. The multiplicity of narratives cannot become the content of a unifying narrative of narratives (even of their failure), since that narrative would in its turn be a narrative. This attention to the particular pragmatics of acts of language appears also in the widespread deconstructive consideration of philosophy as a kind of writing, as the first step in detaching the philosopher from pretensions to the cosmic isolation characteristic of "rational perspective" or "pure perception." Likewise, Derrida's "White Mythology" has made the point that there is no metaphor of metaphor that is not itself a metaphor; there can be no "literal" or "clear and distinct" idea of metaphor.[40] Since narrative is in this sense both constitutive and disruptive of the possibility of representation by concepts, the particularity or singular eventhood of many narratives replaces even the unified narrative of multiplicity (the story of pluralism).

All this affects the way we write. We cannot write history, which means perhaps that we can begin to write historically, with an attention to the temporality of our writing. Thus, Robertson's attention to the differences between Ford's world and ours is the ground of his reading rather than the gap it spans; likewise, Readings acknowledges the risk of his being caught up in the acceleration that he reads. So we are not despairing, or miserable. We do not tell the story of the failure of narratives, but say that we must judge, without determinate criteria, what to say now. As Lyotard has put it, postmodernism is not a break with modernity, but a radical rewriting, asking what phrase to link to modernity, what to put next.[41] Hence, for example, DiPiero's scandalous juxtaposition of *La Princesse de Clèves* and *The War of the Roses*. This is the question that historical time poses in the postmodern condition. The absence of determinate criteria, once we have become incredulous with regard to grand narratives of legitimation, means that the adding of our phrase to those preceding (our "linkage," in Lyotard's term) itself takes on the quality of an event. This amounts to saying that criticism may actually become historically responsible. We must say something (even to keep silent is to "say something") and we cannot say everything; so injustice is inevitable: there is no "right phrase." The worst injustice is the assumption that there is no alterity for which our phrase cannot "make room," no difference we cannot understand as variety, represent to ourselves. The worst injustice is to claim that we can find the "right phrase," overcome differences. How then can we find the phrase that makes a difference without at the same time offering to put an end to difference? How can we silence neither the past nor the future, avoid modern mastery? We can offer no rules, we can only work. This makes the question of what we say political, historical, in the sense that our statements cannot be exhaustive or definitive: "the nature of the social always remains to be judged."[42] We have given up on finality. You must judge. Any apparent logical incoherence to the linkages in this book should be considered as potentially marking a displacement of the unified first-person subject of history.

In this book, we are concerned with the difference that events of writing and reading make to the writing and reading of history. Modernist history, as a critical field or science, is founded by and stems from the establishment of a discrete break or cut between a past, the time about which the historian writes, and a present, the time of writing. The modernist historian is not a chronicler, a mere appendix to the story "he" writes but the absolutely privileged and secure site grounding the possibility of the story. Modernism presents a rigid division, a binary opposition. On one side, the present, modernity, the moment (temporal space) of overview, of research and writing, secure in its self-presentation precisely because it is modern; on the other side, the past, a history that surrenders itself to the gaze of modernity. Postmodernity is not the overcoming of modernity but of the division that founds and secures it over and against the past.

History is not a panoply of past events, written about in an unhistorical present. We think that writing and reading cannot be understood as merely contingent or secondary in their effects upon the history to which they happen. On the contrary, we think that they structure history in ways that upset the understanding of it as a procession of moments independent of acts of inscription. Nor, however, do we think that history is a purely present act of inscription (nothing other than "what is said about it now"). On the contrary, we think that the "it" of historical difference uncannily haunts the "now" of the historian's discourse. We inhabit neither the distant past nor the distance of the present. Confronting the modernist conception of historical time with the time of its inscription gives rise to just the sort of anachronisms that this book traces. The time of inscription comes both after history and before it, since history is in a sense constituted by the possibility of being re-transcribed.

Our anachronisms are not falsehoods, but the thinking of the unaccountable and yet necessary phrase-events upon which every act of historical recounting or epistemological accounting is based. This is a denial of a certain history, but it is also a rigorous thinking of temporality, a refusal to think of time as something that befalls phrases. History is no longer an envelope or medium within which things happen; our historical awareness is of the conventional modernist account of history as the effect of a certain unacknowledged arrangement of phrases. It is this awareness, which comes both after modernism and before it, that we pose "across the ages." Modernism bases its claims to legitimacy on the distancing of the knowing subject from the paratactic succession of historical phrases ("and then . . . and then . . . and then . . . "). We want to ask, how long must it take to arrest time and make it an object of knowledge? What linking of phrases establishes the silent detachment of the observer's distanced survey? We do not think that these questions can be answered by any more perspicacious modernist history.[43]

We thus move to an understanding of aesthetics that is prey to the incommensurable, where art objects or phrases become singularities or particularities. The art object is not in history, but marks a gap in historical time in the sense that it seems to inhabit at least two temporalities at once: an unthinkable future history and a past become uncannily present. The reading of that aporia would begin with a recognition of the constitutive impossibility of history, as temporally divided between its status as "what is written" (about events) and "what happens" (events themselves). A sketch of the terms of such a reading can be found in de Man's remarks on the extent to which literature is divided from itself in "Literary History and Literary Modernity" in *Blindness and Insight*.[44] De Man traces the writer trapped between the desire to be modern (to make writing into an event, a presentation of itself) and a self-referentiality constitutive of the literary (a coterminous recognition of the writing of the event as *re*presentation of itself). The desire to forget the past is the only sign that the lesson of the past (that it is necessary to be modern) has been learned.[45] De Man identifies the figural turn as the attempt to evade the unbearable predicament of being divided between the time of writing (presentation) and the writing of time (representation).[46]

Postmodernity is thus the recognition that history as "giving voice" to the past would be inversely split between the event of writing history and the writing of the historical event, the representation of the past that relegates it to the status of what is repeated (*re*presented). The history of voices forgets the voice of history, and vice versa. History, like literature, becomes the site of the recognition that something cannot be said. To this incommensurability the aesthetic may testify, though it has no language that would not reduce that incommensurability to the compatibility of a single voice. In literature the sign of this constitutive impossibility appears as figure (trope) or as affect (sublimity), in history as affect (enthusiasm) or as figure (apostrophe, prosopopoeia).[47] This postmodern sense of history, as a double scene inversely analogous to that of writing, is what this collection investigates.

We began to think the conditions of possibility of modernist knowledge or aesthetic practice by investigating the narrative pragmatics of the production of knowledge. That was a way of refusing to abstract knowledge from the conditions of its production. It meant not merely thinking about historical context but asking what kind of story we tell when we invoke history. History can no longer be abstracted from the conditions of its inscription. Likewise, postmodernism insists that we cannot continue to separate the conditions of aesthetic production from art as an institutional practice. Thus, if early modernist art looks like life and avant-garde modernist art looks like art, postmodern aesthetic production refuses even the solace of recognition in the gallery: it does not look like art resembling life, nor does it look like art resembling art. It does not look like, or resemble, anything. There is no resemblance, no mimesis. Sherry Levine "steals" other people's photographs, Richard Serra leaves pieces of factory finished steel lying around in Federal

Plaza blocking traffic, Jenny Holzer produces slogans like "Abuse of Power Comes as No Surprise" on billboards in Times Square.[48]

A digression on the periodization of modernism here may put an end to a certain confusion. The term modernism covers both the Enlightenment's (or St. Augustine's) opposition of ancients to moderns and the avant-garde productions of abstract expressionist painting or literary modernists. What links Austen to Auden, Diderot to Rothko, is a dwelling within representation. What shifts is the object of representation: from the objective world to either the artist's subjective experience of making or the self-reflexive purity of the form. In each modernity there is an assumption both of resemblance (whether mimetic fidelity is to the world or to the art form) and of a subject for and of that representation. Art must look like art. The avant-garde of modernist painting or literary modernism[49] disrupts the recognizable world, but still offers the solace of recognizable form. It remains within the museum; it is still art for and of a subject. This is why postmodernism is not simply the project for a fully annotated edition of *Finnegans Wake*, the better to comprehend Joyce's genius.

Let us return to the question of postmodernism. This is the question of what this book is, or might be, once de Man has sounded the death knell of the literary history that literary modernity implies. As we have seen, the art work is left in the grip of a literary temporality that is inhuman, but inhuman in the sense that its aporia is the alterity that modernism seeks to foreclose by introducing the grand narrative of humanity. This inhumanity renders the art object unrecognizable for the historical tradition of the humanities. That the humanities have difficulty in dealing with an art whose temporality has become inhuman is perhaps hardly surprising. Here lies the source of all those laments for what poststructuralism and postmodernism are doing to the songs of the academy. The texts this book produces do not look like the texts described to us when we were young moderns. Holly traces the influence of Freud on Piranesi, or Grossman reads Samson before Milton, not vice versa. Likewise, for Schaber, Boccaccio understands Giotto by way of Lacan; for Readings the thought of *Paradise Lost* demands an attention to temporality that we owe to the movie theater. That is to say, we find that the artwork does not inhabit the temporality to which modernism has assigned it.

We will go too far; we will claim that postmodernism represents nothing less than (and nothing more than) the sense that the artwork cannot simply be an object within history or an object with a history. Rather, the art object makes a claim upon what remains of us. That claim involves both displacing the discourse of history (the disposition of events under the rule of determinate meaning) and disrupting the position of a subject (that might be the site of that synthesis). We will find an artistic event that deconstructs representation in its testimony to an idea that is, on the contrary, radically indeterminate, inaccessible to the rule of representation (and *a fortiori* to commodification). The names of these indeterminate ideas might include a justice that cannot be reduced to a sociology of power, an object that cannot be reduced to a commodity, a thought that cannot be captured by the *ratio* or proportion of conceptual or symbolic reason, an unconscious that cannot finally be translated into the hidden content of consciousness or the proportions of a predictable or reversible second-order distortion of conscious form.

The Question Returned to the Disciplines

The stakes here are significant: the postmodern thought of the *différance* of the event displaces the twin poles of the institution of humanistic studies: the panoply of historical procession and the transhistorical subject to whom it is offered. The academy can no longer be organized by the idea of the revelation of human nature, of value, or even of the social determinations of culture. And this is not the grounds either of despair (the last resort of the modernist as scoundrel) or of relativism (the grand narrative of a subject so detached and transcendent as to be totally *in*different to events). Rather it must provoke a reexamination of institutional practices, not in the name of the final revelation of an idea of the literary (yet another nature), but in the name of reading, or readings—reading as an impossible profession, like education, government, and analysis.[50] In the postmodern, reading will have to become a work, neither a recognition nor a hermeneutics. The study of what are now the humanities may become historical in a rigorous sense, a reading that attends to the event and refuses to put it to rest as part of an objective historical representation (a world) or as a subjective understanding of history (a knowledge): postmodernism across the ages, history as a sense of the irrepresentable, a demand we must hear and must not drown with the sound of our own voices, with claims to represent history as the property of a subject.

This is not a book for experts, if only because the condition of our postmodernity has finally made clear to us that expertise names, in the words of Michel de Certeau, an "operation which 'converts' competence into authority." Beyond its epistemological claims, expertise consistently transforms itself into the everyday language (which it can only simulate from a place supposedly beyond and safe from it) of power and tactics. Expertise abuses knowledge, but always in the name of some discipline or field that lends it the aura of verisimilitude and veracity. We would stress the postmodern as a wager toward a competence beyond expertise, an autonomy beyond authority.

Following the argument framed by de Certeau, the expert can be understood as the "generalized figure" organizing the cultural, political, and epistemological régime of "modernity."

> Ever since scientific work had given itself its own proper and appropriable places through rational projects capable of determining their procedures, with formal objects and specified conditions under which they are falsifiable, ever since it was founded as a plurality of limited and distinct fields, in short ever since it stopped being theological, it has constituted the *whole* ["everyday life"] as its *remainder;* this remainder has become what we call culture. This cleavage organizes modernity.[51]

The expert, then, as the figure for this modernity, is that person who understands the world of everyday life as a delimited "remainder" posed against the "whole" of her or his discipline. The expert looks to culture as if at a foreign country whose language, customs, and history she/he views and masters from afar. The foreigner who is at home everywhere, the expert is the great systematizer of modernity.

The historican, with her or his critical methodology, her or his protocols of research and prescriptive modes of writing, will provide an example of the disciplinary expertise founding modernity as well as affording a first glimpse toward the postmodern. Postmodernism implies a historian who is no longer a foreigner at home everywhere, but a writer who feels the past as a certain "foreignness at home" (to once again cite de Certeau), a stranger in the house of modernity. This foreignness-at-home is what Freud called *Das Unheimliche*, the uncanny.[52] Postmodernism across the ages writes not the history of the uncanny but the uncanniness of history. Postmodernism must experience the past, therefore, in the mode of an imbrication or invasion. The past is what troubles the present; it is given the force of a question posed to modernity. How does this entrance of the question mark into the midst of modernity come about? To answer this in a cursory and preliminary fashion, we shall once more turn to Freud.

In 1911 Freud added, as a kind of coda, a final paragraph to *The Interpretation of Dreams*. He had originally suppressed this paragraph, no doubt for fear of falsifying the whole in the eyes of the scientific community.

> And the value of dreams for giving us knowledge of the future? There is of course no question of that. It would be truer to say instead that they give us knowledge of the past. For dreams are derived from the past in every sense. Nevertheless the ancient belief that dreams foretell the future is not wholly devoid of truth. By picturing our wishes as fulfilled, dreams are after all leading us into the future. But his future, which the dreamer pictures as the present, has been moulded by his indestructible wish into a perfect likeness of the past.[53]

What this astonishing intermixing of tenses opens up for us is precisely the question of temporality as representation: the future, "pictured" (*vorstellt*, represented) as present, "moulded" (*gestaltet*, structured) by an "indestructible wish into a perfect likeness" of the past. The price to be paid, therefore, for a "knowledge of the past," for the historical knowledge with which the dream privileges us, is its representation as a future made present. To put it another way, the ground of historical representation for a subject who would have some purchase on it, is an "indestructible wish," the atemporal representation of desire.

The difference to which Freud appeals in order to produce history, to delineate the space in which a discourse or representation of history might take place, is not therefore the difference between past and present, or between the historical and the fictive. It is the difference gaping within the subject because he or she is first and foremost a subject of the unconscious. History, like the dream, is one possible representation of this difference; but the representation of history is not finally secured by an appeal to the discipline of history but by an appeal to language itself, to what might simply be called writing.

Freud makes this clear in his discussion of analytical reconstructions of the past.

> The delusions of patients appear to me to be the equivalents of the construction which we build up in the course of an analytic treatment—attempts at explanation and cure, though it is true that these, under the conditions of a psychosis, can do no more than replace the fragment of reality that is being repudiated by another fragment that had already been repudiated in the remote past. It will be the task of each individual investigation to reveal the intimate connections between the material of the present repudiation and that of the original repression. Just as our construction is only effective because it recovers a fragment of lost experience, so the delusion owes its convincing power to the element of historic truth which it inserts in the place of rejected reality. In this way a proposition I originally asserted only of hysteria would apply also to delusions—namely that those who are subject to them are suffering from their own recollections.[54]

Once again it is a question of erasing a difference, seemingly given in advance and traditionally maintained by medical discipline, between the analyst's construction and the patient's delusion, or between the doctor's theoretical ("explanation") and therapeutic ("cure") work, in order to establish it *somewhere else*. And what is at stake here is not truth per se but conviction, assent given to something taken or mistaken for truth. An "original repression," a "fragment of lost experience," "historic truth," all these find themselves represented, inserted, "in the place of rejected reality." The relation here is one of replacement, of imbrication. One does not simply construct a past but repudiates a fragment of the present in order to clear a space for the reappearance of a repressed past.

It is the space of this re-appearance, of a return of the passion of a recollection, structurally (although not always pathologically) hysterical, that enables the doubling back of Freudian insight upon the claims of "postmodernism across the ages." Three points, at least, must be taken into account.

1. Freud does not pose himself as an expert whose doctrinal or disciplinary purview might establish the truth or falsity of his statements. Instead, because he gives the patient's utterances a theoretical force equivalent to his own, those utterances take on the force of questions posed to theory, not simply empirically contingent checks, but poignant revaluations. In short, Freud's discourse is not organized according to the "régime of modernity," an enforcing of the cleavage between scientific or critical statements and everyday language (albeit delusional). The two interpenetrate and call each other into question.

2. Theoretical curiosity or speculation, what Freud calls "explanation," is not only the precondition for pragmatic, analytical utterances, for what he calls "cure." The distinction of the theoretical from the therapeutic collapses—theory itself becomes pragmatic, even as the pragmatic action of analytical utterances becomes itself theory (for example, Bertha Pappenheim's coining of the term "talking cure").

3. The condition for analytical practice as well as theoretical or metapsychological writing is, in the words of Blanchot, "an infinite attention to the other."[55] Representation and, a fortiori, writing are effects of an encounter with some other (the analyst, in fact, cannot represent himself except as other than himself). The truth of this encounter can only be established in relation to the discourse that supports it. Analysis, as theory or clinical practice, always leads back to the economy of writing or speech as such. No appeal to disciplinary protocols or doctrinal rules can assure the truth of the analytic encounter. The authority of analyst and patient alike can only be drawn from the analysis itself, not from some supposed competence instantiated in a certificate-granting institution. Certifi-

cation is a lure; analysis must undo its spurious authority and claims to metalinguistic power.

In short, the lesson that "postmodernism across the ages" draws from psychoanalysis (and not from the psychoanalytic institution) is that there is no metalanguage. There is no language beyond language, especially in the already constituted disciplines, to guarantee the truth of our readings and writings. We have deprived ourselves of the discursive supports promised by disciplinarity, supports granted the sole authority for writing history under the régime of modernity. The essays in this volume are notable for a certain scandalous disregard of disciplinary proprieties: the promise of eighteenth-century penology is kept only with the arrival of the shopping mall; the Fall takes place only after the opening credits in *Paradise Lost*; the truth in painting is revealed only by a toddler in a dark Viennese room; the secret of commodities realizes the commodification of secrets for the aptly named Ford. In similar fashion, the boundaries that separate "high" and "low" culture are transgressed: De Quincey is forced to negotiate with the market; Umberto Eco is asked to speak to Barbara Cartland; Kathleen Turner becomes an eighteenth-century French princess.

We did not have to turn to Freud to learn this about disciplinarity; he is a convenient, if striking, example. And in fact the essays in this volume turn toward a multiplicity of names, ages, places, periods, and disciplines, if only to test their boundaries. We have no desire simply to reconceive them, to write new versions of the ages, of literary or historical periods. Instead, implicit within this project is the renewed attempt by intellectuals to find a place in community and begin once more to speak its language, as ephemeral as it may be.

Let us be clear about this; we are not entertaining some naive notion of a return to roots within a common culture or common language. We are not here to bear witness or give testimony, especially if that means either once again leaning on the great narratives that inevitably and tacitly form the precondition of testimony, or founding our discourse in the absolute autonomy of a subject. The following essays (or assays) remain pragmatic and hence deeply skeptical, where skepticism might be understood not as the property of a subject but as a writing attentive to some other upon whose response it depends. This other "that I am and am not, that I don't know how to be, but that I feel passing, that makes me live,"[56] is the stake of this book. Hence Diane Elam castigates Umberto Eco's phrasing of the postmodern precisely because it silences the woman upon whom it ultimately depends, with the effect that the phallus and the commodity preserve their age-old sovereignty over the empire of the same.

The following essays pose themselves against this sovereignty and its subject—that concept we thought a stop-gap that has turned out to be the safety valve that keeps an entire metaphysics intact. Hence the polemical or provocative tone of this introduction. "There is some other," we seem to say, over and over. It is simple enough to say; not so easy to do. That is where we begin our ethics and our politics—and our writing. That is where we end as well. But is it the same place?

Notes

1. Sigmund Freud, *The Standard Edition of the Complete Psychological Works*, ed. and trans. James Strachey (London: Hogarth, 1966) 7:222 (henceforth SE).

2. We distinguish between scholars such as Stephen Greenblatt or Louis Montrose, influenced by Foucault and Bourdieu, whom we call New Historicists, and Althusserian Marxists such as Alan Sinfield or Jonathan Dollimore, often grouped with them but perhaps more properly thought of as cultural materialists.

3. See J. A. Burrow, *The Ages of Man* (Oxford: Clarendon, 1986).

4. This marks Freud's companionship with Nietzsche's *Untimely Meditations*, trans. R. J. Hollingdale (Cambridge: Cambridge Univ. Press, 1983), especially the meditation "On the Uses and Disadvantages of History for Life".

5. See Michel Foucault, *The Order of Things* (New York: Random House, 1970), 387: "If those arrangements were to disappear as they appeared, if some event . . . were to cause them to crumble . . . then one can certainly wager that man would be erased, like a face drawn in sand at the edge of the sea."

6. Jan Kott, *Shakespeare Our Contemporary* (Garden City, N.Y.: Doubleday, 1964).

7. Jules Michelet, *Nos Fils* 5:2 (1869), trans. Richard Howard, in Roland Barthes, *Michelet* (New York: Hill & Wang, 1987), 199.

8. For the discipline to hear an emergent voice, to speak its emergence, is only for another silence to be marked at its margins by the discipline that speaks.

9. The claim that deconstruction evades politics and history is frequently made; cf., e.g., Barbara Foley, "The Politics of Deconstruction," in *Rhetoric and Form: Deconstruction at Yale*, ed. Robert Con Davis and Ronald Schleifer (Norman: Univ. of Oklahoma Press, 1985), 113–135. For a refutation of this claim, see Bill Readings, "The

Deconstruction of Politics," in *Reading De Man Reading,* ed. Lindsay Waters and Wlad Godzich (Minneapolis: Univ. of Minnesota Press, 1989) 223–244.

10. Jacques Derrida's *The Post Card* (trans. Alan Bass [Chicago: Univ. of Chicago Press, 1987]) would probably have been a postmodern novel. We have not yet finished reading it.

11. Arthur Kroker and David Cook (*The Postmodern Scene* [New York: St. Martin's Press, 1986], 27) are actually talking about hyperrealism or ultramodernism most of the time. The gloss of the hyperreal "reveals" the moment as cliché, as photographic simulation of a moment which is already a simulation, photographed precisely because it achieves the prepackaged, the commodified. And the theorization of this hyperreal moment can only be itself a further simulation in the chain of infinite regression. We do not call this postmodern, since it reduces all events to the indifferent order of simulation. The time of the cliché may disrupt progress, yet the clichés form a succession of images offered to a distanced subject who is the site of their synthesis (the epistemological structure implied by modernist accounts of temporality). The succession of moments is thus modelled spatially rather than temporally, a matter of levels rather than historical progress. Hyperrealism challenges modernity not by assassinating the model of modernist experience (despite Lyotard's *L'assassinat de l'expérience par la peinture: Monory* [Paris: Le Castor Astral, 1984]), but by transferring it into a spatial arrangement, in which the temporal is arrested by the snapshot.

12. Linda Hutcheon, *A Poetics of Postmodernism* (New York: Routledge, 1988), 4.

13. Cf. Ihab Hassan, *The Postmodern Turn* (Columbus: Ohio State Univ. Press, 1987), where postmodernism remains, as in chap. 4, very much a concept.

14. Linda Hutcheon, *A Theory of Parody: The Teachings of Twentieth-Century Art Forms* (London: Methuen, 1985), 4.

15. Charles Jencks, *The Language of Postmodern Architecture* (New York: Rizzoli, 1984), and *What Is Postmodernism?* (New York: St. Martin's, 1987).

16. Jean Baudrillard, *America,* trans. Chris Turner (New York: Verso, 1988). Baudrillard's writings on symbolic exchange should have warned him against the attitude of the flâneur or tourist, denotative of modernism since Baudelaire.

17. Quotation marks here refer to the mélange of Bakhtin with American ego psychology current in the literary critical academy.

18. Hutcheon, *A Poetics of Postmodernism.*

19. As Lyotard puts it, modernism, not an epoch but a mode of thought about time, rests upon two elements: time as succession and an ultimately atemporal subject. The discourse of history is thus structured as a narrative sequence around an "I" dedicated to possession and control of nature and itself through the organization of time as a sequence of phrases. The first person is thus the position of mastery of speech and meaning in modernism (*Le postmoderne expliqué aux enfants* [Paris: Galilée, 1979], 46–48).

20. Hutcheon, *A Poetics of Postmodernism,* 4.

21. Jencks, *What Is Postmodernism?,* 10.

22. Ibid., 14.

23. Jameson, "Postmodernism and Consumer Society," in *The Anti-Aesthetic,* ed. Hal Foster (Port Townsend, Wash.: Bay Press, 1983), 111–125. Foster, *Recodings* (Port Townsend: Bay Press, 1985).

24. Foster, *Recodings,* 7.

25. We disagree with Bruce Robbin's assumption (in his "Afterword" to this volume) that this means a "permanent deferral of action." Our refusal of the logic of political accountability, of the "last instance," commits us to embrace political responsibility most rigorously, since we must act without criteria that prejudge the case. We are responsible, since we cannot appeal to a truth elsewhere in whose name we act. For a detailed account of this politics of indeterminacy, see Readings, *Introducing Lyotard: Art and Politics* (New York: Routledge, 1991).

26. Hutcheon, *A Poetics of Postmodernism,* xi.

27. E.g., E. Ann Kaplan's reference to the "significant cultural break we could call postmodernism" in her introduction to *Postmodernism and Its Discontents,* ed. Kaplan (New York: Verso, 1988), 4. She distinguishes between "utopian" and "commercial" postmodernism (ibid., 3). We sense an opposition here between the writerly and the readerly, between the producer (good, Stakhanovite) and the consumer (bad, brainwashed) that is surprising in someone fond of using the word "deconstruction."

28. Hutcheon, *A Poetics of Postmodernism,* xiii.

29. Ibid., 231.

30. *SE* 1:233.

31. The postmodern is not the age of psychoanalysis in that its disruption is not the revelation of the unconscious speaking as a nature (the unconscious become conscious). We are neither for consciousness nor against it, hence not interested in a claim that the unconscious may speak for itself, as a consciousness.

32. Lyotard, "What Is Postmodernism?," in *The Postmodern Condition,* trans. Geoffrey Bennington and Brian Massumi (Minneapolis: Univ. of Minnesota Press, 1984), 81.

33. This "history" refers specifically to the modernist conception of historical time that organizes the disciplinarity of the humanities at present.

34. Lyotard, *The Differend: Phrases in Dispute,* trans. George Van Den Abbeele (Minneapolis: Univ. of Minnesota Press, 1988), 79.

35. We follow Lyotard in using "phrase" for the minimal element of language.

36. Derrida's "Signature Event Context" (in *Margins of Philosophy,* trans. Alan Bass [Chicago: Univ. of Chicago Press, 1982], 307–330) grounds a general account of language as an economy of "iteration" or repetition-as-different. He points out that the founding condition of the linguistic mark is its capacity to be cited, or repeated in a different context. That difference of context will alter its meaning, leaving it no longer the "same" mark. Structured by the possibility of repetition is another context, the linguistic mark is thus constitutively different from itself. Likewise this capacity to be cited elsewhere disrupts the terms in which the linguistic mark can inhabit or be determined by any one context. This sense that no original identity or finally determinable context can pin down the functioning of linguistic marks leads postmodernists to use quotation marks so much. Our language, like our architecture,

is haunted by citation, by a sense of meaning or form become uncanny. Context and history speak with an otherness that cannot be kept in its place.

37. *The Postmodern Condition*, xxiv.

38. Briefly, no more speculative or rational history after Auschwitz (which is both real and irrational), no more historical materialism after Prague 1968 (which pits workers against the party), no more parliamentary liberalism after Paris 1968 (when the people rise against the representative institution), no more economic liberalism after the crises of 1911, 1929, and 1974–79 (when market forces no longer give rise to general increase of wealth) (*Le Postmoderne expliqué*, 53–55).

39. See *Le Postmoderne expliqué*, 41. It is a pity that a certain literary invocation of "Bakhtin" on the carnivalesque as the ground of a transgressive assertion of popular culture has sought to strike while the iron is hot, forgetting that everything comes to one who waits.

40. Derrida, "White Mythologies," in *Margins of Philosophy*, trans. Alan Bass (Chicago: Univ. of Chicago Press, 1982), 207–272.

41. See Lyotard, "Re-writing Modernity," in *The Inhuman*, trans. Geoffrey Bennington and Rachel Bowlby (Stanford: Stanford Univ. Press, 1991).

42. Lyotard, *The Differend: Phrases in Dispute*, 140.

43. On the dream of modernist historiography, including the "new history" of the *Annales* school, which announced itself as the cliometrics of "total recall," see Colin Lucas's introduction to *Constructing the Past*, ed. Jacques Le Goff and Pierre Nora (Cambridge: Cambridge Univ. Press, 1985), 1–11.

44. De Man, "Literary History and Literary Modernity," in *Blindness and Insight* (Minneapolis: Univ. of Minnesota Press, 1983), 142–166. On De Man's engagement with history, see Kevin Newmark, "Paul de Man's History," in *Reading De Man Reading*, 121–136.

45. Recent revelations about a personal past De Man spent his academic career trying to forget throw his modernism into the harshest light. Detractors who use this as an excuse to "forget" De Man—along with writing apologists—buy into a modernist version of history as a process of revelation of embedded meaning ("now we are aware that, all along . . . ") that ignores the historical problematic of modernity De Man raised. We do not think De Man was in the grip of history, personal or social ("youthful folly," "the spirit of the times"). On the contrary, we think the horror of his early writing is the product of a modernist attempt to take a grip on events that his later work is concerned to disbar.

46. See De Man, "Literary History and Literary Modernity."

47. See Lyotard, "The Sign of History," in *Post-Structuralism and the Question of History*, ed Geoffrey Bennington, Derek Attridge, and Robert Young (Cambridge: Cambridge Univ. Press, 1986), 162–183.

48. For examples, see Brian Wallis, *Art After Modernism* (Boston: Godine Books, 1984).

49. In the literary curriculum, only literary avant-gardists from Henry James through the early Beckett are called modernists. We refer to these figures as the avant-garde, although they follow the Enlightenment.

50. See Freud, "Analysis Terminable and Interminable," *SE* 23:211–253.

51. Michel de Certeau, *The Practice of Everyday Life* (Berkeley: Univ. of California Press, 1984), 6.

52. See "The Uncanny," *SE* 17:217.

53. *SE* 5:621.

54. *SE* 23:268.

55. Maurice Blanchot, *The Unavowable Community*, trans. Pierre Joris (Barrytown, N.Y.: Station Hill Press, 1988).

56. Hélène Cixous and Cathérine Clément, *The Newly-Born Woman*, trans. Betsy Wing (Minneapolis: Univ. of Minnesota Press, 1986), 85–86.

Part One

The Middle Ages

2

Alexander, Biologist

Oriental Monstrosities and the
Epistola Alexandri ad Aristotelem

JAMES ROMM

Humanity's dominion over the natural world is in many ways defined by the ability to categorize and catalogue the enormous diversity of that world, as Michel Foucault has demonstrated in his study of Renaissance taxonomic science *The Order of Things*.[1] The power to assign names, and with them genera, to the beasts of the field is delegated to humankind in the Biblical account of creation as a mark of hegemony and control. Beyond the bounds of the Edenic and hierarchical "kingdom" of nature, however, lie regions that do not submit to humanity's overlordship. In them the system of categories or names developed in the home world seems to be entirely overthrown. For Western cultures prior to the discovery of the Americas, these zones of biological rebellion were traditionally situated in the far East, especially in the lush tropical jungles of India— where even the most lordly of human suzerains, Alexander the Great, had found himself overwhelmed by the intractability of nature.

The anxiety and fascination generated in the West by this perception of the eastern landscape can be clearly felt in much of the Greco-Roman and medieval literature surrounding Alexander's march into India. The fact that the great conqueror had not completed this march, but had been forced to turn back at the banks of

the river Hyphasis by an incipient mutiny among his troops, left a
door open to the swarms of hostile and disordered creatures
thought to inhabit the Asian hinterland; and this aperture grew
increasingly problematic as the Roman Empire fell into senes-
cence without having surpassed, or even equaled, the extent of
Alexander's eastern domain. For a society that liked to see its own
political and authoritarian structures superimposed upon the natural world—a vision articulated in dozens of Roman poems pre-
scribing the techniques of farming, hunting, and fishing—the
indomitability of India posed a serious dilemma, requiring that the
most highly respected of taxonomists, Aristotle himself, be brought
in to help frame a solution.

The efforts of western writers in late antiquity and the early
Middle Ages to impose their scientific order on the eastern landscape present a number of features that can be usefully examined
from a postmodern perspective. On one level these efforts reveal a
literary construction of geographic space that clearly anticipates the
imperial and colonial mythologies of more recent centuries, depicting the conquest of the East as a mission or crusade for "enlightened" European leaders. Second, the proliferation of such literary
constructs of geography in the later Roman Empire suggests how
much political power in this period relied upon cognitive control, as
traditional Romans, who were quickly ceding dominion to other
peoples in military and economic matters, increasingly defined
themselves as champions of scientific knowledge that in itself con-
ferred cultural superiority. In particular, the text examined below, a
pseudonymous letter from Alexander to Aristotle concerning the
discoveries made in India, shows taxonomic science being co-opted
into the service of military and political domination.[2] Finally, the use
of the Alexander myth to explore issues more commonly associated
with descriptive and scientific writing creates an interesting disso-
nance between literary modes, as if some modern-day Captain Kirk
were suddenly removed from the realm of romance and forced to
narrate a public-television documentary program.

The *Epistola Alexandri ad Aristotelem* was one of the most
widely diffused fragments of the Alexander legend that later antiquity passed on to the Middle Ages. Based on a Greek epistle inserted
into the so-called Alexander Romance of the second and third centu-

ries A.D., the *Epistola* later circulated in an independent Latin version and in several vernacular languages as well (including an Anglo-Saxon version, which appears to be the earliest Alexander text in England).[3] The wide diffusion of the *Epistola* becomes even more striking, moreover, if we link it with similar wonder-letters, including the letter of Pharasmanes (or Fermes) to Hadrian,[4] first attested around the eighth century, and the more famous letter of Prester John, which swept through Europe in the twelfth century.[5] Even if not lineal descendants,[6] these later epistles share with the *Epistola Alexandri* a common geographical orientation in that all purport to describe the wonders of the East for the benefit of the political and scientific leaders of the West. It is, in fact, in this shared "orientation"—the word inevitably becomes a double entendre here—that we should base our reading of the Indian-wonders epistles and our explanation of their longevity and popularity.

To put the *Epistola* into a more complex context, however, we must begin at the roots of the Hellenic experience of India, and of Africa as well—since those two regions are frequently treated as a single land mass by ancient geographic writers. Thus when Pliny the Elder, for example, remarks that "India and Africa are especially noted for wonders," we sense that he is discussing, if not a single place, at least a single literary tradition.[7] Both continents formed worlds unto themselves, defined by the peculiar character of plant and animal life, by the bizarre behavior of streams, springs, and rivers, and by alien races; and both became the locus of a genre of descriptive literature that specializes in such exotica. As a result, this literature, though known collectively as the Indian wonders or wonders of the East, often includes Africa, as in Herodotus's *Histories*. "The land westward of Libya is extremely hilly, and wooded, and filled with wild beasts; in this region there are giant snakes, and bears, and vipers, and asses with horns [unicorns], and dog-headed men, and headless men with eyes in their breasts (thus they are described by the Libyans), and wild men, and wild women, and other beasts in huge numbers, not at all fabulous" (*Histories*, 4.191). The aim of such quasi-scientific literature is, to quote Jean Céard in *La Nature et les Prodiges*, to portray a region in which "la nature parait . . . jouer avec la distinction des espèces. . . . Livrée à une fécondité inépuisable, elle s'amuse à créer de nouvelles formes, à diversifier ses oeuvres, elle s'abandonne à une séduisante et terrible anarchie."[8] That is, these accounts depict the landscapes of the far East and South as "free-play" zones in which nature's generative force was unleashed in all its wonderful, and terrible, power. The Greeks, in fact, coined a proverb to express their sense of how nature had run riot in distant lands: *Aei ti pherei Libué kainon.* "Libya always brings forth some strange, new thing."[9] Although in its immediate application this saying refers to Africa and not India, we should understand *Libué* metonymically for both South *and* East,[10] the two regions in whose tropical landscapes nature seemed to exfoliate in a limitless series of new and unexpected forms. To judge by its use in a comedy by the fourth-century poet Anaxilas,[11] moreover, the proverb seems to represent a resigned shrug of the shoulders, a layman's acknowledgment that certain phenomena transcend the scientist's power to explain them: "The arts, like Libya, produce some new beastie [*thérion*] every year," perhaps an equivalent for our "That's progress for you."

Despite this etiological confusion, though, there were those who attempted to explain why *aei ti pherei Libué kainon* in rational, scientific terms. Aristotle, for instance—whose system does not easily tolerate open questions in matters of causation—analyzes the phenomenon in the *De Generatione Animalium,* in discussing the process by which two members of different species can interbreed to produce a third type. "The proverbial expression about Libya, that 'Libya always nurtures some new thing,' has been coined because of the tendency for even heterogenous creatures to interbreed there. On account of the paucity of water, different species encounter one another at the few places which possess springs, and there interbreed."[12] The same theory of poolside miscegeny is also adduced in an interpolated section of Aristotle's *Historia Animalium,* as part of an explanation for the fact that "in Libya all creatures are exceedingly diverse in form" (*polumorphotata*).[13] And finally, a similar (but less well articulated) theory regarding the proliferation of southern and eastern wildlife is put forward in the first century B.C. by Diodorus Siculus.

> [In the eastern portion of Arabia] arise goat-stags and antelopes and other types of biformed creatures, in which parts of animals

which differ widely by nature are combined. . . . For it seems that the land which lies closest to the equator takes in a great deal of the sun's most generative force, and thus gives rise to species of fine beasts. It is for this reason that crocodiles and hippopotami arise in Egypt, and in the Libyan desert a huge number of elephants and variegated snakes . . . and likewise in India, elephants of exceptionally great number and bulk, as well as strength.[14]

Unscientific though such explanations may appear from our perspective, they nevertheless succeed in connecting the biological diversity of Asia and Africa to an indigenous climatic feature, the heat of the sun.[15]

While a handful of thinkers like Aristotle may have puzzled over the cause of "Libyan" diversity in nature, however, other naturalists and ethnographers were content to leave it a mystery. For them, the awe such diversity could inspire could only be dampened by etiological or teleological explanations, and the eastern landscape assumed its most striking aspect when presented as an inexplicable or incomprehensible fact. Hence the Indian wonders are typically recorded in catalogue format: bare, reductive lists that strive for impressive panoramic effects but avoid all discussion of cause.[16] To this tradition belong the great *Indika* of Ktesias of Knidos in the early fourth century and, insofar as we can judge, the writings of the historians who accompanied Alexander into the East or who followed in his footsteps: Megasthenes, Deimachus, Onesicritus, and others.[17] From this school as well come such encyclopedic efforts as the medieval bestiary, derived from the late Greek *Physiologus,* and their descendants in the *Liber Monstrorum* and *Liber Creaturarum.*

The great encyclopedia that collects and subsumes all Greek pseudoscience, Pliny's *Natural History,* would seem at first glance to be a part of this catalogue tradition; in fact it contains the longest of the extant wonder-lists, compiled in book seven under the rubric noted earlier ("India and Africa are especially noted for wonders"). But Pliny also reintroduces Aristotelian etiology into his retelling of the wonders of the East; and the context in which he does this will be important for later Indographic literature, especially the *Epistola Alexandri ad Aristotelem.* Hence it is in Pliny that we may trace the next step in the evolution of our central text.

Readers of Pliny's great wonder-catalogue are struck first by its extreme density and lack of elaboration. Pliny does not explain or even comment on the phenomena he recounts, but tosses each new item paratactically into the great grab-bag of wonders.[18] Moreover, the pace of the list is frenetic, even when measured against Pliny's normally clipped and unceremonious prose; the reader scarcely has time to absorb any single item before being hurried on to the next.

> There are satyrs in the easternmost mountains of India (in the region said to belong to the Catarcludi); this is a very fast-moving creature, going at times on all fours and at other times upright, in human fashion; because of their speed only the older and sick members of the tribe can be caught. Tauron says that the Choromandi tribe are forest-dwellers, have no power of speech yet shriek horribly, have shaggy bodies, grey eyes, and dog-like teeth. Eudoxus says that in equatorial India the men have cubit-long feet, while the women have such small ones they are called the Sparrowfeet. Megasthenes says that a race living among the Nomad Indians has only holes instead of nostrils, and is club-footed; they're called the Sciriate. (NH 7.2.24–25)

This mad dash through the Oriental landscape continues, without pause, for more than seven pages of octavo text, before Pliny finally draws breath and moves, in a more sober frame of mind, to his next topic.

The effect created by this hypertrophy of facts and images is not only striking in itself but crucial to the larger goals of the *Natural History,* to judge by the programmatic introduction and conclusion with which Pliny frames it. He prefaces this catalogue by remarking on the kaleidoscopic diversity of these two lands, which he compares to a leopard's spots and the variegated features of the human face; it is at this vast diversity, he says, and not at individual phenomena, that we must look when we consider the wonders of the East (NH 7.1.6–7). He then repeats this idea at the end of the wonder-catalogue, suggesting that only by surveying the whole of nature can we experience its truly awesome multiplicity. "In her cleverness nature has created these and other, similar things as playthings for herself, and as miracles for us. Moreover who has the power to list the individual things she creates every day, nay, almost in every hour? Let it suffice that her power is revealed by the fact that the races of men are among her marvels" (*NH* 7.2.32). The Indian landscape, as Pliny sees it, only exemplifies the near-infinite diversity inherent in all natural forms,[19] a diversity Pliny celebrates as the source of a sublime sense of wonder.

In the eighth book of the *Natural History* Pliny again turns his attention to the wonders of Asia and Africa, this time in connection with the animal kingdom rather than the family of man. Here, too, the frenetic pace drives the narrative forward, as in chapters thirty and thirty-one,[20] where Pliny retails many of the animal legends made famous by Ktesias's *Indika*.[21] Nevertheless, Pliny sees himself as the direct heir not of Ktesias but of Aristotle. In discussing the African lion, for instance (*NH* 8.17.44), he pauses to comment on the Greek adage "Libya always produces something new," and repeats Aristotle's theory that the random gatherings of species by scarce watering holes accounts for this array of hybrids.[22] Directly following this discussion, moreover, Pliny cites Aristotle more explicitly, rejecting a piece of lore concerning the lion in the following terms.

> Aristotle relates a different account; and his opinion I see fit to place first, since I shall follow him in the greater part of these inquiries. When Alexander the Great became inflamed with a desire to learn the nature of the animal world, and assigned this pursuit to Aristotle, a man who excelled in every field of study, then it was ordered to the many thousands of men in the territory of all Asia and Greece to obey him: All those to whom hunting, birding, and fishing gave sustenance, and all who were in charge of pens, flocks, beehives, fishponds, and aviaries, were not to let any living thing escape his notice. And by questioning these men he laid the foundations for those nearly fifty brilliant volumes on biology. These have been summarized by me, along with some items that their author was ignorant of; I ask that my readers give them a warm reception, and, with my guidance, wander at leisure amid the universal works of nature and the central passion of the most illustrious of all rulers. (*NH* 8.17.44)

This collaboration between Aristotle and his one-time student, Alexander, implies that Aristotle (rather than Ktesias) had been in possession of full and accurate knowledge concerning the wonders of the East; and Pliny, as heir to that knowledge, takes upon himself the mantle of lofty scientific authority that it confers.

The legend recounted here by Pliny has only the most tenuous basis in historical fact, as I have discussed elsewhere.[23] Although Aristotle probably did serve as tutor to the adolescent Alexander at the request of the latter's father, Phillip of Macedon, the relationship between the two men had probably been severed well before Alexander came to control much of Asia. Whatever the story's veracity, it is important for our purposes that Pliny has used it to make tractable the otherwise chaotic disarray of the wonders of the East. Through the legendary partnership of Alexander and Aristotle, Pliny asserts, a cognitive dominion over the East has been established by the West, allowing the penetrating light of Hellenic science to shine under every rock and into every dark, forbidding thicket.

Pliny provides the best glimpse of the imaginative context in which the *Epistola Alexandri ad Aristotelem* and other late antique Alexander texts[24] must be read. Here, in particular in the *Epistola's* sentimental prologue, the partnership of Alexander and Aristotle is staged as a high scientific drama taking place against the backdrop of the remote and terrifying East. The two men have been paired as an immensely powerful research team, the greatest of explorers serving as the collecting and investigating arm of the greatest of zoologists, extending the reach of empirical science into regions where it had never before been able to go. But in this case the drama also becomes a horror story, in that the Aristotelian system does not stand nearly so firm as it had for Pliny. Instead nature shows the dark side of her wondrous diversity: a nightmarish power that threatens at every moment to overwhelm the recording scientist.

We should consider the form in which these letters originally circulated. The Alexander epistles, although known to the Middle Ages largely by way of those that found their way into the Alexander Romance, seem, according to our best evidence, to have originally formed a book-length collection of letters, perhaps an epistolary novel.[25] Thus although the longest of these epistles, the text on which this discussion focuses, was eventually published in Greek in the ß version of the Alexander Romance[26] and in a separate

Latin edition, probably in the second and third century A.D.,[27] we should nevertheless bear in mind that it was part of a much larger epistolary tradition focused on the scientific partnership of Alexander and Aristotle. In fact the Alexander who speaks in the *Epistola Alexandri* describes it as one of a series. "In my previous letters I have already spoken to you concerning the eclipses of the sun and moon, the fixed positions of the stars and the presages of the weather; I sent these to you after setting them out in a careful exposition, and now I shall combine with them these new accounts and set down everything on paper."[28] Extrapolating from this statement we can reconstruct the original setting of the *Epistola* as a compendious cycle of missives from Alexander to Aristotle, examining all aspects of the "New World" in the East from the perspective of Old World biology and teratology.

The reconstruction is supported, moreover, by the degree to which the *Epistola* and the other letters describing Alexander's journeys into the land of wonder,[29] portray their hero not only as a military conqueror but also as a beleaguered champion of experimental science. He constantly expresses a "desire" (*pothos*)[30] to see new lands and new creatures, and refuses to allow even the most dire warnings and portents to deter him from this quest. And when he does encounter such novelties, his first impulse is to investigate, experiment, or take samples for later study. In an episode described in a letter home to his mother, Alexander, after coming upon a species of tree that grows tall in the morning but shrinks to invisibility in the afternoon, orders his men to collect its sap (an effort cut short by an unseen hand which attacks the army with whips and threats).[31] In another extraordinary episode, Alexander, having come upon a primitive man in the Indian wilds, conducts a crude test of sexual taxonomy. "He ordered a beautiful young girl to be brought, and when she was brought Alexander said to her: 'Approach that wild man so that you may observe his condition and see whether he has an entirely human character in him.' This she did, and when the man turned around and saw her, he picked her up and straightaway began to eat her" (*EA*, 2.33). Although his efforts end in grisly failure, the episode is nevertheless significant in that it casts Alexander as Aristotle's investigating arm—the same role as that created for him by Pliny's *Natural History*.[32]

The prologue to the *Epistola* gives a clearer sense of the terms
in which this communiqué between field researcher and labora-
tory scientist was conceived. Here Alexander expresses himself
nostalgically to his former teacher, and lays out his scientific objec-
tives.

> I am always in mind of you, my dearest teacher and nearest to
> my heart (after my mother and sisters), even amidst the hazards
> of war and the many dangers that threaten us; and since I know
> that you are dedicated to philosophy, I decided I must write to
> you concerning the lands of India and the condition of the cli-
> mate and the innumerable varieties of serpents, men and beasts,
> in order to contribute something to your research and study by
> way of my acquaintance with new things (*per novarum rerum
> cognitionem*). For although your prudence is wholly self-suffi-
> cient, and your system of thought, so fitting both for your own
> age and for future times, needs no support, nevertheless I thought
> I had better write to you about what I have seen in India . . . so
> that you would know of my doings (you always follow them so
> closely) and so that nothing here would be foreign to your expe-
> rience (*ne quid inusitatum haberes*) (*EA*,1)

As a good Aristotelian, Alexander realizes that unaccustomed phenomena (*inusitata*) pose an innate threat to his master's taxonomic
system, and so, having uncovered a vast array of such novelties, he
feels the need to get them transcribed and categorized. There is even
a certain urgency in his tone, as revealed in his repetition of the
phrase "I thought I had better write to you"—a formula that will
recur several times in the body of the letter.

Having thus opened by informing Aristotle that the reigning
taxonomy will need to be revised (while tactfully reassuring him
that the system as a whole remains valid), Alexander goes on to
express the overwhelming sense of wonder and confusion his new
discoveries have inspired. "As I see it, these things are worthy of
being recorded, whether singly or in great, manifold groups; for I
would never have taken it from anyone else that so many wonders
could exist, unless I myself had first examined them all right in front
of my own eyes. It's amazing how many things, both evil and good,
the earth produces, that mother and common parent of beasts and

fruits, of minerals and animals. If it were permitted to man to survey them all, I would think that there would hardly be enough names for so many varieties of things." (*EA*, 2). Here Alexander, in tones reminiscent of Pliny's seventh book, envisions the natural kingdom as a totality, awesome in the near-infinite range of its creations. For Alexander, though, this totality has become more threatening than it had been for Pliny, in that the parameters of taxonomy here seem to be stretched to the breaking point. Indeed, by suggesting that man's supply of names (*nomina*) may not be large enough to denominate nature's bounty, Alexander poses a serious challenge to Aristotle, who often refers to his own taxonomic categories as names (*onomata*). The Aristotelian system may be in danger of overload as it tries to absorb all Oriental anomalies, and Alexander, the man of action who carries that system forward into the world, seems afraid that he will ultimately be unable to hold together the rapid diverging poles of theory and experience.

The shaky sense of control Alexander reveals in this prologue becomes even more tenuous as his army moves across the Indian frontier, encountering swarms of hostile beasts and monsters everywhere. In the first long episode of the *Epistola*, Alexander, whose army has been chronically short of fresh water, decides to bivouac his army beside a stagnant pool. His mistake becomes apparent, however, when swarms of scorpions arrive to drink at the pool and commence stinging the soldiers with their barbed tails (*EA*, 17). No sooner have these pests been driven off, however, than others arrive, so that the night becomes a long series of horrific incursions.[33]

> At the fifth hour of the night the trumpet signalled that those awake on watch should take their rest; but suddenly white lions, the size of bulls, arrived. . . . Also boars of immense size . . . together with spotted lynxes, tigers, and fearsom panthers, gave us a fight worse than any previous plague. And then a huge flock of bats, similar to doves in their form, flung themselves into our mouths and faces, attacking the soldiers' limbs with their man-like teeth. In addition one beast of a new type appeared, larger than an elephant, and equipped with three horns on its forehead, which the Indians call a *dentityrannus;* it has a head like a horse but black in color. This beast, having drunk water, spotted us and made a charge at our camp. (*EA*, 18–20)

This night of terrors sees the entire panoply of the Indian wonders ranged against Alexander's troops, many of whom are wounded or killed as a result. It is as if Pliny's wonder-catalogue had been brought terrifyingly to life, and Alexander set down in the midst of its chaotic diversity. The connection to Pliny becomes even more striking when we take account of the setting for this zoological Walpurgisnacht: beside a watering-hole, ancient science's primary locus for the generation of new animal forms. In fending off the swarming creatures that surround the watering-hole, then, Alexander acts out his role as champion of Aristotelian biology, putting to rout the taxonomic disorder exemplified by that environment and making the world safe for Hellenic science.

The fact that this crusade ultimately fails in this and other episodes of the *Epistola*—or at best seems capable only of fighting a holding action against eastern nature—may seem out of tune with the idealizing, heroic dimensions of the Alexander myth. However we can well imagine why late antique and early medieval readers might prefer the East to remain untamed. Aristotle's dictum, after all, promised that Libya *always* (aei) brings forth new creatures; the orderly structure of European nature seemed to require or to take strength from the zone of disorder beyond it, much as Greek gardeners, even in modern times, will deliberately surround their vegetable patches with a border of unruly weeds. The literary appeal of Alexander's forays into this marginal zone must have lain as much in the confirmation of its indomitable disorderliness as in the resulting attempts to control it. In effect it is Alexander's anomalous experiences in India, as the prologue of the *Epistola* implies, that confirm the validity of Aristotle's system for those back home in the comfortable West.

Much the same, of course, might be said of the early European exploration of the Americas, which was portrayed by some at the time as a recapitulation of Alexander's march into the Orient. Thus Columbus set about looking for monsters shortly after his first landing in the New World; these would furnish proof positive that he had arrived in Asia, since the characteristic feature of Asia, according to two millennia of Indian-wonders literature, was its monsters. Throughout the Renaissance the American "Indies" continued to bear the stamp of this tradition, and remained notorious for savage creatures that, like Shakespeare's Caliban, could be contained though not controlled by their western overlords.

Notes

1. Michel Foucault, *The Order of Things* (New York: Random House, 1970).

2. As the Asian queen Kandaké remarks in *The Greek Alexander Romance* (London: Penguin Books, 1991) 3.22 (henceforth *AR*), not only by might but also by mind did the Greco-Roman world strive to conquer the East. For other examples of intellectual and spirtual encounters between eastern and western societies, see the legends discussed in two articles by André-Jean Festugière, "Trois rencontres entre la Grèce et l'Inde," *Revue de l'histoire des religions* (1942–43): 32–57, and "Grecs et sages orientaux," *Revue de l'histoire des religions* (1945): 29–41. For a brief survey see also Jean W. Sedlar, *India and the Greek World* (Totowa, N.J.: Rowman and Littlefield, 1980) chap. 10.

3. Known in England as early as the eighth or ninth century, according to Kenneth Sisam (*Studies in the History of Old English Literature* [London: Oxford Univ. Press, 1953], 83 n.3). The text (bound into the Beowulf codex, Cotton Vitellius A xv) has been edited by Stanley Rypins in *Three Old English Prose Texts*, Early English Text Society 161 (London: Oxford Univ. Press, 1924), xxix–xliii, 1–50. For the transmission see George Cary, *The Medieval Alexander* (Cambridge: Cambridge Univ. Press, 1956), 14–16; and Friedrich Pfister, "Auf den Spuren Alexanders in der alteren englischen Literatur," in *Kleine Schriften zum Alexanderroman*, Beiträge zur klassischen Philologie 61 (Meisenheim am Glan: Hain, 1976), 200–05.

4. Edited by Henri Omont, *Bibliothèque de l'école des chartes* 74 (1913): 507–15. This letter, like the *Epistola Alexandri*, seems to have been translated into Latin from some late Greek original. See also the letter of Premo to the emperor Trajan, published by E. Faral, *Romania* 43 (1914): 199–215, 353–370.

5. See Francisco Alvarez, *The Prester John of the Indies* (Cambridge: Cambridge Univ. Press, 1961).

6. Cary (*Medieval Alexander*, 15), without citing evidence, states that the *Epistola Alexandri* was "used in the Letter of Prester John."

7. Similarly in the *mappa mundi* described by Herodotus in the *Histories*, trans. David Grene (Chicago: Chicago Univ. Press, 1987), 4.37–42, India (or the somewhat larger province of Asia) and Africa are paired as "down-under" land masses in antipodal opposition to northerly, and normative, Europe. On this confusion, see Sedlar, *India and the Greek World*, 9.

8. Céard, *La Nature et les Prodiges*, Travaux d'Humanisme et Renaissance 158 (Geneva: Librairie Droz, 1977), 14. For a survey of the tradition until the Renaissance, see Rudolph Wittkower, "Marvels of the East," *Journal of the Warburg and Courtauld Institutes* 5 (1942): 159–97. John B. Friedman, *The Monstrous Races in Medieval Art and Thought* (Cambridge, Mass.: Harvard Univ. Press, 1981), focuses on the anthropological dimension of the wonders. For the grounding of these texts in actual experiences

of India, see Jean Filliozat, "La valeur des connaissances greco-romaines sur l'"Inde," *Journal des Savants* (1981): 97–136; and A. Dihle, "Die fruchtbare Osten," *Rheinisches Museum* n.f. 150 (1962): 97–100, reprinted in *Antike und Orient* (Heidelberg: Winter 1984), 47–61.

9. The saying is cited twice in the works of Aristotle (*Historia Animalium,* ed. A. L. Peck [London: Heinemann, 1965], 607a 4–5; *De Generatione Animalium,* ed. H. J. Drossaart [Oxford; Clarendon Press, 1965] 746a 35–36) in ways that imply popular currency. Cf. Athenaeus, *Deipnosophistae* 14, ed. C. B. Gulick (London: Heinemann, 1941), 18.10–12, Eustathius on *Odyssey* 1.66.29, ed. M. Devarius and G. Stallbaum (Hildesheim: G. Olms, 1960). The saying later was associated with evil schemes and contrivances; see Zenobius, 2:51, and Diogenes, 1:68, in E. Leutsch and F. G. Schneidewin, ed., *Paroemiographi Graeci,* 2 vols. (Gottingen: Vandenhoeck and Ruprecht, 1839).

10. The saying is used by Aristotle to explain both African and Asian creatures.

11. *Hyakinthos Pornoboskos* fr. 27, in A. Meineke, ed., *Cornicorum Graecorum Fragmenta* 3 (Berlin: G. Reimer, 1840). See also the explanation of the proverb *Libukon therion* in Apostolius, 10.75, in Leutsch and Schneidewin, 2:507.

12. Aristotle, *De Generatione Animalium,* 746b.7–13. Henceforth *GA.*

13. Aristotle, *Historia Animalium,* 606b.17. Henceforth *HA.*

14. Diodorus Siculus, *Bibliotheca Historica,* 2.51.2–4, ed. Bekker and Dindorf (Stuttgart: Teubner, 1985).

15. Cf. Pliny, *Natural History* (Cambridge, Mass.: Harvard Univ. Press, 1963), 6.35.187: "There is nothing surprising in the fact that monstrous forms of animals and men arise in the extreme reaches of [Africa], because of the molding power of fiery motility in shaping their bodies and carving their forms" Henceforth *NH.*

16. Analyzing the medieval wonders texts, Mary Campbell, *The Witness and the Other World: Exotic European Travel Writing, 400–1600* (Ithaca, N.Y.: Cornell Univ. Press, 1988), esp. 57–75, helps elucidate the importance of their catalogue form. See also Nicholas Howe, *The Old English Catalogue Poems,* Anglistica 23 (Copenhagen: Rosenkilde and Bagger, 1985).

17. Paul Pedech, "Le Paysage chez les historiens d'Alexandre," *Quaderni di Storia* 3 (1977): 125: "La peinture de cette nature, avec ces grandes fleuves, ses forêts immenses, ses animaux inconnus et sa végétation exubérante renouvelait dans la littérature grecque un genre hérité d'Hérodote: l'exotisme."

18. Indeed, this list runs on so much that its Renaissance editors, who elsewhere divided the *Natural History* into brief chapters for reference purposes, could not find any convenient break, and subsumed the entire list within a single, gigantic chapter.

19. On this passage see Céard, *La Nature et les Prodiges,* 16.

20. Examined in detail by Ermino Caprotti, "Animali Fantastici in Plinio," in *Plinio e la natura,* ed. A. Roncoroni (Como: Camera di Commercio di Como, 1982), 42–46.

21. For Pliny's dependence on Ktesias, see Céard, *La Nature et les Prodiges,* 14.

22. Cf. *NH,* 6.35.187, quoted above at n.15; Céard, *La Nature et les Prodiges,* 16.

23. Romm, "Aristotle's Elephant and the Myth of Alexander's Scientific Patronage," *American Journal of Philology* 110 (1990): 566–575.

24. On the enduring power of the Alexander legend to define the Indian landscape for later Greek civilization, see A. Dihle, "The Conception of India in Hellenistic and Roman Literature," in *Antike und Orient*, 89–97.

25. Such is the belief of R. Merkelbach, *Die Quellen des griechischen Alexanderromans*, 2d ed. (Munich: Beck, 1977), 56 n.32, and Lloyd Gunderson, *Alexander's Letter to Aristotle about India* (Meisenheim: Hain), 86–88. The arguments surrounding the origin and accretion of the Alexander Romance as a whole are beyond the scope of this study, but every account of this process indicates that the miracle letters were originally a separate element, deriving more from folk tale and oral saga than from historiography. See B. Berg, "An Early Source of the Alexander Romance," *Greek, Roman and Byzantine Studies* 14 (1973): 382. Erwin Rohde, *Der griechische Roman und seine Vorläufer*, 3rd ed. (Leipzig: Breitkopf and Hartel, 1914), 187, believes the letters represent the oldest stratum of the novel.

26. Alexander Romance, 2.17. On the relationship between the independent Latin letter and the Greek version in the novel, see Merkelbach, *Die Quellen*, 193.

27. There is no good evidence for the date of the Greek original. Gunderson (*Alexander's Letter* 119) argues that this letter is nearly contemporary with Alexander himself, since its prophecies of the fate of his sisters would have rung true only in the twenty years or so after his death; and Merkelbach (*Die Quellen*, 60–62). He also supposes that the historical details of the prophecy would be intelligible only to an audience very close to the actual events. See, however, the review of Gunderson, *Alexander's Letter*, by A. Cizek, *Gnomon* 54 (1982): 810.

28. *Epistola Alexandri ad Aristotelem ad Codicum Fidem Edita*, ed. W. W. Boer (The Hague: Excelsior, 1953), 3. Citations in text are to pages in this edition, as *EA*, because these are keyed to Gunderson's English translation, *Alexander's Letter to Aristotle about India*. A better text for Latinists is M. Feldbusch, ed., *Der Brief Alexanders an Aristoteles uber die Wunder Indiens*, Beiträge zur klassischen Philologie 78 (Meisenheim am Glan: Hain, 1976), laid out to permit a synoptic comparison of *EA* with other, related Alexander narratives.

29. The tradition is admirably summarized and catalogued by Gunderson, *Alexander's Letter*, 32–33, as "miracle letters" reporting "as many remarkable experiences as possible. The setting is always in distant lands. There Alexander and his soldiers fight with monsters and undergo thrilling adventures, they see strange peoples, weird customs, and march through uninhabitable deserts. This is teratological literature" (33). See also the catalogue in Rohde, *Der griechische Roman*, 187 n.1.

30. See Victor Ehrenberg, *Alexander and the Greeks* (London: Oxford Univ. Press, 1938).

31. Recension of *AR*, 2.36. See H. Engelmann, ed., *Der griechische Alexanderroman Rezension, Buch 2*, Beiträge zum klassischen Philologie 12 (Meisenheim am Glan: Hain, 1963).

32. See also the legend of the bathyscaph expedition, in D. J. A. Ross, *Alexander and the Faithless Lady: A Submarine Adventure* (London: Birkbeck College, 1967).

33. On this episode see A. Cizek, "Ungeheuer und magische Lebewesen in der *Epistola Alexandri ad Magistrum Suum Aristotelem de Situ Indiae*," *Third International Beast Epic, Fable, and Fabliau Colloquium, Münster 1979, Proceedings*, ed. J. Goossens and T. Sodman (Cologne: Bohlau, 1981), 78–94, esp. 83–89.

3

The Aesthetics of Deception
Giotto in the Text of Boccaccio

BENNET SCHABER

The following essay was originally a talk intended, first and fore-most, to provoke some response from its audience. This it did, questions being raised about its politics (were there any? were they elided? etc.), about its relation to theory (was it reducing a literary work to an example or confirmation of certain psy-choanalytical tenets?), and about its relation to literary and art history (what kind of history was being presented, since if it was a "social" history, perhaps it was only a social history of reception rather than production). The issue of postmodernism occurs pre-cisely as the temporal problem introduced when one attempts to conjoin all the above concerns in an act of speech (in my case) or of writing (in Boccaccio's). After all, I attempt to connect the temporality of allegorical *figurae* (in Freud's account of the words of a three-year-old boy and in Giotto's frescoes in the Arena Chapel) with the time of dialogue; and those with a certain history of writing art history, all coming to bear on the oft-repeated claim that Giotto somehow marks that founding moment in the West when a true vision of nature was finally revealed. Hence the question this essay ponders: What is the relation to vision of the acts of speaking and writing that claim to reveal precisely the inaugural moment of visual revelation in painting? Can speech and vision be separated, ever? Must eyes be hungry in order to see, mouths blind in order to speak (or eat)?

47

Because accounts of Giotto's discovery or revelation of a natural (and rational) vision are consistently phrased within the tropics of a return or restoration of painting,[1] I have used Lacan's "return to Freud"[2] as a kind of varnish over the entire essay. Lacan's "return to Freud" is monumentally important not only because it returns us to the letter of Freud's texts, but because of its sensitivity to the function of return within those texts, within psychoanalytic theory. I have tried to take this function of return seriously, both as a duty imposed upon writing and as a kind of key to the temporality of the postmodern: a "contraclau," a medieval troubador might say, the counter-key one receives from some other in order to unlock the meaning of one's own riddle.

> Fag ai lo vers, no say de cuy;
> e trametrai lo a selhuy
> que lo m trametra per autruy
> lay vers Anjau,
> que m tramezes del sieu estuy
> la contraclau.[3]

(I've made this verse, I don't know what it's about; and I'll send it to someone who will send it with another toward Anjou; let him send me from his little box the key [to this riddle].)

Like his troubador companions, Guillaume knew, at least, that meaning forms the limit of writing and hence demands a passage through some other, so that meaning might be returned and restored to the one who writes.[4]

In 1905, commenting upon the transformation of libido into anxiety, Freud produced the following footnote.

For this explanation of the origin of infantile anxiety I have to thank a three-year-old boy whom I once heard calling out of a dark room: "Auntie, speak to me! I'm frightened because it's so dark." His aunt answered him: "What good would that do? You can't see me." "That doesn't matter," replied the child, "if anyone speaks, it gets light." Thus what he was afraid of was not the dark, but the absence of someone he loved; and he could feel sure of being soothed as soon as he had evidence of the person's presence.[5]

This little tale is remarkable on a number of counts. First, it foreshadows by fifteen years the "*Fort! Da!*" game in which the problem of libido and anxiety will be given its most striking formulation as the inscription within the subject of an other whose name is death, its sign the abject and dizzying alternations of the repetition compulsion.[6] Second, the little boy in the dark precociously constructs what we might call a *figura*; linking within his demand for a light-giving word both the *Fiat lux* of Genesis and the '*En arche en ho logos* of John, he takes note of a temporal, hence allegorical, problematic within western culture—the relation of the old law to the new—that Freud would rediscover as the temporal problem of the subject itself, the problematical relation of any scene to "the other scene" of the unconscious.[7] Third, here Freud seems to confirm the Lacanian intuition that places "Demand" squarely within the problem of libido and anxiety: Freud seems to be elaborating the drive. ("Demand in itself bears on something other than the satisfaction it calls for. It is demand of a presence or of an absence . . . transmuting it into a proof of love.")[8] The Freudian tale, now become something of a parable, has the advantage of producing, in miniature, a problem that continues to be our own. It might be variously phrased as language and light, speech and vision, text and image, etc.

In what follows, I rehearse this problem, which is both temporal (alternation, repetition, allegory) and historical (re-inscribed anew at various chronological junctures). And since the text chosen for this rehearsal (hardly an innocent word in this context, since it unites both a visual theatrics with the repetitions one re-hears) arrives from the fourteenth century, it might also be placed under the heading of "postmodern medievalism," an unhappy phrase, perhaps, but useful, perhaps.[9] My text is a brief tale from Boccaccio's *Decameron*, a tale that has not been the subject of abundant commentary. It might have remained one of the least remarkable of the one hundred *novelle* had it not, because it took Giotto as a protagonist, found its place in the abundant commentary that history has woven around the famous painter.[10]

The relation of speech to vision is central to the story Panfilo tells. Its explicit point is that "nature has frequently planted astonishing genius in men of monstrously ugly appearance." He explains that one day Giotto and Forese da Rabata, a Florentine jurist, took a trip on horseback together. Caught in a downpour, the two take refuge in the home of a peasant from whom they borrow some old woolen capes and a pair of hats. As they continue their journey, Forese notices how unkempt and disreputable Giotto looks. Forese remarks that if a stranger were to see Giotto now, he would hardly believe him to be the world's greatest painter. Giotto replies that the same stranger, seeing Forese, could hardly credit him with knowing his ABCs.

The fame of this story rests not upon its narrative but upon Panfilo/Boccaccio's comments assessing the greatness of Giotto's craft. In Michael Baxandal's pioneering *Giotto and the Orators*, we find Boccaccio's description of Giotto's craft cited *in toto*, along with the famous three lines in which the writer praises the painter in the *Amorosa Visione*.[11] Again we find the same two passages cited in Vittore Branca's "definitive" biographical study of Boccaccio. Branca sketches out the "vigorous 'vernacular' culture" that forms the context of Boccaccio's achievement and within which Giotto spoke with a "renewed figurative language."[12]

Of course, this "figurative language" might be "renewed" precisely because that is just how Boccaccio spoke of it: Giotto had, according to Boccaccio, renewed, "brought back to light" (*ritornata in luce*), an art "which had been buried for centuries" (*che molti secoli . . . era stata sepulta*). Hence those three irresistible lines in the *Amorosa Visione*, placing the assessment of Giotto precisely within a dialectic of the occulted, the buried, the silent, against the renewed, the revealed, the manifest—this time with nature herself as agent.

> Giotto, al qual la bella
> Natura parte di se somigliante
> non occulto nel' atto in che suggella.[13]

(Giotto, to whom fair nature hid not that resemblance of herself, sealing it in his craft.)

For both Baxandal and Branca, Giotto's paintings "speak": to Baxandal they speak with the voice of a nascent humanism beginning to privilege and praise *natura* at the expense of *exemplaria*; to Branca they speak for a renewed and vigorous culture, this time not in Latin but in the vernacular. But this speech has not itself occasioned any reading. Unheard within a rigorous demand for vision—as if, to return to our Freudian parable, the voice in the dark had brought forth the light without ever being heard—it has remained in place simply to delimit a space in which Giotto's practice might become visible, in which he might cease to hide that semblance of himself from us, as nature had ceased to hide hers from him.

The relation of Giotto to Boccaccio, set out in the *Decameron* through the embedding of one within the text of the other, finds itself, through a history of commentary, reversed. Thus, from within the painted text of Giotto, it is now Boccaccio who speaks. He operates as an immanent eye, and speech procures the visibility of painting. Boccaccio speaks from within painting as Giotto had procured the visibility of nature by placing the eye of painting within nature itself (or, to return to Freud, the way the aunt's response to her nephew brings forth light in response to darkness). This remains to be demonstrated in day six of the *Decameron*. Beyond these metaphors, what takes up my attention here is a relation of vision to speech in which the one responds to the other; and a relation of nature to history, of nature's revelation in history, and the price of that revelation.

"Price" is not only a metaphor, especially in this context. Vasari's "Life of Giotto," still the most famous account of the painter (it includes a notice of Boccaccio's appreciation), uses price as a metaphor, grafted onto Boccaccio's own metaphors, and as an explicit estimation of the painter's worth in the most famous episode of his life, his drawing of a freehand circle, the *tondo*.

> In my opinion painters owe to Giotto, the Florentine painter, exactly the same debt they owe to nature, which constantly serves them as a model and whose finest and most beautiful aspects they are always striving to imitate and reproduce. For after the

many years during which the methods and outlines of good painting had been buried under the ruins caused by war it was Giotto alone who, by God's favour, rescued and restored the art, even though he was born among incompetent artists.[14]

Once again, Giotto is credited with having resurrected an art "buried under the ruins"; and this "rescue" and "restoration" is given as a retrieval of nature, so that art "owes" to both "exactly the same debt." Giotto becomes the singular, inestimable, and inimitable (precisely because he re-founds the imitation of nature) origin of a revitalized art of painting. And this is what is at stake: the production of Giotto as origin and of painting as an original return to the revelation of nature.

Within this context the freehand circle takes on its full meaning, describing as it does (1) a circular return to an origin (nature), (2) the absolute reason or *ratio* of that nature as perfect geometrical figure, as well as (3) a turn away from an "incompetent" art, so that the circle's beginning (medieval art patterned on the facing pages of the *liber* held in figurative relation, or the *speculum*, as found with Vincent of Beauvais) is not the same as its end (the Lucinda, for example, and its rationalizing of pictorial space as monocular geometry). "Giotto had drawn the circle without moving his arm and without the help of a compass," so that in the freehand circle the master's hand, in its natural movement, meets the geometry of nature's absolute reason given as vision. "This showed the Pope and a number of knowledgeable courtiers how much Giotto surpassed all the other painters of that time. And when the story became generally known, it gave rise to the saying that is still used to describe stupid people: 'You are more simple than Giotto's O.'"[15] The ability to discern the genius of the circle, which divided the "knowledgeable" from the "stupid," the reasonable from the unreasonable (the Pope's nuncio was originally baffled by Giotto's circle when the painter submitted it to the Pope as evidence of his talent), becomes, upon its return from the visual field to the realm of popular speech, the rhetorical figure of stupidity.

Giotto's circle, in itself and for the history of art, comes to stand for the origin of art as the visual instantiation of the geometrical reason of nature. But what is elided from this history is the joke that crowns it (the word *tondo*, meaning both a perfect circle and a slow-witted simpleton), as the comic context of Boccaccio's tale is elided whenever his account of Giotto's achievement is cited. Reason and, by extension, art become absolute (originary) when the visual medium becomes divorced from the speech, the discourse, that brings it to light. Vision is established as reason itself, singular, as when the hand becomes a compass and revolves around a central point that becomes the single eye of monocular vision and the vanishing point of perspective.

This brief history of citations brings to light not so much a circle[16] as its collapse upon its axis, its becoming a singular and monological point. The representation of the founding moment of this (natural) art of vision disavows the play of presences and absences in its demand, so poignantly brought out by Freud in the young boy's words. In Freud's story the words, spoken in the dark, could still grasp the light (and love) as homage to a difference (between the boy who speaks and the light-giving Other to whom his words beckon) that would never collapse. We, too, can hold tight to this difference by restoring to Boccaccio's words the comic dialogue that elaborates them. Not in order to establish discourse as capable of exhausting vision, but in order to re-establish within vision the temporal and diacritical gap that all speech makes manifest in its demand for a reply.

The late Middle Ages, especially in Italy, witnessed a positive rage for praising Giotto, especially in literary works. Dante notes that Giotto's fame has "dimmed" that of Cimabue.[17] Petrarch tells us he has become especially famous among the modern artists, *inter modernos*.[18] We can agree with Henry Ansgar Kelly that "commending Giotto was clearly the thing to do in the Italy of Chaucer's time."[19] The name of Giotto, therefore, signals an historical epoch's recognition of itself as a new beginning, as modern. With Vasari the fate of this recognition is sealed, with Giotto's "return" to a prior nature transformed into a new "departure" for modern art. A "before" (nature) comes to represent an "after" (modernity), and the figure for this move is a circle, Giotto's *tondo*. What I insist upon below is that Boccaccio subtly took note of this in his tale, making the tale neither modern nor premodern but postmodern.

In *Word and Image*, as if by historical compulsion, Norman Bryson begins a study of French painting of the *ancien régime* by invoking a problem of medieval art and the so-called "supremacy" there "of the discursive over the figural."[20] In examining the window in the apse of the cathedral at Canterbury, Bryson is at pains to establish its essential invisibility a propos its figural repression by doctrinal, explanatory texts (in actual captions, letters in glass, and in the paradigmatic arrangement of the panels themselves). "The visual information [the window] emits is fully exhausted by textuality," Bryson says—hence the window's essential invisibility and total readability.

Now, Bryson is no doubt right, at least in part, even if the notion of "medieval art" proves untenable.[21] Nevertheless, one need only confront his formulation with an illuminated manuscript to see how far short he falls. For even if the visual text of medieval art presents itself as a "nothing to be seen" and an "everything to be read" (for the historian of art), the illuminated manuscript presents us with a letter whose life is at least as visible as it is readable. From the earliest rune poems, through the literal play of troubador lyric, to the anagrams and acrostics of romance or the poetry of Villon, illuminated letters given volume and opacity, bursting into flower or woven into knot puzzles, the medieval letter not only restores vision within the text, not only incites reading as an effect of vision, but presents itself as irreducible to either discourse or figure.[22] Can it be simply an accident then that, as an epoch we now call medieval, a middle age, comes to close itself, to seal itself—much as Giotto "sealed" nature's resemblance in his art—Boccaccio would give to Giotto the last word of a tale, a last word whose significance is only its letters, ABC, *l'abici?* These letters, like the *tondo* that forms both circle and letter, are both readable and visible; they illuminate themselves in their reading.

Day six of the *Decameron*, a day whose tales are given over to clever responses to rather less clever questions, might itself be figured as a response: to the debate opened up by two servants, Licisca and Tindaro, who argue over whether women are virgins at marriage; and a response as well to day one, itself given over, at least implicitly, to the notion of the story itself as a kind of response. Thus Boccaccio's text doubles back on itself as it begins its second half.[23]

This doubling back of day six onto day one has already been anticipated. Day one ends with a poem whose explicit subject is narcissism, a lover in love with the reflection in a mirror. Day six registers its response to the question of vision with the famous assessment of Giotto's practice as a painter. Now the net effect of the invocation of this practice is not so much to rehabilitate or even undo the narcissistic and *a fortiori* visual/specular knot of day one, as to divert it toward the question of representation *tout court*.

> Giotto was a man of such outstanding genius that there was nothing in the whole of creation he could not depict with his stylus, pen or brush. And so faithful did he remain to Nature that whatever he depicted had the appearance, not of a reproduction, but of the thing itself, so that one very often finds, with the works of Giotto, that people's eyes are deceived and they mistake the picture for the real thing [*che il visivo senso degli uomini vi prese errore, quello credendo esser vero che era dipinto*].[24]

Giotto, who "brought back to light an art which had been buried for centuries beneath the errors of those who, in their paintings, aimed to delight the eyes of the ignorant [*dilettar gli occhi degl'ignoranti*] rather than please the intellect of the wise [*compiacere allo 'ntelletto de' savi*],"[25] is credited with the creation of representations whose very truth as reproductions of nature grounds their status as deceptions, as lures drawing the eyes on to mistake one thing for another. The tale in which Giotto appears revolves around a visual mistake: Messer Forese, the Florentine jurist, in noting the appearance, *apparenza*, of Maestro Giotto—who, we are told, refused the title *maestro*—fails to note, to see, his own.

> As Messer Forese was riding along listening to Giotto, who was a very fine talker, he turned to inspect him, shifting his gaze from Giotto's flank to his head and then to the rest of his person, and on perceiving how thoroughly unkempt and disreputable he looked, giving no thought to his own appearance he burst out laughing, and said: "Giotto, supposing we were to meet some stranger who had never seen you before, do you think he would believe that you were the greatest painter in the world?" To which Giotto swiftly repied: "Sir, I think he would believe it if, after

taking a look at you, he gave you credit for knowing your ABC."

On hearing this, Messer Forese recognized his error, and saw that he had been paid back in the same coin for which he had sold the merchandise.[26]

Forese's error is rectified, repaid, when he first hears, then recognizes, and finally sees: *Il che Messer Forese* udendo, *il suo error* riconobbe, *e* videsi *di tal moneta pagato quali erano state le derrate vendute* (my emphasis).

Two points must be taken into account here. The first is that the price of vision, of seeing, is the recognition of error, a recognition that is an effect of hearing. The second point, intimately related to the first, is that what Forese hears, echoing from a visual mistake, is his own message returned to him by Giotto, inverted. Echo answers Narcissus, only this time the response takes—because vision is exposed as a second seeing, a postvision.

Noting Giotto's appearance, Forese bursts out laughing, *comincio a ridere*. He laughs because, as with any joke, he has engendered a metaphor; that is to say he has substituted another place for the one from which he sees. This second place has not yet seen even a first time: "supposing we were to meet some stranger who had never seen you before [*venendo di qua alla' ncontro di noi un forestiere che mai veduto non t'avesse*]."[27] Giotto's response, returning words for laughter and bringing about a new vision, adds joke for joke. He adds a further vision to a second vision taken for a first (Forese's stranger), this time a point of view from which Forese sees himself seeing. Forese's visual mistake derives, therefore, from his belief that he can position himself outside the dialogical couple he forms with Giotto. By identifying himself with a third party, with the Other, stranger or foreigner (*forestiere*), he believes that his own position as second, as other to Giotto, simply disappears (like a child who covers his own eyes in order not to be seen by another). But by replying to him in his own words, Giotto makes clear that this third party would see both men. Hence, to imagine a truly first, primordial moment of sight, Forese must imagine himself as someone else seeing "as if" for the first time.

The idea of a true, original, monocular vision is only the attempt to make good on the lack of truth qua third term within dialogical duplicity. Giotto's reply insists that there is no pure position of a first, true vision. The first vision would always be a failed recognition, a "missed encounter" with the object supposedly seen. Forese seems to know this but he needs to re-learn it from his interlocutor. To imagine a first vision would be to imagine someone seeing me seeing, that is, seeing through my eyes. Hence this supposedly first moment would already be a second, a (failed) recognition. True vision depends upon its confirmation (in words) by the seen other, not upon some pure and therefore unseen position. The temporality of vision, therefore, is that of the future anterior: one always "will have seen." Forese will have seen for the first time only after Giotto has disabused him of a "first," erroneous vision.

This is why the metaphor of return associated with Giotto's reproduction of nature, used by Boccaccio himself and inaugurating a history of its own repetitions, is absolutely and in principle correct. For if seeing is always a second seeing, a postvision, is not nature, as something seen, reproduced and represented, also and always a second nature, a return of nature, a postnature? And equally then, the site of a mis-take, a second time mistaken for a first. This is why Giotto, credited with bringing back to light an art buried for centuries, is said to please the wise rather than the ignorant; for who are the wise if not the ignorant twice over, those capable of being "deceived," of "mistak[ing] the picture for the real thing [*quello credendo esser vero che era dipinto*]"; that is, of mistaking the picture for the truth.

This is what makes Boccaccio's episode so different from Vasari's. The latter's wager was to originate modern art in a point both monological and monocular. Boccaccio, on the other hand, places Giotto within a scene both dialogical and specular. Forese can only locate the origin of his gaze, the seemingly monocular origin of vision and (here legal) truth in an Other, an Other made manifest by the real other Giotto becomes for him as a reply in speech. Speech and vision de-originate each other; who can say which was first? Both are found, or rather re-found, to be double, divided against themselves. Truth arrives from the locus of an Other, not a singular point of origin. This is why it is so difficult to tell the wise from the ignorant: the truth of a vision or an utterance must await its reply, therefore partaking of the vexed and uncanny temporality of deferred action, *Nachträglichkeit*, a temporal and diacritical conundrum we might call postmodern.[28]

Let us, once more, return to Freud. He mentions Giotto only once in his entire oeuvre; but even here Giotto is associated with a return, not the return of nature but Freud's own return to Padua and Giotto's frescoes in the Arena Chapel there.

> During later years, when I was already deeply absorbed in the study of dreams, the frequent recurrence in my dreams of the picture of a particular unusual-looking place became a positive nuisance to me. In a specific spatial relation to myself, on my left-hand side, I saw a dark space out of which there glimmered a number of grotesque sandstone figures. A faint recollection, which I was unwilling to credit, told me it was the entrance to a beer-cellar. But I failed to discover either the meaning of the dream-picture or its origin. In 1907 I happened to be in Padua, which, to my regret, I had not been able to visit since 1895. My first visit to that lovely University town had been a disappointment, as I had not been able to see Giotto's frescoes in the Madonna dell'Arena. I had turned back half-way along the street leading there, on being told that the chapel was closed on that particular day. On my second visit, twelve years later, I decided to make up for this and the first thing I did was to set off towards the Arena chapel. In the street leading to it, on my left-hand side as I walked along and in all probability at the point at which I had turned back in 1895, I came upon the place I had seen so often in my dreams, with the sandstone figures that formed part of it. It was in fact the entrance to the garden of a restaurant.[29]

As elsewhere, Giotto marks the site of a return, the return of a picture, of grotesque (*grotesk*) figures glimmering in a dark space, themselves a return, via etymology, from grotto to Giotto. The recurring dream image only pays homage to a failure, a mistake, where the signifier "grotto" displaces "Giotto" at the exact place where Freud fails to encounter the frescoes he has travelled so far to see. And if the dream fulfills a wish, is it not the wish to see, given to Freud as recurrent vision, but vision of the wrong thing? And so Freud returns, in person, to the site of oneiric returns, if only, once again, to mistake the dream vision for the real thing.

What did he see, then, that second time? He doesn't tell us anything about that. But, his eyes traversing the paneled frescoes until they reach the altar where, among the trumpeting angels of the last judgment, another rolls back Giotto's layers of paint as if they were a scroll, to reveal, at history's end and judgment's beginning, he might have seen nothing but painting, the return of painting—post-painting.

"The signifier," says Lacan in the seventh seminar, "introduces two orders into the world: the truth and the event [*Le signifiant introduit deux ordres dans le monde: la vérité et l'évènement*]."[30] We might take this as incisive commentary upon the episode Freud recounts. For here the signifier, "grotto," noted at the moment of a signifying incursion, a stopping and a turning round, itself turns round, tropes itself ceaselessly on the other stage of the dream as recurring event awaiting its truth to emerge from the darkness of a grotto (also the obscurity of a word, or more minutely, a letter), buried for twelve years and finally returned to light—*ritornata in luce* (as Giotto and *giardino*, garden).

Freud knew Boccaccio's *Decameron:* he mentions it in a note to the case of the Wolfman, in connection with the ability to see while remaining unseen; but he does not seem to recollect Panfilo's tale here. Nevertheless he returns us to its exact dynamics (and even its vocabulary). From Lacan's *deux ordres* to the Freudian *désordre,* perhaps all that is emphasized, as it was with Boccaccio, is a certain "confusion of tongues" lurking in the midst of vision. For if Giotto returns to Forese his own message in inverted form, is it not in order that the *che vuoi?* that issues from the place of Giotto, no longer *maestro* but analyst *avant la lettre,* might trump the law, the lawyer, the judge and judgment, with the letter, the *abici*?[31]

Boccaccio's tale attempts to take account of Giotto's craft as the re-emergence, in history, of a pictorial form of representation that itself emerges (or, better, has prepared for it the space of its possible emergence) from a certain dialogical repartee, whose ground is a visual moment of *méconnaissance.* I use this word in order once again to invoke Lacan, whose work has prepared the space for my own, although Lacan never claimed that his work was anything more than a reemergence, a return to Freud. And Freud's work, as I have tried to demonstrate, is inscribed within a dialectic of returns, made possible by a certain inscription of the letter in the unconscious.

This structure of return is fundamental. It founds the subject of the Freudian parable opening this essay, a subject founded upon its own disappearance into the dark when the voice of the Other brings light (*"Fort! Da!"*). For the allegorical *figura* linking Genesis and John in the child's words gives not the origin of the world, but of the subject who speaks and whose first words receive their meaning (as the subject receives its being) from the reply to their demand. The last shall be first, the after comes before. As in a sentence, the first word secures its position as first only after the second has granted it a meaning (a first signified is only the effect—not the original cause—of a second signifier). In the *"Fort! Da!"* game, *"Fort!"* cannot primordially signify absence until *"Da!"* comes along to mark the loss of the word *"Fort!"* *"Fort!"* will signify absence only upon its first repetition; the "truly first" instance of *"Fort!"* will not signify at all. It will have been nonmeaning, pure loss itself.

If this temporal matrix, in a sense, transcends history, the problem it poses (that an origin is only originary retroactively, an original repetition) can only be reckoned historically—with the historically determinable and specific representations ready to hand. The story Boccaccio tells is not quite the same as Vasari's, not quite the same as Freud's. Nonnegotiable questions, negotiable answers, as one author has put it.[32]

The name of Giotto, therefore, in Boccaccio's text and my own, marks a moment in the history of representation when its essence as a history of deceptions, of errors, is exposed, but only insofar as that exposure itself becomes liable to the deceptions inherent in all representation.[33] This moment might be called "postmodern." It calls history into question as both representation of history and a history of representation—a history of mis-takes on history from which even nature is not exempt—if nature is given as signifying in advance, a representation whose first time is a second.

Postmodernism, then, wherever it appears, may be seen as a first chance at history—a history no longer reducible to "cliometrics," to use Sol Yurick's term for the history that puts a past economy of information to work in consolidating the present.[34] Postmodernism would stand for a new writing of history, one that divides the present against itself and makes possible a return of the past that would pressure its own narcissistic and masterful gestures. This new writing would not be so new after all, since the hands of Giotto and Boccaccio, at least, have already preceded, but not pre-empted, us. Post-history, perhaps, that will post-date us, and return to us.

Notes

1. See, for example, Giorgio Vasari, *Lives of the Artists,* trans. George Bull (London: Penguin, 1985).

2. See Lacan, *Écrits* (Paris: Seuil, 1966).

3. Guillaume Neuf, in *Lyrics of the Troubadours and Trouvères,* ed. Frederick Goldin (Gloucester: Peter Smith, 1983), 24–27.

4. These lines, a coda to Guillaume's poem, were loosely translated by Umberto Eco at the conclusion of *The Name of the Rose,* trans. William Weaver (New York: Harcourt Brace Jovanovich, 1984), 610. For a more extended discussion of their relation to postmodernism, specifically its use of irony, see Diane Elam's essay in the present volume.

5. Freud, *Three Essays on the Theory of Sexuality,* in *The Standard Edition of the Complete Psychological Works of Sigmund Freud,* ed. and trans. James Strachey (London: Hogarth, 1966), 7:224. Henceforth *SE.*

6. *SE* 18:14–18. The *Fort!-Da!* game involves Freud's grandson throwing a cottonreel on a string over the wall of his cot and pulling it back. Its appearance is greeted by the cry *Da!,* its disappearance accompanied by the cry *Fort!.*

7. For *figura* see Erich Auerbach, "Figura," in *Scenes from the Drama of European Literature* (Minneapolis: Univ. of Minnesota Press, 1984), 11–79. On the way *figura,* in allegory, effaces a primal diacriticality and deciphers it as deferral and narrative, see Joel Fineman, "The Structure of Allegorical Desire," in *Allegory and Representation,* ed. Stephen J. Greenblatt (Baltimore: Johns Hopkins Univ. Press, 1981), 26–61.

8. Jacques Lacan, "The Signification of the Phallus," trans. Alan Sheridan, *Écrits, A Selection* (New York: Norton, 1977), 286.

9. I borrow "postmodern medievalism" from Stephen Knight, *Geoffrey Chaucer* (Oxford: Blackwell, 1986), 3. He associates it primarily with deconstruction qua method. Although, as a Marxist, he is happy with locating a certain dialectical movement within medieval texts, he is not willing to acknowledge a postmodern moment in any way immanent in (even if not reducible to) them. In his reading of *Troilus and Criseyde,* sexual difference, gender, is reduced to and analogized with the dialectical play of public and private spheres. Here a conceivably postmodern moment intervenes, creates a temporal and structural problem, a radical questioning, that culture seems to solve everywhere but where it lodges in the subject. Gender is not dialectical without the inscription of a phallic term to effect its *Aufhebung;* hence the danger

of dialectics where gender is concerned.

10. Giovanni Boccaccio, *Decameron*, Day Six, Fifth Story (Bologna: Nuova Casa, 1985), trans. (modified) G. H. McWilliam (London: Penguin, 1987), 493–95.

11. Michael Baxandal, *Giotto and the Orators* (Oxford: Clarendon, 1971), 74.

12. Vittore Branca, *Boccaccio, The Man and His Works* (New York: New York Univ. Press, 1976), 38.

13. *Amorosa Visione*, 4.16–18.

14. Giorgio Vasari, *Lives of the Artists*, trans. George Bull (London: Penguin, 1979), 57.

15. Vasari, *Lives of the Artists*, 65.

16. The joy at the discovery of the circle can nearly be read in the etymology of the name of the one who drew it: Gioia and O—Giotto.

17. *Purgatorio*, 11.94–96.

18. Petrarch, *Epistolae ad rebus familiaribus*, 5.17.

19. Henry Ansgar Kelly, "Chaucer's Arts and Our Arts," in *New Perspectives in Chaucer Criticism*, ed. Donald M. Rose (Norman, Okla.: Pilgrim Books, 1981), 111.

20. Norman Bryson, *Word and Image* (Cambridge: Cambridge Univ. Press, 1983), 5.

21. Cf. Kelly ("Chaucer's Arts"), who notes that the medieval *ars* is not identical with our own visual estimation of "art."

22. On the letter and medieval textuality within a Lacanian frame, see Roger Dragonetti, *La Vie de la lettre au moyen âge* (Paris: Seuil, 1980).

23. Boccaccio makes of the book itself a problem of doubling back and difference whose aspects relate to class, religion, time, but predominately gender. Hence the problem of virginity: the women claim that men delude themselves when they believe in a first instance, on any of these fronts.

24. Boccaccio, *The Decameron*, 494 (translation modified).

25. Boccaccio, *The Decameron*, 494.

26. Boccaccio, *The Decameron*, 495 (translation modified).

27. Freud, in *Jokes and Their Relation to the Unconscious*, SE 8:99–102, argues that jokes require three "persons," the third being an inhibiting force, the inscription of an other that divides the first into two. He even notes that this third can be language itself, which then functions as a lure, what he calls a "take-in."

28. See the introduction to this volume.

29. *SE* 4:15.

30. Lacan, *Le Séminaire, 7: L'Éthique de la psychanalyse* (Paris: Seuil, 1986), 308.

31. For the *che vuoi?*, the question of desire posed from the "locus of the other," see Lacan, "Subversion du sujet," *Écrits*, 793–827.

32. Hans Blumenberg, *The Legitimacy of the Modern Age* (Cambridge, Mass.: The MIT Press, 1983).

33. All exposures suggest some Other who exposes something for me. But what guarantee can there be that this Other is not deceiving me?

34. Sol Yurick, *Metatron, the Recording Angel* (New York: Semiotext <e>, 1985), passim.

4

"The Miller's Tale" in Chaucer's Time

NICHOLAS ROYLE

A mockery. Here she comes, sweet as apples, lovely as a pig's eye. There's the husband, short-sighted as an astrologist, superstitious enough to believe a story about the imminence of an apocalyptic flood, the revelation of God's secrets—an opportunity for the young scholar to sneak off to bed with the young wife, scarcely a woman, as blissful to look at as an early-ripe pear-tree in blossom, ecstatic melody and revelry being the result, apparently for both parties, together with a broken arm and a fall into unconsciousness on the part of the ludicrous husband who thinks the end of the world has come and cuts the cord supporting his flood-proof tub up in the rafters and down he crashes. Everyone laughs and laughs.

Who tells the story? Hende Nicholas? Geoffrey *in propria persona*? Which story?

It is not that everyone laughs but that everyone laughs and laughs. It's just too much. It's not clear whether we can take it, whether anyone can.

"The Miller's Tale" is a joke.[1] But who tells it? And who's laughing? It's extremely serious. It's all elaborated, constructed, fabricated, as if by a fictive carpenter and her or his assistant, him or her or neither (since there will not have been much space for sexual opposition or difference in the postmodern), a demonic other, who is intent on discontructing it, disregarding or taking all the frames to pieces, letting no narrative frame stand in the way, allowing everything to fall and break, in suspense. There are narratives within narratives within narratives and this, among other things, is the abyssal irony of the Chaucer-text, leaving us with a phantasmagoric carpentry of storytellers: Geoffrey Chaucer, the narrator, the Miller, John the carpenter, Nicholas . . . Abyssal and phantasmagoric because there is no means by which to judge the tone of "The Miller's Tale," its voice, the place or identity of its narrator, or of its listener or reader. Ironic, then, in the (of course ironic) sense outlined by Paul de Man—with reference, that is, to the systematic undoing of understanding.[2] Phantasmagoric is the so-called man, that "stout carl for the nones" from the General Prologue, the "short-sholdred," "brood," "thikke" Miller for whom (as we are told in the General Prologue: 550–51) "Ther was no dore that he nolde heve of harre, / Or breke it at a rennyng with his heed," whose name is Robin, in other words who appears to have a demonic other, a double, another Robin, who turns up in the course of the narration of "The Miller's Tale," described as "a stout carl for the nones" (3469), and who breaks into the tale charged with breaking down a door. "And by the haspe he haaf it of atones; / Into the floor the dore fil anon" (3470–71). This is not so much the teller in the tale as it is the putative narrator (Robin, the Miller) being filed into a position on the threshold, taking away the door, weirdly heaving into suspense the frame or boundary distinguishing the inside and the outside of the tale, the narrative and narrator, but also the narrative and itself, the narrator and "himself." Truly the milling of a tale.

But all this, in any event, is in another voice, at the same time, undecidably dubbing it, the voice of the narrator who "moot reherce" (3173) the tale he has supposedly heard from the Miller. It's extremely serious—with all the seriousness necessarily marking the prescriptive statement purportedly governing our understanding of "The Miller's Tale": "And eek men shal nat maken ernest of game" (3186). A paradoxical seriousness, then, that (however much it remains finally unreadable) will not prevent us from believing that we can negotiate the hurdles of these multiple frames; that we can follow a certain univocality, as well as a certain unified narrative voice in the tale; that we know how to listen to the soundtrack, in spite of its polytonal, polyvocal and even "panauditory" dimensions; in short, that we can put all the milling, the polyphony, and undecidability in the background, and attend to the telling of the tale.

A paradoxical seriousness, then, that does not mean the tale is not also frightening, maddening, deadly, hilarious.

It is the strange seriousness of a panopticon, a panopticon which, like any other, turns out deceptive.[3] The panopticon would be the visual counterpart to the explicit and ubiquitous emphasis given to sound and voice in the tale: it parallels the kind of panauditory register whereby we seem to hear everything, from the "soun" of the "dronke" narrator (3138) to the "semy soun" of a character's cough (3697). It is the panopticon with which we are apparently presented, the panopticon generated by the multiplicity of forms of so-called dramatic irony, constituted out of the delusion that we can see everything—the gulling of John the carpenter, the lovemaking of Nicholas and Alisoun, Absolon's wooing of Alisoun—a delusion or misprision heightened by what we perceive as idiotic blindness. They cannot see but we can see everything: the dramatic irony of this panopticon is hilarious, even if it, too, will have proved to be abyssal. For in this spectacle, this Chaucerian cinema, everything is on show, including madness and death. There are moments when characters in the tale also appear to be in possession of a privileged view, as for example when Robin goes to Nicholas's door and "cride and knokked as that he were wood" (3436), till finally he takes a peep at that other seeming lunatic:

> An hole he foond, ful lowe upon a bord,
> Ther as the cat was wont in for to crepe,
> And at that hole he looked in ful depe,
> And at the laste he hadde of hym a sight.
> This Nicholas sat evere capyng upright,
> As he had kiked on the newe moone. (3440–45)

Or at the so-called end of the tale when all the townsfolk "kiken" or peer into the roof, laughing at the carpenter who is "holde wood in al the toun" (3846). Death, too, is part of the parade. Thus the shocking materialization as witnessed by the carpenter:

> This world is now ful tikel, sikerly.
> I saugh today a cors yborn to chirche
> That now, on Monday last, I saugh hym wirche. (3428–30)

Everything will have been summoned up in the eerie but perhaps also hilarious gravity of that "now."

We are told that men—and doubtless women—"may dyen of ymaginacioun" (3612). But we see it all for what it is, the apocalypse is a joke, nothing can gull us. The last thing in the world we would identify ourselves with would be a figure like that of the clerk who, as the carpenter's mininarrative has it,

> walked in the feeldes, for to prye
> Upon the sterres, what ther sholde bifalle,
> Til he was in a marle-pit yfalle;
> He saugh nat that. (3458–61)

There are holes all over the place—the hole revealing Nicholas in his room or this "marle-pit," for instance, or when Nicholas orders John to "breke an hole an heigh, upon the gable, / Unto the gardyn-ward, over the stable" (3571–72). But they are holes into which we can look. We see them and are given access to what secrets they may contain. The same goes for all the other secrets in the text. The truth of what is "deerne" (3278) or of what others should not "(e)spye" (3566, 3729), everything in any way concerned with secrets or "pryvetee" (3201, 3276, 3295, 3454, 3558, 3603, 3676, 3802): in keeping with the logic of the panopticon, all of these things are made visible. Everything is revealed.

"The Miller's Tale" make a mockery of the Bible, in particular the Book of Revelation. However difficult it may be to distinguish the voice of Nicholas, superimposing itself on other, already indeterminable voices, in his mininarrative within that other mininarrative known as "The Miller's Tale," a certain parody of a Biblical tone irresistably suggests itself. For example, commanding the carpenter:

> But whan thou hast, for hire and thee and me,
> Ygeten us thise knedyng tubbes thre,
> Thanne shaltow hange hem in the roof ful hye,
> That no man of our purveiaunce spye.
> And whan thou thus hast doon, as I have seyd. (3563–67)

Nicholas's "sermonying" (3597) has the most serious, the most properly apocalyptic purpose in the world: it offers the revelation of the apocalyptic flood and links this revelation to that of "Goddes pryvetee," to secrets of which one must not have knowledge. "Men sholde nat knowe of Goddes pryvetee" (3454). We have been warned. And Nicholas, though apparently himself one of the cognoscenti, tells the carpenter, "Axe nat why, for though thou aske me, / I wol nat tellen Goddes pryvetee" (3557–58). But if this Chaucerian Book of Revelation, "The Miller's Tale," seems to offer us a presentation of apocalypse, a true uncovering (*apokalypsis*), a revelation of the final truth, of God's "pryvetee" (secrets, secrecy, private affairs but also private parts[4]) or of the "pryvetee" of "God," it is perhaps in the image or figure of the hole itself—and, more specifically, that of an asshole. Everything rounds on the figure of the "toute," on the "naked ers" (3734) of Alisoun or the "ers" (3802) of Nicholas.

For the text is, after all, an extraordinary joke. When Absolon takes revenge on Alisoun and the thunderously farting Nicholas by smiting the latter in the "toute" with a "hoote kultour" (3812), Nicholas's scream of "Help! water! water! help, for Goddes herte!" (3815) is what inaugurates the apocalypse for the carpenter. The revelation of the flood is the revelation of the final truth, of the final truth as a joke. To the extent that there is a revelation of "pryvetee" (divine or otherwise) in the tale, to the extent that there is a central image on which the panopticon is trained, it is an asshole. The final revelation is based on the revelation of Nicholas's "ers"; it is a revelation forged between the explosive sounds of a blinding fart and a scream for "water!" The revelation is marked, literally, by the marking, burning, or branding of an asshole, and by the paronomasia of "water" to which this marking immediately gives rise. The carpenter "herde oon crien 'water' as he were wood" (3817), cuts the cord and crashes to the floor. After which everyone laughs and laughs. In considering "The Miller's Tale" itself as an extended joke, everything turns on the "water," which operates as a source of laughter with a remarkable power of condensation. The two separate narratives—of John-Alisoun-Nicholas and Alisoun-Nicholas-Absolon—are brought together in this single word.

In a recent essay entitled "Laughing in the Meanwhile," Samuel Weber provides a brilliant analysis of Freud's *Jokes and Their Relation to the Unconscious*.[5] He explores Freud's emphasis on the need for the diversion of attention in the course of the telling of a joke and notes that, for Freud, "Consciousness is not absent while the joke is being told and heard, it is present, but in a peculiar way, this presence is at the same time 'held far away,' *ferngehalten*, from what is really 'going on' in the joke" (701). The Chaucerian theater will have been practicing a work of concealment, or diversion of attention, after all.

What is the time of all this? Weber is particularly concerned with Freud's use of the word *unterdes*—"in the meanwhile." It is a question of the temporality of a joke, and the time of laughter: "just as we begin to think back about what has been going on, 'we are already laughing' [as Freud puts it]" (702). Our attention has been, in Freud's phrasing, *überrumpelt*. And Weber glosses this word: "not merely 'caught unawares,' as Strachey translates it, nor even simply 'overwhelmed': the German word *rumpeln* signifies, onomatopoetically, a rumbling, rattling noise. The mind of the listener has been overcome by a sound that disorganizes it; we 'come to' and find ourselves engulfed by laughter. Impossible to say just where or how that laughter 'began': no sooner do we begin to think back, *nachzudenken*, than we discover that it is already 'over,' indeed all over a body that no longer does our bidding" (702–3). The space of this "in the meanwhile," the time of laughter and the laughing body are, for Weber, precisely "insignificant," posing a dislocation of meaning from which "psychoanalysis draws back" (706) but which the Freudian account of jokes has nevertheless made conceivable or at any rate perhaps inscribable. Weber's essay could be described as postmodern in the Lyotardian sense that it serves to "[put] forward the unpresentable in presentation itself": in its evocations and analyses of the time of laughter it could be said to be searching, in Lyotard's terms, "for new presentations, not in order to enjoy them but in order to impart a stronger sense of the unpresentable."[6] For after all, who is *there* to enjoy? What could be the identity of such a laughing subject? Or of a body, by definition insignificant, not even signifying in the way in which an hysterical body might be said to signify?[7]

It would be possible to show in greater detail how "The Miller's Tale" works with, out of, and through the uncanny time of laughter. In particular we could listen to this text, listen to the amazing outpouring of what the Reeve calls the phantasmagoric Miller's "clappe" (3144), listen to the seemingly panauditory Chaucerian soundtrack, to all its music, bell-ringing, singing, talking, snoring, coughing, knocking, and farting, and try to attend to what fascinates our attention. We might attempt to analyse the ways in which Chaucer's poem seems to play out a certain unpresentable rhythm of erotic "melodye" (3306, 3652) and hallucinatory silence, and to generate its own kind of rumbling or rattling. In terms of attending to "The Miller's Tale" as a joke, however, it would be a question of the impossible, of attending to the thought of a temporality and of a rumbling or rattling that is unpresentable. It is what is (impossibly) figured in the thought of "The Miller's Tale" as a multiple sound-track that can—with a "clom!" and a "clom" (3638–39)—offer the hushful vigilance of the carpenter "Awaitynge on the reyn, if he it heere" (3642) but at the same time leave this attention in a suspense of noise: the carpenter, we are told, is snoring, he "routeth" (3647). Laughter will have already engulfed, like a flood: there can be no pause before this laughter, no time for it, nor any way of presenting what was "happening"—"in the meanwhile"—in order for it to come about. Laughter will have already overwhelmed, already risen over, in a flood of sound. Chaucer's poem exploits an awareness that, for the purposes of a joke, there can be no place for silent laughter: laughter must involve noise.

But "The Miller's Tale" is also more than a joke, it is beyond a joke. It mocks. It simultaneously mimes and ridicules. It makes a mockery of jokes. In its ending, which is really no ending at all, it proleptically incorporates the response of the audience, promulgating figures of overwhelming noise and manic laughter. We are plunged once more, again or further, into the milling of a tale, into a seemingly endless dispersion of voices into overwhelming noise and manic laughter. No way of knowing how to judge this "jape" (3842), this hilarity and uncanniness, this mad laugher at madness, this mockery of sound. No one can or will hear what the carpenter is saying: "For whan he spak, he was anon bore doun / With hende Nicholas and Alisoun" (3831–32); no matter what "this carpenter answerde, / It was for noght, no man his reson herde" (3843–44). For "every wight gan laughen" (3849). This does not complete the joke, rather it ensures a certain suspense and undecidability. It complicates and heightens the sense of what is unpresentable. Nothing is being filled out or finished, even if this is precisely what is implied by the flat peremptoriness of the final five lines:

> Thus swyved was this carpenteris wyf,
> For al his kepyng and his jalousye;
> And Absolon hath kist hir nether ye;
> And Nicholas is scalded in the towte.
> This tale is doon, and God save al the rowte! (3850–54)

Focusing once more on the image of the asshole, we may wonder at the truth or significance of this "nether ye." It is, perhaps, the first eye that looks back at us. In any case it scarcely figures the completion of a panopticon, but more an inversion or torsion of otherness, suggesting precisely that the panopticon could never be complete, nor ever be presented. As such it may be read as a further imperceptible wink or flourish of undecidability and suspense, of the unpresentability of laughter, which is the unpresentability of what we could now call, in the most provisional and peirastic fashion, Chaucer's time, the postmodern.

Notes

1. All Chaucer citations and line-references are taken from *The Works of Geoffrey Chaucer*, ed. F. N. Robinson (London: Oxford Univ. Press, 1957).

2. See Paul de Man, *Allegories of Reading: Figural Language in Rousseau, Nietzsche, Rilke, and Proust* (New Haven: Yale Univ. Press, 1979), 301.

3. My use of "panopticon" is intended partly in the Benthamite sense (1791; *OED*, la) of an edifice or construction (esp. a prison), every part of the interior of which is exposed to the privileged position of an all-seeing eye, but also in the more general, figurative sense (in keeping with the ancient Greek *panoptos*, "fully seen or visible") of "A place where everything is visible" (*OED*, lb). It is aimed in particular at exploring the double notion of fiction as panopticon and panopticon as fiction. The strangest, most dramatic, and most suggestive figuring of a panopticon in Chaucer's poetry is perhaps at the end of *Troilus and Criseyde* (see book 5, 1808–20), in which we are offered the description of the ascent of Troilus's "lighte goost" up into "the holughnesse of the eighthe spere":

> And down from thennes faste he gan avyse
> This litel spot of erthe, that with the se
> Embraced is, and fully gan despise

This wrecched world, and held al vanite
To respect of the pleyn felicite
That is in hevene above; and at the laste,
There he was slayn, his lokyng down he caste.

4. For another account of "Goddes pryvetee" in this sense, see Laura Kendrick, *Chaucerian Play: Comedy and Control in the "Canterbury Tales"* (Berkeley: Univ. of California Press, 1988), 5–19. She focuses particularly on the unavoidable double or triple reading of the lines from "The Miller's Prologue": "An housbonde shal nat been inquisityf / Of Goddes pryvetee, nor of his wyf" (3163–64). Stressing that "The late-fourteenth-century denudation of God the Son was a pan-European phenomenon" (11) in contemporary visual art, she explores not only the double meaning of "Goddes pryvetee" but also notes ambiguity in the word "his," which she suggests can be read as referring to God's or Christ's wife, i.e., Mary. Kendrick highlights Chaucer's poem as a tale "putting the lowest possible interpretations on sacred images and texts" (16). She also cites, in apparent innocence, the delightful and apparently innocent description proffered by Alfred David, in his *The Strumpet Muse: Art and Morals in Chaucer's Poetry* (Bloomington: Indiana Univ. Press, 1976): "In the fabliau, attempts to get to the bottom of the mysteries of life usually backfire" (99). In the so-called end, Chaucer's poem indeed will have touted itself as such a homonymic tale, as a joke with an indeterminable but.

5. Samuel Weber, "Laughing in the Meanwhile," *Modern Language Notes* 102:4 (1987), 691–706 (further page-references appear in the text); Sigmund Freud, *Jokes and their Relation to the Unconscious,* trans. James Strachey, ed. Angela Richards, Pelican Freud Library 6 (Harmondsworth: Penguin, 1976).

6. Jean-François Lyotard, *The Postmodern Condition: A Report on Knowledge,* trans. Geoff Bennington and Brian Massumi (Minneapolis: Univ. of Minnesota Press, 1984), 81.

7. Weber makes this point: "For the body, laughing is far more difficult to assimilate to an economy and to a temporality of representation than is the hysterical body, which, as symptom, is still significant" (706). Thus even Lacan's suggestion about the question at the base of hysteria ("Am I a man or a woman?" Jacques Lacan, "A Love Letter" in *Feminine Sexuality,* ed. Juliet Mitchell and Jacqueline Rose, trans. Jacqueline Rose (New York: Pantheon, 1982), 149–62) would seem to have no place in the temporality of this laughter.

Part Two

Postmiltonism

5

The Hyphen in the Mouth of Modernity

Marshall Grossman

Postmodernism Across the Ages. The title suggests both persistence in and movement through time. One wants to take its "postmodernism" in a singular and unitary way, as some substantive formation enduring endlessly in an ocean of history, washing up, wearied but intact, on the pebbled shores of diverse ages, shaking off the brine and supplementing, with its tearful eyewitness, the account of itself that it finds already oft told in this strange place. However, in this age—if it is, when it is done, to have been an age—though one may think postmodernism, one sees postmodernisms, diversely rooted in their particular discursive histories.

From the window of my Brooklyn apartment, I find recently imposed on my vision a sixteen-story, polygonal building of red brick. Its oddly angled facets rise in slabs topped by what I take to be a fake-copper mansard roof, to which is added, on one side, a small, fake-copper pyramid. On each side of this roof is a stone facing, containing—like a clock lacking a dial—a red neon circle.[1]

I take the copper to be fake because the day it was put up, its color approximated—in a way—the green copper-oxide color that *real* copper acquires as it weathers. I say approximated in a way, because the material in question, whatever it is, doesn't imitate a weathered appearance but rather seems to take a stab at what the familiar color of weathered copper would look like if clean and new, excepting the fact that clean and new copper is an entirely different color.

The building, which obscures and dwarfs the two-story public library that had previously organized the site, was put there, in
the face of community objections, by the Morgan Stanley Bank,
which I know to be, in another register (that of the multinational
financial operator and master of the transcendental tender offer)
a postmodern entity, or, to impart to my meditation the rigor
of Jurgen Habermas's translated discourse, an operator of
"postmodernity."[2] So, its allusions to a building material that constructs the nonexistent newness of an aged coinage metal and the
absence of the clock hours within the neon circles of finance give
the building an absolute monumentality. Insofar as a monument
marks the place, localized in time and space, at which something
has been transferred from space and time to memory—has become, in effect, a tradition—this building, which by its bulk asserts
hegemony over its neighbors and the nearby Williamsburg Savings Bank Tower (to which its empty clock faces allude), razes the
buildings whose style it expropriates from their contexts in the
history of Brooklyn (a venerable history by American standards),
and absorbs the motifs of the past and the archeological strata in
which they reside into its own decontextualized allusiveness. As
an *absolute* monument the mode of its remembering is oblivion and
the extent of its reach limitless. It encumbers the future by turning
back to a past that it preserves only as what is lost, just as the
green roof points at once to its always already-aged quality with
respect to its models and the loss of the historical process of
weathering by which ageing occurs.

I know this building to be an example of postmodernism, and I
wonder if the temporal disruptions of its clockless clocks and not
exactly pre-aged, not-quite-copper roof might be clues to the temporality of postmodernism, or at least to the defining attributes of
postmodernism as a specifically temporal situation. I will return
later, in a very different context, to the definition of a specifically
postmodern monumentality and temporality.

First, tempted as I am to read the view that my window frames
more or less synchronically, and to derive from it a postmodernity
that would bind to a finite and specifiable set of attributes the
postmodernities I see there, I am stopped by my casual knowledge
that the postmodernity of the building ought to be situated

diachronically with respect to the great age of the Bauhaus and architectural modernism against which it reacts, or to which it alludes, while the postmodernism of Morgan Stanley must be understood in relation to the age of industrial capitalization it has passed through, the time when its function was to underwrite the productivity, as opposed to the performativity, of American capital. As for the burial of the 1950s social realist branch library beneath this conglomerate pile, I must meditate on the fact that the library had, prophetically, in the time before Morgan Stanley, converted half its space to "the Brooklyn Business Library."

Although these transitions of style and changing modes of production seem to be connected, I would hesitate to assimilate the two histories and modes of change. I fear that would lead to a totalizing idealization in which a virtual master code, operating at or near the modes of production, would appear to govern and rationalize the internal developments of the historically distinct (though intertwined) disciplines involved. I suspect that my hesitation is itself an instance of the postmodern moment in criticism.

Thus each of the postmodernisms that appear in my window seems more integral with its own immediate modernism than with something dragging its cunning self, intact, across the ages. So too would it seem that postmodern literature, painting, and music stand in a more determinate (if not necessarily more determinable) relationship to each of their disciplinary pasts than to each other.

Since my interest in postmodernism is theoretical, an interest not in the beings of postmodernism but in its possibilities of being, I propose to leave aside for the moment the empirical patterns that insist through my window, and, beginning with the term "postmodernism," to sketch something of a conceptual morphology. My question, then, is not what is postmodernism through the ages but what might a postmodernism, properly so called, be?

I come to this question from a particular age, the Renaissance, and with a particular obligation to engage the possibility of postmodernism in the age of Milton. I begin, therefore, in the manner of a Renaissance rhetorician, by making a three-fold division of the subject, addressing in turn: the semiotic function of the "post-," a contextual definition of "modernity," and Milton's canonicity in relation to modernism and postmodernism.

What precisely is transacted across the conjunction of "post-" and "modern"? While the "post-" carries us past what follows it, it retains, by virtue of its lexical attachment, precisely that which has been passed in time. The use of compounds like "post-war" or "post-structuralist" depends on the persistent significance of the war or of structuralism in the contexts they are used to address. Thus the *post-* form is transitional; it distinguishes the moment at which something that had been experienced as currently unfolding is felt—not as ended, rather as a more or less institutionalized presence. When a succeeding configuration gets its own name, what it supersedes may be regarded as other in a way that is directly impeded by the *post-*formation. There is thus a double dependence of the postmodern on the modern. Early modern people, as those who lived in the Renaissance are now properly called, were evidently and indisputably aware of their modernity, but they do not seem to have conceived of themselves and their works as post-medieval or even post-Dark Ages. On the contrary, they often worked hard to obscure their ruptures with the immediate past and to represent them as pervasive continuities.[3] Modernism eventually constituted the Middle Ages as an otherness that lay behind it, and it seems now to have constituted postmodernism not as an otherness that lies before it but as the ever-recursive image of its own exhaustion.

The *post-* form, then, indicates not the othering of the modern, in the way that the Renaissance achieved the othering of the Middle Ages, but rather establishes a moment after the modern during which we seem to be bound in a present that is present only as the presence of a present that is lost, that is belated, and that remains. In so far as modernity is the way of the "now," postmodernism installs that "now" as a remainder, or, more properly, a memory. In the postmodern, then, what is present is present as past, as a reminder of its own monumentality. Thus the empty circles of neon decorating the odd faces of the Morgan Stanley building refer at once to the nearby clock tower of the Williamsburg Savings Bank (by which generations of Brooklyners told time) and to the belatedness of clock time itself in the digital realm of Morgan Stanley. Similarly, the weatherproof, "weathered copper" of its roof remembers without being in the time in which a copper roof's durability inheres, the time in and through which it acquires the protective cover of copper oxide that eventually stabilizes it in and over time. Through such elements the postmodern incorporates the past without recycling it, retaining it rather as an out-of-phase aspect of the present, as memory—or, what amounts to the same thing, an allusion. Thus the hyphen, invisible or expressed, that joins "post" to "modern" funcitons as a mouth, for the transaction that takes place at this hyphen is the sucking inside of the world, so that experience may be retained, in its loss, as a property of consciousness, that is, as memory. Memory installed in this way is best called nostalgia.[4] In it the markers of different times—public clocks, copper roofs, asymmetrical edifices—are held out of time in an expansive, yet dimensionless present, a present that remains absent to itself by virtue of its having been given over to recollection.[5]

If the world that is swallowed and internalized by the *post-* of postmodernism is the modern world, then it remains to define the period of that modernity by defining a contextually relevant modernism. Having referred to the Renaissance as the early modern period, I have already tipped my hand about the broad historical parameters my definition will entail. In proposing this broad definition of modernism, I forgo any attempt to characterize the variety of modernisms that articulate the various local regions of its career. My intent rather is to describe a signal rhetorical move, a trope, that formalizes the variety of modernist moments and, at the same time, limns, by coming into and receding from view, the dimensions of a modernist epoch: What characteristic might encompass and unify, in some restricted, yet contextually relevant way, the expanse of Western cultural development from, say, Shakespeare to Joyce? I take my examples from the restricted field of English literature, but similar examples could be found in other arts and other venues.

> Seems, Madam? Nay, it is. I know not "seems."
> 'Tis not alone my inky cloak, good mother,
> Nor customary suits of solemn black,
> Nor windy suspiration of forced breath,
> No, nor the fruitful river in the eye,
> Nor the dejected havior of the visage,
> Together with all forms, moods, shapes of grief,
> That can denote me truly. These indeed seem,

> For they are actions that a man might play,
> But I have that within which passes show;
> These but the trappings and the suits of woe.[6]

Thus Hamlet tells Gertrude to disregard the legible signs of his state of mind and to equate Being precisely with that which once having been taken in can never be securely brought out.

"Welcome, O life! I go to encounter for the millionth time the reality of experiences and to forge in the smithy of my soul the uncreated conscience of my race," writes Stephen Daedalus, in a diary or record not of the world but of the world lost and epiphanically transferred into a personal and invisible cognitive possession.[7]

With these two literary historical moments as a temporal frame, I would propose that modernism records the adventures of an ethical subject, determined and self-identified, according to its cognitive possessions. By ethical I mean one whose story or mythos is represented (to itself) as having been shaped by its own choices and decisions, and whose character is to be deduced from the genre of story so shaped. In short, the subject of modernism is the subject whose being resides in his or her, generally proprietary, knowledge and whose knowledge is the summation of his or her experience.[8]

Remaining, for now, within the confines of a formal analysis, I would suggest that the swallowing of the world signified by the *post-* of postmodernism is a second ingestion of what modernism itself had already swallowed when, around the time of Shakespeare, for whatever reasons, the relation of Being to its symbolic representations became competitive; that is to say, the being of representation itself began to intrude upon its referential function.[9] For the modern subject any immediate relation with the world (that is, its *Umwelt*) is subject to an epistemological reservation. What one sees are "actions which a man might play," but what one knows is "that within that passes show."

Where the being of things is hopelessly doubtful, the relation to one's own knowledge is secured as the familiar hegemony of the individual consciousness. Thus the trajectory of modernism can be seen as a progressive interiorization of the world of experience, ranging from the language games of Shakespearean postepideictics to the internalization of oceanic nature in Molly Bloom's interior monologue, or, in a theoretical register, T. S. Eliot's bizarre comparison of the mind of the poet to a platinum filament catalytically converting individual emotions and feelings into objectively correlative art objects, in which the continual sacrifice of the self to the objective world ensures, ironically, the publication of one's own experienced emotions in the form of an objectively evoked and effectively universalized feeling.[10]

When the processes of postmodernity, however, put in question the security of even this epistemological subject—making present to it its various disseminations and the paucity of its future—the functional substitution of knowledge for Being becomes, itself, a memory. This memory reproduces, or remembers, the two forms of an older epideixis, the encomium and the execration, as nostalgic reverence and nostalgic travesty respectively. In practice these two logical possibilities for postmodern representation are often combined: in the closing scene of Kubrick's film *Full-Metal Jacket*, U.S. Marines, stunned and battered by the Tet offensive, sing the "Mickey Mouse Club Song," as they fan out over a Vietnamese landscape (constructed, one might add, on an English location).

What distinguishes this mixed nostalgia from the phenomenological presence of modernism is a disruption in narration. Hamlet cannot reliably make visible "that within which passes show," because the black clothes, teary eyes, and dejected facial expression that might signify his inner reality are "actions that a man might play." But the inner truth can be written out in a person's life and perceived retrospectively in the narrative that life generates. When the action is completed and all its embedded plays have been played out, each episode receives its meaning and the "rest is silence." Narrative, when it closes, converts all its included actions into elements in an atemporal design, each element deriving its meaning in relation to the whole structure. Thus it represents the plenitude of knowledge as a terminal retrospection, the journey of its subject, through time, to the proprietary truth that rewards its efforts. Hamlet knows that "murder, though it have no tongue, will speak / With most miraculous organ" (2.2.605–6), and that to make it speak, he must present it to itself as already known: first in dumb show, and then displaced into the appropriated banalities of an old script: "The stoy is extant, and written in very choice Italian" (3.2.268–69).[11] The price of this recursive speech is the end of Hamlet, his conversion from a life raveling out into time to a story bounded on each side by silence, a bare stage, hard covers.

By the time of Milton the crisis of being that opens before Hamlet's inability to identify himself with his observable actions was being recuperated by the conversion of questions of being into narratives of knowing. Milton is a canonical author precisely with respect to the literary historical endurance of his consolidation, particularly in *Paradise Lost*, of the modernist subject as the subject of ethos, the subject of the story of the choices it has made and will make on the basis of what it knows.[12]

Milton engaged this modernist subject directly in a permutation of the *grand récit* of the Christian West, the story of creation, fall, apocalypse, and resurrection. For reasons both formal—his exhaustive working out of the rhetorically possible situations from which this subject could issue—and pragmatic—the production of his major works in the immediate aftermath of the failure of the English revolution—he also located, with considerable precision, the postmodern moment embedded within the formal possibilities of the ethical subject.

Take, for example, the 1671 volume in which *Paradise Regained* and *Samson Agonistes* first appeared. The Jesus of *Paradise Regained* is the highest of modernists. He acts in utter privacy to forge in the smithy of his soul the uncreated conscience of his race, and his acts are undertaken in a state of totally illuminated anticipation, a completely epiphanic unity of "light" and action. Moreover, the change he effects, though it will transform the world, is presented as wholly interior and private: a transformation of the self that will empower and enable others to be similarly transformed. Having "said, and stood" (4.561), Milton's Jesus is proclaimed by angels to have reached the fullness of time: "'on thy glorious work, / Now enter, and begin to save mankind"' (4.634–35), but in the poem's final lines, "he unobserved / Home to his mother's house private return[s]" (4.638–39).[13]

"To which is added," as it says on the title page, not the triumphant spectacle of the Passion, as we might well expect, but rather *Samson Agonistes: A Tragedy*. In contrast to the celibate Jesus, we meet, posteriorly in the volume, his profligate and uxorious prefiguration. Positioned in this way, presented as the failed *imitatio* of an as yet unborn Christ, Samson's story is, we might say, post-Hebraic, and, Samson's nazerite vow (the word "nazerite" *now* unable to shed its anticipatory whisper of Nazareth) suspends him, as a post-Jew, between the exhaustion of the law and the belatedness of spirit.[14]

More Hamlet than Jesus, Samson suffers from the hopeless inmixing of his motives—indistinguishably divine and libidinous—and he is driven to express the putative divinity of his inner knowledge by all too literally pressing out what remains inside.

Dr. Johnson's famous censure is very much to the point. "It is only a blind confidence in the reputation of Milton that a drama can be praised in which the intermediate parts have neither cause nor consequence, neither hasten nor retard the catastrophe."[15] The subject of an ethos depends upon the proleptic narrativization of its experience; its self-identity through time is constituted retrospectively and continuously in a mimesis of its actions, and this is what is missing from *Samson Agonistes.* However, this structural absence, analogous to the absence of the trace of the weathering process in the Morgan Stanley Building's ersatz roof, attains a thematic insistence within the poem, for only *blind* confidence in Samson could allow Manoa, or the chorus, or the reader, to be more than agnostic with regard to Samson's ability to distinguish his own suicidal desires from the inward speaking voice of God. Unlike Milton's reputation as a poet, Samson's reputation as a judge instills no such confidence.[16]

The events of Samson's life, especially the judgments and choices of his married life, vary drastically and inexplicably from the story announced by divine intervention at his birth. Unable to author a story to fit the authorized story, Samson loses the light of a cognitively secure and private interior knowledge—he loses himself. Unable to act because the story of his acts has become destructured in this way, Samson becomes prematurely his own monument: "Myself, my sepulchre, a moving grave" (102).

As Stanley Fish points out, it is only by dying and thus removing his excessive self from the stage that Samson can become the monumental narrative he seeks to generate.[17] Even then, the Israelite uprising he sought to inspire never occurs; God fails to validate Samson's invisible ethos by writing it out as the mythos of history. No Fortinbras comes on stage to clear away the bodies and call flights of angels to carry him to rest. On the contrary, Samson remains, strangely installed in his posterior position in Milton's volume, as that which is added to the story of the perfected warrior who succeeds him. The orthodox Christian reading of the Samson story points out that Samson's failure conduces to and explicates the glory of Jesus's success. Milton's volume complicates this facile typology, reversing the expected order and situating Samson, as it were, in the shadow of that unknown thing, which he cannot remember—because it has not yet occurred—and for which, in the exigency of his circumstances, he cannot wait.

As a drama, *Samson Agonistes* bears a certain resemblance to the Morgan Stanley building. It tells and retells a tale of timely action from which time—the medium in which human ethos is written on the world—has been expunged. It refers to a future that can only arrive as its own revision, its post-. Moreover, Samson, who was his own sepulcher, brings down on himself and his audience the temple in which classical heroism plays its scene. Henceforth he is to be contained within and supplemented by the tomb his father proposes as a memorial to inspire the Hebrew youth. The memorial marks also the scene of a catastrophic conversion from drama to narrative, from presence to story. Milton's play is thus a monument to Samson's monumentality. It marks at once the becoming of memory of a certain scene of heroic human action in the world and the Greek drama in which its ethos was preserved as the working out of a series of causally related events. As the theater collapses, so too collapses the duration of ethos, the dialectic of ethos and mythos for which Greek drama stood and which Christ is made to reject in *Paradise Regained* (3.285–364).

The story Milton needs to tell is one not of the strength that follows enlightenment but of historically urgent action in the dark, the problematic discovery that "strength is not lost, though light denied." To tell his story, Milton chose a classic form, Euripidean tragedy, but the material he put into that form cannot but travesty what the form reveres.[18] Undermining the twin pillars of Aristotelian poetics and Christian historiography that were to hold it up, it brings the temple down, installing the memory of its ruins to mark the place where what will be was. It may be in this place, rather than any specifiable time, that we might best situate the postmodern moment.

Notes

1. *The Morgan Stanley Building,* 1 Pierrepont Street, Brooklyn, N.Y. Haines, Lundberg, Waehler, Architects. The building is owned by its developer, Forest City Development of Cleveland. The Morgan Stanley Bank is the principal tenant and the prime mover behind its construction. The neon circles are part of the building's lighting and are the responsibility of the owner, not the architect. In response to my inquiry, the architect's spokesperson reports that the roof was designed to "reference the skyline," that the material used is "just metal," and that copper or slate would have been preferred but are now too costly to use.

I would like to thank Ms. Jane Cohn of Haines, Lundberg, Waehler for her help and cooperation. Thanks are also extended to Bill Readings for suggesting the title of this essay.

2. "Modernity versus Postmodernity," *New German Critique* 22 (1981): 3–14.

3. Looking ahead to our discussion of Milton, we might take as an example the way in which the Reformation, in order to claim its continuity with the "primitive" Catholic church, situated the Roman church and its history as a corrupt parenthesis opened at the Constantinian Donation and now to be closed.

4. Thus, for example, this postmodern moment in politics: "Republican strategists believe that Reagan's popularity stemmed in part from the fact that by last fall he had become a nostalgic figure; by the time he left, he had in effect been gone for some time" (Elizabeth Drew, "Letter From Washington," *The New Yorker,* Feb. 27, 1989, p. 77).

5. Augustine catches this absence of memory to itself in the famous discourse on time in book 11 of the *Confessions:* "For if there be times past, and times to come; fain would I know where they be: which yet if I be not able to conceive, yet thus much I know, that wheresoever they now be, they are not there yet: if there also they be past, then are they not there still. Wheresoever therefore and whatsoever they be, they are not *but as present* [*non sunt nisi praesentia*]. Although as for things past, whenever true stories are related, out of the memory are drawn *not the things themselves which are past* [*non res ipsae, quae praeteriereunt*], but such words as being conceived by the images of those things [*sed verba concepta ex imaginibus earum*], they, in their passing through our senses, have, as their footsteps, left imprinted in our minds" (my emphasis). *St Augustine's Confessions,* trans. William Watts (1631), 2 vols., Loeb Classical Library (London: Heinemann, 1931), 2: 247–49.

6. William Shakespeare, *Hamlet,* ed. Edward Hubler (New York: New American Library, 1963), 1.2.76–86. Subsequent references are given parenthetically.

7. James Joyce, *A Portrait of the Artist as a Young Man* (London: Penguin, 1975), 253.

8. There is not space now to elaborate in a useful way the relationship of this identification of the self and its accumulated knowledge to the emergence of protocapitalist and then capitalist modes of production, but one could usefully refer to the discussion of *Areopagitica* in Christopher Kendrick, *Milton: A Study in Ideology and Form* (London: Methuen, 1986), 17–53, for the lineaments of such an argument.

9. For a discussion of the emergence and canonization of this specifically Shakespearean representation of the speaker as the subject of his or her own verbal duplicity, see Joel Fineman, *Shakespeare's Perjured Eye: The Invention of Poetic Subjectivity in the Sonnets* (Berkeley: Univ. of California Press, 1985).

10.

What is to be insisted upon is that the poet must develop or procure the consciousness of the past and that he should continue to develop this consciousness throughout his career.

What happens is a continual surrender of himself *as he is at the moment* to something which is more valuable. The *progress* of an artist is a continual self-sacrifice, a continual extension of personality.

. . . . I, therefore, invite you to consider, as a suggestive analogy, the action which takes place when a bit of finely filiated platinum is introduced into a chamber containing oxygen and sulphur dioxide.

"Tradition and the Individual Talent," in *Selected Essays*, new ed. (New York: Harcourt, Brace & World, 1960), 7–8 (my emphasis). See also, Eliot's comparison of the poet's mind to "a receptacle for seizing and storing up numberless feelings, phrases, images, which remain there until all the particles which can unite to form a new compound are present together" (Ibid., 8).

11. The appropriation of *The Murder of Gonzago* as the miraculous organ that makes Claudius speak what is in Hamlet's mind reduplicates the situation of *Hamlet*, an old story, known in the choice French of Belleforest, and appropriated to Shakespeare's uses from an earlier version, played on the London stage in the 1580s and now lost.

12. I argue the case for this reading of Milton in *Authors to Themselves: Milton and the Revelation of History* (Cambridge: Cambridge Univ. Press, 1987).

13. All citations of Milton refer to John Milton, *Complete Poetry and Major Prose*, ed. Merritt Y. Hughes (Indianapolis: Odyssey, 1957).

14. On the ideology of the Christian as post-Jew, see Marshall Grossman, "The Violence of the Hyphen in Judeo-Christian," *Social Text* 22 (1989): 115–22.

15. *Lives of the English Poets*, ed. George Birbeck Hill (Oxford: Clarendon, 1905), 1:189.

16. For scholarship on Samson's lack of trustworthiness, see Joseph Wittreich, *Samson Agonistes: An Essay on Interpretation* (Princeton: Princeton Univ. Press, 1985). Dr. Johnson's use of the adjective *blind* is particularly pointed, not just for its sly reference to Milton's affliction, but because it would be sight that, taking in its scene all at once, would perceive the lack of a unified design and challenge the continuity of a story presented to the ear. Recalling the Greek derivation of *theory* from *theorein*,

we could say that, lacking a visible set of causal relations to link episode to episode, Milton's tragedy remains insufficiently theorized.

17. "Spectacle and Evidence in *Samson Agonistes*," *Critical Inquiry* 15 (1989): 556–86.

18. To return one last time to Brooklyn: We might distinguish the pathos of blind strength in *Samson Agonistes* which, as Herman Rapaport has pointed out, mourns and celebrates the passing of classical tragedy along with the darkness of its hero (*Milton and the Postmodern* (Lincoln: Univ. of Nebraska Press, 1983) and the Morgan Stanley Building's bathetic assertiveness as two distinct modes of the postmodern, corresponding respectively to the reverent encomium and travesty execration modes of postepideictic nostalgia.

6

Milton at the Movies

An Afterword to *Paradise Lost*

BILL READINGS

Time is not what is lacking to consciousness. Time makes consciousness lack itself.

J. -F. Lyotard

What follows moves very fast, in order to raise a question about the modernist temporality of accelerated revelation. I run the risk that the price of that questioning is acceleration without revelation. Certainly, no enlightenment is proffered. In its place, I attempt to sketch some contours of what must become a larger reading of Milton, concentrating on the intersection of vision and femininity in the filmic and specifically concentrating on the temporality of the filmic: Milton's postmodernity lies in his relationship to time. In concentrating on the question of temporality, my turn to the movies leaves aside the vast corpus of theoretical work on film as narrative. I am not concerned with understanding the activity of film by means of the differentiation between story and discourse in the structuration of the succession of filmic signifiers, as in the exemplary works of Christian Metz, Seymour Chatman, Stephen Heath, or Linda Shires and Steven Cohan.[1] The visual projection of history in Milton's work does not quite fit this model, unenlightened as he was by the brothers Lumière. In order to understand why, we need to consider the difference between the cinematic account of "suture" and Milton's account of passivity.[2] If film theory gives us an experience of viewing in which interpellation is animated by the desire to see, Milton's is explicitly a cinematics of blindness, for Adam "now enforc'd to close his eyes," for Samson, for Milton himself in Sonnet 16 ("When I consider how my light is spent"). The analogy of contemporary film theory's developed analysis of the image does not apply to the filmic revelation at the end of *Paradise Lost*.

At which point, why call it a cinematics at all? Because the analogy of cinema is helpful insofar as it leads toward a phenomenology of temporal experience. Film theory has tended to elide the experience of watching by thinking the viewer inscribed within the filmic image, interpellated or sutured as a point in the apparatus. The viewer thus appears to theory as captured within, and captivated by, the apparatus to which he or she is blind. The alternative I wish to propose is not a sociology of reception but an attempt to think "they also serve who only sit and watch."[3] A phenomenology of the temporality of cinema is not an account of what it is really like to see a movie, but of the conditions of experience that cinema imposes. Hence my titular preference for "movies" over film: the apparatus does not simply impose a meaning on the viewer, it implies a viewing.[4]

In the case of Milton's epic, it is very hard to pin down any particular experience of reception at all. The postmodernity of *Paradise Lost*, as opposed to any presumptive intention to ignore history, lies in the fact that the Fall itself appears as an unaccountable event. That the Fall doesn't "take place" either in eternity or in history becomes apparent to anyone who tries to teach *Paradise Lost* to undergraduates accustomed to cliff-hangers. Students are always better readers than one thinks, and tend almost unerringly to ask, "Where's the beef?" In a poem supposedly about the Fall, the "central" event simply isn't narrated as a climax. This is not merely the effect of our preoccupations: it is marked as anticlimactic within the text.

After the Fall, at the beginning of the modern times that Milton's writing inhabits, comes history. More precisely, history as the modernist account of the temporality of the movies: Adam's vision. The importance of the cinematic quality of the revelation given to Adam lies in the kind of temporal discipline it imposes on the eye, an eye that blinks at twenty-four frames per second and yet calls this a stable or uninterrupted vision.[5] Then, lest this modernist temporality become too material, the eye is closed and the project explicitly inscribed elsewhere, within the soul of man. In each case, it remains an explicitly historical project of revelation. Meaning as such, truth itself, will be revealed at the Second Coming of Christ, when Christ will be a pure signified, "all in all," without further use for any material signifier of his power.

> Then thou thy regal sceptre shalt lay by
> For regal sceptre then no more shall need,
> God shall be all in all.[6]

Note the erasure not merely of the material marks of power but also of worldly subjectivity. Christ will lay himself "by" along with his sceptre, entering into the passive anonymity of "no more shall [be] need[ed]," moving from "shalt" to "shall," "all in all" *as* God rather than merely *with* God. Until then, we have to make do with worldly signifiers, which speak truly only insofar as they do not dazzle us with their tinsel trappings, only insofar as they make us aware at the same time both of truth and of the historical deferral of that truth.[7] Thus, even if the eye is relinquished in the transition between books eleven and twelve of *Paradise Lost*, the modernist version of the temporality of the filmic is retained, in that the revelation of "a paradise within thee, happier far" (12.587) is achieved through the contemplation of historical sequence.

Milton's poetic project imagines the opening of modernity at the historical moment of the genesis of the capitalist nation state. A displacement of this project, a displacement I call either postmodern or poetic, takes place as the work of *Paradise Lost* evokes, willy-nilly, the problematic of the event against the claim to lend meaning to the succession of moments. And it would only be by virtue of a modernist conception of temporal succession (of time as a succession of discrete moments linked by an understanding of history as meaningful project) that is irrelevant here that we might be tempted to call Milton prescient. My account of Milton's postmodernity shares Herman Rapaport's sense of a destabilization of the relationship of language to meaning.[8] However, Milton's poetic work is not simply the negative moment of the modernist project; it is the radical disturbance of an assured relationship between language and time. Milton, that is, is not Saussurean *avant la lettre*, but one who, by virtue of a certain poetic labor, poses the question that the letter may have no *avant*, who insists upon the difficulty of the time of writing, the irreducibility of the event of writing to the modernist writing (description) of the event within the framework of a single history. In what follows I focus on the play at work in both the filmic and the figure of enjambment as an example of the way in which *Paradise Lost* is divided between two temporalities, modern and postmodern.

The time of modernism is that of a sequence or succession of moments, the time of the new, organized as a project of universalization. The potential achievement of universalization in *Paradise Lost* is the time of heaven. The link between modernism and heaven depends upon the opening of moments to the possibility of being thought in terms of universal concepts. Meanwhile, modernism is the moment of capitalism, in that the rule of the market is the rule of universal exchangeability grounding the project of total emancipation.[9] The currency or universal language of the capitalist market is time. Production is valued as labor time; capital is stocked or stored labor time. This allows us to understand why the service industry is capitalized as "*fast* food." Capitalism's contradiction is thus the simultaneous drive to "gain time" while understanding time as value: hence the paradox of "saving time"—where does time go when it has been "saved"? This contradiction drives the system in that time must be saved but can not be spent. That is, time is "gained" when capital accrues surplus value. Time can only be "stored" as more capital. To store time as capital, however, does not balance things, but speeds them up more. Capital is not stored labor so much as stored time, the application of which results in exponential acceleration. Computer technology is the organization of energy as pure temporal switching: the best computer is the one that works fastest. Matter becomes information (e.g., electric money, "sound bites") as it is reduced to the most minimal temporal elements, a succession of pulses (on/off, 1/0). Capitalism should thus be defined as the drive to accountable time.

A resistance would have to introduce a temporal alterity, an unaccountable time. In the philosophical work of Lyotard, this is the time of the event; for textual studies, this is the time of reading (as opposed to all hermeneutical devices for extracting meaning in the shortest time possible).[10] Reading is not a Luddite resistance to the world, but an insistence on the literary event as irreducible to an exchangeable moment. Insofar as it is the rigorously thought temporality of the future anterior ("it will have been"), reading opens the possibility of just such an unaccountable time. The taking place of the event must be thought as incommensurable to the commodification of the event as moment. The determination of the meaning of an event recuperates it as a moment in the development of a structure or system, and the distinction of event from moment is that the event as such cannot be commodified in this sense (represented by a determinate concept): it is unaccountable. Milton's resistance to the modernity of rhyme introduces the undecidability of enjambment and insists on just such an unaccountable temporality. Postmodernism would thus be the possibility of reading Milton's temporality as more than either reactionary eschatology or the false modernity of chiliasm's project for a new age through worldly failure and heavenly millennium.

I can only sketch this problematic at the broad thematic level in Milton, as the problem of time thought as a simple succession of moments, the time of the movies, both within the narrative of *Paradise Lost* and in the time introduced in the last three books. Denis Danielson, in *Milton's Good God*, points out that prelapsarian Eden is ameliorative.[11] In our terms, Eden is a modernist project: obedience and good gardening would cause Adam and Eve to rise to the status of the lower angels and so on up the ladder, "by gradual scale sublimed." Adam and Eve are to be rewarded for giving a good account of their time. The Fall puts an end to that: the fallen world is "postmodern," in the sense of the modernist critique.

The condemnation to history is thus to a pointless succession. The history into which man falls is a postmodern temporality, an endless treadmill of struggle. Michael informs Adam that he must leave Paradise for quite another kind of agricultural labor.

to remove thee I am come,
And send thee from the garden forth to till
The ground whence thou wast taken, fitter soil. (*PL*, 11.260–62)

Adam must now work upon the very soil out of which he was created and that is thus more suited to him. And however hard he may work, however much he may till the soil to make it "fitter," it will remain the same soil from which he came. He is condemned to work to transform the earth, to make it fitter, and at the same time to stay where he is, not to progress from the point at which he began. The paradox of postlapsarian labor is to toil without hope of actual improvement. Work thus changes to take its place in a history that is mere succession, without any hope of meaning as a result of accumulation. History simply happens, again and again, without adding up to anything, in meaningless contiguity. This is a world of deferral, not simply of dispersal, since the originary or concluding term is radically displaced.

The effect of the last two books of *Paradise Lost*, with their historical vision, is to return man to Edenic modernity. The difference is that in Eden mankind gained in the direct presence of godhead, grew more godlike. The revelation of divine truth took place in man. In modern times the revelation of divine truth is indirect because it is historically mediated. Godhead is not revealed simply in the world, for the world is fallen and "venial discourse unblamed" (*PL*, 9.5) is impossible. Divine truth can only be understood by contemplation of wider historical processes. Now we can understand why the Bible is understood by Milton as preeminently historical, as "written *records* pure" (*PL*, 12.513).

What I want to do is affirm postmodernity, a world of reading, of unaccountable time, by distinguishing between the poetic work that *Paradise Lost* performs and the conceptual result that the poem enjoins as its project. The latter is the revelation of divine truth. The former is a transformative evocation of materiality, a labor. My own endeavors can thus be understood as materialist—if we recognize that the resistant complexities of materiality and history are betrayed in the conceptual reductions effected by any historical materialism. In fact, historical materialism stands on the side of Milton's modernist historical project, except that it seeks to inscribe the proletariat in the place of the divinity that is Milton's revealed "truth of history." My argument thus resists Milton's use of God, or Kerrigan's of the unconscious, to explain away literary postmodernity as an effect of something else.[12] Both amount to recuperating the loss of origin by appeal to another, true, origin. Milton offers God in place of human endeavor, Kerrigan offers the unconscious in the place of Milton's intended deity.

Thus we begin with the Fall in *Paradise Lost* as a fall into history that itself has no history; the immediate postlapsarian condition is to be embroiled in history without content, in a meaningless succession of events. There is no metanarrative. The history into which Adam and Eve fall is thus a postmodern temporality. The only resolution of succession is an end of history that will reduce temporality to meaning as history. Yet it cannot take place, it cannot succeed. To serve the end of history is to stand and wait, with a passive constancy that is not part of the history upon which it waits. Thus, the poem passes from an atemporal fall into temporality to a temporality that can only wait upon the atemporal.

Adam and Eve fall, and once they lose the inital "high" brought on by the fruit, they fall to "fruitless" argument. This is different from their contretemps before the Fall (concerning separation) in that it is a disagreement wagered against time, *contre temps*.

> Thus they in mutual accusation spent
> The fruitless hours, but neither self-condemning,
> And of their vain contest appeared no end. (*PL*, 9.1187–89)

Book nine ends with "no end": the conditon of the fall is endless succession. Book ten begins with "Meanwhile," and lines 1–229 discuss the reaction of Heaven to the Fall. Another opening "meanwhile" at line 229 introduces the response of the forces of Hell to the Fall. Our attention is then switched back to Sin and Death with another "mean while" at 585. Meanwhile, God is watching, and at 613 he intervenes with a running commentary on the actions of the hellish pair. The angels sing "while the creator" (649) orders several of them to alter the constitution of the earth so that it will be subject to change, to the temporal passage of weather and seasons. Then we turn at line 715 to Adam and Eve's responses to the changes, which are clearly ordered in temporal succession: "whom thus afflicted *when* sad Eve beheld" (863). There is a movement from things happening all at once in the superhuman sphere to the succession of events on Earth. Time is now accounted for, synthesized in order to be understood in terms of meaning, only in heaven. This reverses the synthetic fusion of temporal difference traced in the description of the Creation (which was also introduced with a "mean while" at 6.192).

Books eleven and twelve consist of historical synopsis, making clear that the Fall is a fall into the predicament of temporality, into history as predicament. They seek to resolve this predicament as History, as the progressive revolution of a deferred meaning, a truth that is not present in the succession of events but animates it from elsewhere—a metaphysics. And yet the Fall as pivotal event cannot be accounted for, cannot be related as history, in *Paradise Lost*. The original moment that might lend meaning to history itself is outside history. The Fall cannot take place in any history it inaugurates.

The Fall thus marks the passage from accountable to unaccountable, postlapsarian, postmodern time. This might seem to make *Paradise Lost* a manual for the avoidance of postmodernity. Except that the Fall itself takes place unaccountably. The division between modernist and postmodernist time is itself unaccountable. The dismissal of postmodernism as merely the nihilistic succession of images, presided over by women, as "effeminate slackness" (*PL*, 11.634), is one we hear from Habermas in our day as from Milton in his. Yet that reading from within modernism (for Habermas) or from the side of Heaven (for Milton) can only render its account of postmodernity by forgetting the quality of the event that must divide modernism's universal present from itself. That event is the time of the new, the "it happens" that cannot be accounted for by the universal present meaning that the project of modernism must inaugurate. Milton must think this unaccountable event in reverse, as it were, in the Fall that marks the end of Edenic modernism and that will itself be reversed at the Second Coming.

To return to the opening of this essay, the Fall is an unnarratable event. As we've seen, the Fall has consequences in Heaven, Hell, and Earth, but it is not itself an event of epic dimensions. This is not simply because "Lady Eats Fruit: Everything

Changes" is poor headline material, but because of the structure of the Fall as an event: it is an event without content; it takes place in no time. One is here close to Christopher Kendrick's wide-ranging analysis of Milton's use of suspense, in noting that *Paradise Lost* cannot be a suspense narrative because the Fall is suspended.[13]

The divided, self-differing temporality of the Fall is apparent if we try to pin down its occurrence. When Eve eats the fruit, Nature marks the fall with "signs of woe" (*PL*, 9.783) that Eve disregards, just as Adam does when nature gives a "second groan" (9.1001) at his own fall. The voice of nature canot be heard at the time it speaks of the Fall. Afterwards, when they become aware of what they have done, they turn to an explicitly "fruitless" argument (9.1188). The pun points not only to the loss of the psychotropic effects of the fruit, but also to the extent to which they are removed from the moment of the Fall, plunged into the temporality that succeeds it. The Fall occurs as the failure to bear fruit, the failure of the moment to ripen in its season. Thus, the Fall can only be known in another place, in another book, "meanwhile" in Heaven in book ten. So it is that only in book eleven do the couple begin to take cognizance of the Fall. Nature's sighs have been strangely incommunicative, and more signs are given: a hunter chasing a pair of creatures appears both in the sky and on the ground. These signs constitute a "double object" that bears the meaning of the Fall and yet they are explicitly "mute" (9.194). First nature groaned but spoke without content and went unheard. Now nature is mute, gives silent signs, and the meaning of the Fall can be interpreted. Either the Fall is given a voice that says nothing, bears no meaning, or the Fall is spoken, supplies mute or silent signs that can be understood after the event, in the discourse of another. Furthermore, although Eve provokes the signs, Adam must interpret them before they are "shown" to her, in the words of the Argument.[14] The signs become visible to their cause only in a doubly mediated after-time. Nature is silent, after the Fall: the production of signs is explicitly divided from the moment of their understanding. The content or meaning of the Fall can appear only after the event in signs that are "mute" and thus postdated by their own understanding.

To sum up, the Fall has no content, at the time. And when it has content, it has no time. In the same way, the "sin / Original" is not complete until it is repeated. The word "Original" occurs only in the description of the second consumption. And the "sin original" condemns man to temporality as repetition of sin. That temporality is itself without origin, since the Fall is not an event but the beginning of repetition and succession as such. And this history has no origin, no first case that is not already marked by repetition: by the time the Fall is original, it has already taken place. As we have seen, the text gets quite confusing about the first signs of the Fall. Likewise there is a problem about when God judges the Fall: either the promised judgment and sentence of death takes place as a moment without content (punishment is delayed) or it has content (instant death) yet does not take place (the moment is delayed).

The temporality into which mankind falls is filmic. It is postmodern in that history is the site of representation as distinct from reference: history as a field of simulacra. If for films to represent history would be modernist, postmodernity offers the movie as a sterile or fragmentary temporal succession. In *Paradise Regained* cinematic projection appears as a Satanic device, working in the demonic element of air. In *Paradise Lost,* although the projection may be an "object divine," it is distinguished by the fact that Adam necessarily misreads it: it must "needs impair" human sense, and that impairment is linked to the seduction of visual representation, appearing as the figure of woman. This seductive temporality is gendered: women appear frequently in the film of book eleven; history takes place entirely between men in book twelve.

A visuality that appears as a disconcerting remainder over the prophetic vision of truth is constantly at issue for Milton. This is perhaps unsurprising for the man to whom his daughters read in his blindness, the man for whom the mediation of women came to mark the loss of vision. Adam misunderstands the women he sees, Samson has to be blinded before he can deal with Dalila properly, Eve is seduced by her own image in the pool in book four. She must be admonished to turn from the simulacrum to the substance. Visuality raises an uncanny difference, that of sex, which must be erased in order for genders to fall into the correct ratio. Eve sees herself in the pool and falls in love, Narcissus-like. The voice admonishes her to turn to Adam, but initially rejects him as less "soft" than the "smooth watery image" (*PL,* 4.479–80). She is admonished again, this time by Adam, and acquiesces, finding in him "substantial life" (*PL*, 4.485). What is the difference that arbitrates this choice between two objects? Eve is made in the image of Adam, "manlike, but different sex" (*PL*, 8.471). Sexual difference is thus a difference between two things that are "like," and Eve's choice is between the male substance whose image she is, and her own image, the image of an image, the simulacrum. Adam, as substance, is less visible than Eve, and the lessening of visibility is the opening of humanity to its true substance. The vision of Adam to which she cleaves is the rejection of visuality for substance.

> with that thy gentle hand
> Seized mine, I yielded, and from that time see
> How beauty is excelled by manly grace
> And wisdom, which alone is truly fair. (*PL*, 4.488–91)

What she "sees" is how not to see, how to reject visuality for the grasp of substance. The vision of truth is an optics of blindness, as Adam finds when Raphael closes his eyes so that he may understand history. Thus Satan's flattery of Eve is different from the general respect accorded to humanity by animals in that it consists of praising her as a representation; he makes her accept her appearance as truth, take her representation for the reality of her status. His offer is that the fruit will make her a God. This is explicitly set up in his initial praise of her as "Fairest *resemblance* of thy maker fair" (*PL*, 9.538).

The Fall is the product of Eve's deciding that she is equal with a God (and may eat the fruit), and the effect of the fruit is that Eve thinks she has become a God. For Eve to think herself a God is not just hubris, it is the confusion of her appearance, her image (made in the image of God), with what she is: she comes to think herself a "goddess among gods" (*PL*, 9.547). As she says to Adam, she finds her fruit-filled self "growing up to godhead" (*PL*, 9.877). Hence Fowler's emendation of "eat" to "ate" in his Longman's edition at 781 seems to me infelicitous, precisely because the verb is stressed. The early editions of *Paradise Lost* give us the actual report of the Fall as marked by an eye rhyme.

> So saying, her rash hand in evil hour
> Forth reaching to the fruit, she plucked, she [eat]:
> Earth felt the wound, and nature from her seat (*PL*, 9.780–83)

The transgression of the Fall introduces a transgressive rhyme into this explicitly unrhymed poem. And rhyme enters at the level of the visual, of the text considered as visual rather than discursive artifact.[15] The Fall is an eye rhyme, a transgressive leap placed within the field of vision. And this transgression into visibility is also its effect. The serpent tells Eve that after eating the fruit he "Considered all things visible in heaven" (PL, 9.604). The possibility of this line as endstopped marks the effect of the Fall. Eve is seduced by the serpent because he leads her to "consider all things visible," to understand all things in heaven or earth in terms of their visibility—to mistake the represented appearance of things for their reality. And when Eve doubts, the serpent replies, "*look* on me" (PL, 9.687). Her eyes will be opened, but the internal eye that reads the text of divine prohibition will be shut: the opening of eyes is not a gain in knowledge but a fixing of knowledge at the false level of mere seeming, mere representation. As at the pool, so in the Fall, Eve is tempted by representation to understand herself within a field of representation, to take her own appearance as her reality. This is the threat of visible history (movies) to historical vision (understanding) that woman represents (as herself) throughout Milton's oeuvre.

The postmodern temporality of the fallen world, the succession of simulacra without origin or closure, is the time of movies insofar as they present the figure of woman to the eye. At this point woman becomes no longer the image of man, but makes a claim to represent herself. To put it another way, woman loses interest in the substantial rule of reality so as to behave as if she were real, an "as if" that opens meaning to the seductive play of tropes. Eve at the pool makes the mistake of understanding Adam and her reflection as both images of herself and of choosing the one most like her, and most like an image, the "smooth" reflection, not the rough Adam. She is more like the reflection because she is herself an image, of Adam. To choose her reflection is to choose the simulacrum, the image of an image. The monstrous regiment of woman is the rule of the image, *eikon* become *basilike*. We can thus hear "basilisk" in *basilike* and think Milton's feminized Charles I as Medusa. The rule of woman is the placement of the image as center in a world divorced from origin: history become the succession of images detached from the underpinning of a first instance.

The link between women and an unhistorical visuality (the condition, after all, of literary theory) is reinforced in the visibility of the "fair bevy" of women and the error they induce in Adam as he responds to events with "the taste / Of lustful appetance" (*PL*, 11.617) rather than knowing them historically, in context. After the Flood, when God introduces the historical consciousness of a project by making a promise, women disappear and history takes place between men, as it is related in discourse between men. So Adam mistakes the movie he is shown, fails to understand it by virtue of his seeing it. And that failure to understand is an effect of the visibility of woman, her excess over the vision of truth.

Woman as pure image (subjectivity defined by the image of a subject) occupies a visual field divorced from the substantial meaning that inhabits the potentiality of the divine Word: she is the figure of history as a predicament for linguistic signification. The visual, that is, marks the potentiality of signification as mere appearance divorced from real being, the play of signifiers divorced from substantial signified meaning. History is a linguistic predicament in that it is constitutively misunderstood: if history is taken as real it is misunderstood. History, woman, the visual are tropes of the condition of a discourse, a language, that does not participate in being, that is not proper to meaning.[16]

The shift to angelic dictation in book twelve is accompanied by two other moves: from history as temporal succession or filmic sequence to the passion of patience; from the seductive figure of woman to the steadfastness of ignorance. *Paradise Lost* offers three solutions to this representational predicament: the forgetting of women; the return from the visual field to the Word; and the proleptic understanding of the end of history through waiting. Forgetting women and waiting are more properly effects of the acceptance of the rule of the Word. The change from vision to narration in book twelve brings history under the aegis of a divinely inspired Word that suppresses the (visual) surface effects of historical appearance.

> the rest
> Were long to tell, how many battles fought,
> How many kings destroyed, and kingdoms won, (*PL*, 12.260–63)

Instead of the play of historical succession, the Word focuses on the ahistorical truth of the end of history. Adam responds to Michael's reduction of historical events as a relief from the predicament of history.

> now first I find
> Mine eyes true opening and my heart much eased,
> Erewhile perplexed with thoughts what would become
> Of me and all mankind; but now I see
> His day, in whom all nations shall be blest, (*PL,* 12.273–77)

Adam is no longer perplexed by becoming. The giving up of the visual has been the *first* "true" opening of his eyes in rejection of the dazzling play of historical surface in favor of the awareness of the apocalyptic end of history, the day that will mark the end. The eyes are opened truly only when we stop looking at images, at women, at temporal succession. And this opens the solution to the representational predicament of history—waiting. They also serve who only stand and wait in steadfast ignorance of the unaccountable temporality of postlapsarian history, of women, of images, accepting only the accountable. The temporality of the eye, caught up by the figure of woman, is rejected in the shift to the biblical word in book twelve, yet returns as the strange time of the poetic word variously subject to endstopping or enjambment.

As we have seen, the Fall cannot be accounted for, and thus displaces the possibility that postmodern temporality can simply be ignored as "of no account," since the division of the unaccountable from the accountable project of modernism is itself both necessary for, and unaccountable by, modernist time. The Fall is a pocket of unaccountable time that refuses the rejection of unaccountable time as merely "fallen." Nor is this merely one error: the time of reading that the Word inhabits is itself irreducible to an accounting in terms of originary or final meaning. And *Paradise Lost* stages the unaccountability of the time of reading the Word in the necessary undecidability of the temporality of enjambment, of the poetic "membrane, joint, or limb" that presumably does not affect the tongues of angels, whether functioning sexually or poetically (*PL,* 8.625).

A schematic example: Milton introduces the fallen angels in book one at what looks like the inception of a project. His statement seems to close off the possibility of revisionary reading that has been at the forefront of critical troubles at least since Blake.

> Though of their names in heavenly records now
> Be no memorial blotted out and razed
> By their rebellion, from the books of life.
> Nor had they yet among the sons of Eve
> Got them new names, till wandering o'er the earth. (*PL*, 1.361–65)

In what time are we, *in medias res?* After the past, before the future. This would seem to be the universal present in which modernism forms and grounds its projects, the now that may engender the new. And yet the time of a reading does not inhabit this present. We are not, it seems, reading the book of present life (if we were, we might question even the anonymous presence of the demons). To inhabit the time of the present would allow the reading of line 362 as endstopped, in the absence of punctuational guidance.[17] And so, against all reason, sense, and theology, the wild optative arises: "[Let there] Be no memorial blotted out and razed." Nor can this be dismissed as a merely incidental aberration, given the way in which play between enjambment and endstopping is crucial to the possibility that the deity may stand as both synchronically and diachronically revealed in the poem, as in the appearance of God to Messiah in book six.

> He said, and on his Son with rays direct
> Shone full, he all his Father full expressed
> Ineffably into his face received. (*PL*, 6.719–21)

Again there is an absence of punctuation that allows the lines to offer both the endstopped revelation by Christ in the world ("he all his Father full expressed") and the incarnation of divine meaning in Christ, read by enjambment ("he all his father full expressed / Ineffably into his face received"). The incarnation and revelation of divine meaning are "simultaneously" present. And yet that simultaneity can only be recovered in the posterior temporality of a divided reading, a reading that is divided by giving two different times (the endstopped and the run-on) to the lines. In order to present meaning in the unified moment, the troubling temporality of reading must be forgotten. The decision "between" at least two readings cannot be made in a unified moment of reading. The relationship between reader and text is displaced. Something is happening. And it must be allowed to happen before it can become clear what will have happened. To proffer a comprehension of the text that simply determined what happened would be unjust to the text as event. Milton seeks to introduce an idea of deity that will fuse the text as both object (what happens—description) and process (the happening of the event). The effect of this is that *Paradise Lost* finds itself as constitutively failed prophecy, prophecy that can be said to have succeeded insofar as it is out of joint with its time. This is the fissure around which William Kerrigan has read the text.[18] In an age too late for prophecy, Kerrigan and others find a new deity for humanism in the unconscious. This seems to me a very faithful reading. It also seems wrong, because it effectively forecloses the text as event by reducing it to the effect of another object, a grounding ahistorical nature, producing temporality as a flawed fiction.

Postmodernity means the possibility of reading the text as an event that will not be foreclosed, of reading the problematic temporality of the literary work as not an effect of anything other to itself. Rather than having an origin elsewhere, it may be that the event-effect, which we shall name literary for now, is the recognition of temporality as a process of deferral that the thought of origin can only belie or betray. The rage of philosophers and priests against literature, that is, may itself be an effect of the extent to which the time of textuality is divided in a way that resists the determination of becoming as an effect of being, history as an effect of origin or conclusion, the event as an effect of meaning.

Literature thus demands that there can be no invocation of originary intention (even unconscious) or final solution that will decide between enjambment and endstopping, between the structures of meaning in which an event may participate, because the event as such does not participate in a structure of meaning, but is radically incommensurable with such understandings. Judgment is demanded, but it is never given in advance. The letter can have no

avant. Its event places judgment as inevitably posterior. That troubling or divided temporality, which is that of the postmodern or
future anterior, of what "will have been" said, is the product of the
extent to which the performative event of writing cannot finally be
determined as the content of the descriptive writing of the event. We
can never finally say what *Paradise Lost* means, because it issues a
demand that we say that. This demand constitutes the possibility of
its meaning at all, but can never be part of that meaning. The moment of understanding may be made the matter of another history,
but that history can never be its own, can never occupy the temporality it orders and disposes. This temporal self-division is more
than a corrective to pretensions to total historical knowledge; it insists that the poem is realized as literature by certain writing effects
which that project both requires and is unable to account for. To read
Paradise Lost is to pay attention to what cannot be said or written,
yet is necessarily being said or written: that the devils' names must
not be blotted out, for instance. "History" is one name that has been
applied in an attempt to reduce this non-self-identity within language. The poetic work of *Paradise Lost* is postmodern in that it does
not claim either language or history as originary.

Notes

1. Christian Metz, *Psychoanalysis and Cinema: The Imaginary Signifier,* trans. C.
Britton, A. Williams, B. Brewster, and A. Guzzeti (London: Macmillan, 1982); Seymour
Chatman, *Story and Discourse: Narrative Structure in Fiction and Film* (Ithaca, N.Y.:
Cornell Univ. Press, 1978); Stephen Heath, *Questions of Cinema* (Bloomington: Indiana
Univ. Press, 1981); Steven Cohan and Linda Shires, *Telling Stories* (New York: Methuen,
1989).

2. On "suture," see Heath, *Questions of Cinema,* 76–113.

3. Milton, Sonnet 26, line 14: "They also serve who only stand and wait."

4. I give this sense to the term "movie" following Stanley Cavell, whose
Pursuits of Happiness (Cambridge, Mass.: Harvard Univ. Press, 1981) understands
cinema without thinking the philosophical implications of the apparatus in purely
formal terms.

5. As Jean-François Lyotard puts it in "L'Acinéma," "To write in movements,
to be a cinematographer, is conceived and practiced as an incessant organization of
movements. Spatial localization is governed by the rules of representation, the
instantiation of language by the rules of narration, sound-time by the form of 'film-

music.' The so-called impression of reality is a real oppression of orders [of experience]," *Des Dispositifs Pulsionnels* (Paris: Bourgois, 1980), 52 (my translation).

6. Milton, *Paradise Lost,* ed. A. Fowler (London: Longman, 1971), 3.339–41. All further quotations are from this edition, referred to henceforth as *PL.*

7. See Marshall Grossman, *Authors to Themselves* (Cambridge: Cambridge Univ. Press, 1987), for an extensive and lucid account of the thematics of historical revelation in *Paradise Lost.*

8. Herman Rapaport, *Milton and The Postmodern* (Lincoln: Univ. of Nebraska Press, 1983).

9. In his afterword to this volume, Bruce Robbins dismisses the notion that there is anything "inherently capitalistic about the rationality of counting or accountability." My claim here is slightly weaker than the one he imputes to me: to say that capitalism is the economics of accounting is like saying that the USA is the land of the motor car, which denies neither that cars exist elsewhere nor that Americans may at times have recourse to other modes of transport. Drawing on sect. 4 of chap. 1 of vol. 1 of *Capital,* I think that the capitalist mode of commodification rests upon the imposition of exchange value as the universal abstract form of value. Thus commodities, if they could speak, would say "we relate to each other merely as exchange-values" (Karl Marx, *Capital: A Critique of Political Economy,* trans. Ben Fowkes [London: Penguin, 1976], 177). Like Marx, I'm inclined to turn to the literary example of Defoe's *Robinson Crusoe* to find capitalist man characterized as a bookkeeper, the logical result of believing that value speaks the universal language of exchange (170). The process of commodification and capitalist exchange, as Marx analyzes it, is nothing less than the translation of all human social relations into the universal language of exchange value to allow "the common expression of all commodities in money" (168), money being thought as the "universal equivalent form" (183). This is less an argument against "counting" per se than against the notion of a universal language that might permit total accountability. This does put me at odds with traditional Marxism's tendency to invoke "history" as such a universal language.

10. On Lyotard and the event, see the introduction to this volume.

11. Denis Danielson, *Milton's Good God* (Cambridge: Cambridge Univ. Press, 1979).

12. William Kerrigan, *The Sacred Complex* (Cambridge, Mass.: Harvard Univ. Press, 1983), passim.

13. Christopher Kendrick, *Milton: A Study in Ideology and Form* (New York: Routledge, 1986), 215.

14. "Adam shows to Eve certain ominous signs" (Argument to book 11).

15. Fowler does claim, in defense of his emendation, that the word may have been pronounced "et", which perhaps allows some assonance between "eat" and "seat". However, the rhyme is primarily visible (John Milton, *Paradise Lost,* ed. Alastair Fowler, 484n.).

16. Here I find myself in substantial agreement with Marshall Grossman's argument that modern subjectivity is divided between appearance and Being, in his essay, "The Hyphen in the Mouth of Modernity," in the present collection, 75–87.

17. Stephen Orgel and Jonathan Goldberg do supply a comma after "memorial," presumably because they feel that the original is "patently incorrect, . . . confusing or misleading," since these are the criteria for emendation that they quote (Orgel and Goldberg, eds. *John Milton* in the Oxford Authors series [Oxford: Oxford Univ. Press, 1990], xxxi).

18. Kerrigan, *The Sacred Complex,* esp. 3–8.

Part Three

The Postmodern Eighteenth Century

7

A Discourse of One's Own

Thomas DiPiero

D anny DeVito's film *The War of the Roses* depicts scenes of brutal domestic violence accompanying the divorce proceedings of Oliver and Barbara Rose, played by Michael Douglas and Kathleen Turner. Unable to reach a mutually satisfactory property settlement, the Roses continue to share the mansion they inhabited during their marriage, mapping out color-coded regions to designate private and common territory. The initially acrimonious verbal wars between the Roses mount to sadistic physical violence as each attempts to persuade the other to give up the house. Food fights and verbal abuse give way to full-scale war in which ordinary domestic objects, automobiles and trucks, and even the family pets serve as weapons to destroy tens of thousands of dollars worth of property and, finally, the Roses themselves.

One might consider *The War of the Roses* an example of black slapstick comedy that, thanks to increasing studio budgets and technological advances, escalates the classic pie fight into full-scale commodity wars endangering not only clothing, coiffures, and dignity but real estate and human life as well. One might also draw parallels between *The War of the Roses* and other films such as *Fatal Attraction* and *Ruthless People* that depict relationships gone awry and the violent excess of women who are every bit as capable as their male partners of maiming and killing. Two features distinguish *The War of the Roses* from cinematic slapstick physicality and tales of marital strife, however. The first of these features is the steadfast refusal of Turner's character to allow her own voice and desire to be stifled by her husband's financial or sexual blackmail. The second is the relegation of the film's principal narrative—the story of the Roses' divorce and the domestic violence that leads ultimately to their deaths—to a series of flashbacks: the Roses' tale is told by their attorney (played by DeVito) to a voiceless young man who has come to him seeking a separation from his wife. These two distinctive features compete to legitimize conflicting ideological positions in the film. On the one hand, Barbara Rose gets the last word in the lawyer's story. This extenuates her use of violence as the only means available to her of making herself heard. On the other hand, by putting the tale into the lawyer's hands, the film undermines the legitimation of Barbara's violence and mocks her attempt to dispute the universality of reason that ascribes to her a position that she rejects outright.

I plan to confront Mme. de Lafayette's *La Princesse de Clèves*, a novel published in 1678 and the object of a modicum of critical scorn, with DeVito's *The War of the Roses*. This confrontation is not simply a comparison. It will not be a question here merely of epitomizing synthetic similarities between the two narratives in order to allow the texts to speak to one another across the gulf of three centuries. Instead, I attempt to discover what process of abstraction within the narrative production of knowledge in Madame de Lafayette's time led to the construction of a master narrative in which the human subjects taking part in that narrative were reduced to generic individuals whose lack of differentiation legitimized one of the dominant discursive modes of the seventeenth century. I turn to DeVito's film to show how the suppression of a particular voice in *The War of the Roses*, specifically that of Barbara Rose, reveals in its censorship the point of articulation of a congruent voice in *La Princesse de Clèves*, a voice that failed to speak not because it was not permitted to but because it did not yet have a language. Mme. de Clèves is a young woman who dreads the possibility of resembling other women, and her refusal to speak their language ultimately costs her her life. Mme. de Lafayette's contemporaries interpreted the princess's death as the result of an admirable if incomprehensible faithfulness to her dead husband's memory. I will argue that her demise signaled a refusal to be assimilated into the economy of male desire—an argument others have already made[1]—but that it also expressed the concomitant repudiation of the subject constructed as a figure of equivalence uniting specifically aristocratic individuals. *The War of the Roses* ironically invokes history in its mutation of the feud between the houses of Lancaster and York in fifteenth-century England into a feud over a house in the United States in 1989. Its nominal appropriation of history correlates a similarly titular arrogation of history and its uses in *La Princesse de Clèves*. I argue that both works rupture unilinear constructions of historical knowledge in order to dispute specific sites of subjectivity and epistemology.[2]

The Roses begin their eventually tortured existence together when Oliver Rose spots the beautiful young Barbara and, taken with her beauty, pursues her and wins her.[3] The film chronicles their life together from their impoverished but romantic life on a law student's budget to their acrimonious coexistence in the regal splendor of the stately mansion they finally die fighting over. As the narrative progresses, the Roses' positions are more and more clearly demarcated: he is the rising young and articulate professional and she is the uncultivated and directionless housewife who dedicates her energies to the house (and later to a fairly successful home catering business). Oliver never listens to his wife: he asks her questions and ignores her responses; incites her to relate anecdotes in front of his senior colleagues and then, embarassed at her inarticulateness, takes over for her; and, perhaps most crucially, he will not take no for an answer when he wants to have sex and she does not. It is Barbara who lands the first blow in the film, but only after being goaded to do so by her husband (he refuses to let her verbal responses frustrate his desire). In one of the film's most violent scenes, the two wind up in each other's arms after a brutal fight; Oliver begins sexual foreplay and his wife resists. When he continues, however, she feigns interest and kisses him on the shoulders and chest, continuing downward until her head moves out of the frame. Suddenly, the look of pleasure on Oliver's face turns to one of excruciating pain. Barbara then wheels him around on his back and pushes him headlong down a flight of stairs. Landing at the bottom, Oliver collects himself and asks, "Was it good for you?"

Oliver's question is clearly charged with irony yet it reveals his adamant refusal to accept even the most unambiguous of his wife's responses. By responding to Barbara's unequivocal refusal to have sex with him with the archetypically banal "Was it good for you?" Oliver effectively denies that they did *not* have sex and he affirms the ascendancy of his own desire in the encounter. Unwilling to accept Barbara's responses unless they happen to coincide with his own, Oliver persists literally until his dying breath in expecting his wife to respond in programmatic fashion to his demands. The final sequence in the Rose story, however, gives her the last word. Oliver and Barbara are perched precariously on their crystal chandelier. When the fixture gives way, they plunge to their deaths and finish their battle lying in a crumpled heap amid broken glass. Oliver struggles to place an affectionate hand on Barbara's shoulder, and with her last energy she removes it.

Although the close of the Roses' story gives Barbara the last word in depicting her ultimate refusal to let Oliver impose his will one her, two considerations mitigate her somewhat dubious victory. On the one hand, she is never allowed simply to speak but must use violence to make her voice heard. While it might be argued that the same is also true of Oliver, their unequal financial positions as well as their disparate access to legitimate power structures make their positions anything but equivalent. As a wealthy attorney, Oliver is better able than the majority of people to manipulate the discursive structures of power outside the domestic sphere. He makes his living by exploiting his privileged ingress to those structures. He seems unable, however, to negotiate the theoretically equal footing that couples in a domestic arrangement share. Consequently, Barbara's recourse to violence, which Oliver literally advises in an early scene in their bedroom, is her last attempt to make Oliver listen to her. Since most of their encounters involve not brute physical strength but cunning, ingenuity, and the use of household technology, their ingenious brand of domestic violence places them on more or less equal footing.

On the other hand, the film represents Barbara Rose's ultimate acquisition of her own voice at the expense of her life and it presents the story of that acquisition as a didactic tale somewhat implausibly emanating from an attorney who acts as a family counselor against his own financial interests. The attorney labors well into the night spinning the lengthy tale of the Roses' divorce and subsequent deaths in order to dissuade another man from entering into a similarly dangerous situation. The affective register of the lawyer's protracted exemplary tale consequently resides in the masculine camaraderie and master/disciple relationship that cause one man to forego his professional fees for the benefit of another, less experienced man. Dissuading the potential client, the attorney speaks to him not as a professional but as one of the guys when he warns that in divorce and negotiating with women, "There is no winning, only degrees of losing."

The use to which the attorney puts the Roses' tragic tale of domestic violence is specifically encoded for the financial—and health—benefits men can derive from it. On a more general level, however, the film's mixing of different narrative modes universalizes the Roses' story and inserts it into the register of an unequivocally accurate history of events of near universal significance. The conceit of the flashback, in which events from the past are related from the point of view of a specific character involved in those events, is common in virtually all forms of narrative. In *The War of the Roses,* DeVito's lawyer continually relates events he witnessed as Oliver's friend and as the Roses' attorney, but he also narrates situations in the Roses' life that he could only have had access to in narrative form— that is, private matters between Barbara and Oliver that the latter must have related to him. I do not quibble over a narrative convention that has traditionally lent expositional economy to complex sequences of events; I do, however, want to point out that when the attorney relates as personally experienced those events to which he had access only in narrative form, he not only reproduces a master narrative designed to disparage gender equality but he contributes to legitimizing it as well.[4] That is, he removes his story from the subjective domain of a tale told by a family friend and inserts it into the register of universal truth revealed by an omniscient narrator who uses his own access to truth to provide a didactic significance to the events related. The most striking example of the lawyer's construction occurs during the death scene I elaborated above in which Barbara sternly removes Oliver's hand from her shoulder (as the scene is shot it apparently takes place without witnesses).

The significance of the lawyer's unilinear historical construction lies in its subtle recasting of the events in the Roses' specific circumstances into a general, master narrative of feminine treachery and masculine powerlessness in the face of such guile. By molding the Roses' story into a categorized moral exemplum, the lawyer—played, we must keep in mind, by the film's director—divests it of its specificity and appropriates it as a professional tool that, in the context of a legal consultation, earns legitimacy precisely because it is told by a lawyer to a client. This didactic tale is all the more powerful and even shocking because a professional litigant uses it to advise a potential client that in some cases—cases involving women's relationship to property, duplicity, and having the last word—dispute, whether legal or personal, is doomed to failure.

Consequently, by mixing narrative modes and giving the last word to a woman who dies for the right to speak it, *The War of the Roses* satirizes women's relationship to power. It rehearses the sardonic cliché that in their roles as domestic dictators women whip their husbands into complete submission and there's nothing men can do about it except to go grudgingly along with whatever their wives want. The lawyer's tale acquires its perlocutionary force through its application of models of verisimilitude and universality to a narrative that logically cannot support them because most of the events it contains occurred unobserved on a purely intersubjective level. His tale consequently delegitimizes Barbara Rose's voice by applying in the ostensibly professional context of a legal consultation the locker-room wisdom that all women are bitches. His tale, in other words, reduces the specifics of a sequence of events whose historical accuracy remains inaccessible to us to a master narrative of feminine duplicity.

The narrative construction by which *The War of the Roses* invalidates feminine difference and construes it instead as violent opposition can help elucidate a similar annihilation of difference operating in Mme. de Lafayette's *La Princesse de Clèves*. At the time of the novel's publication, its detractors seemed unable to apprehend the critical contribution it made to the developing genre of prose fiction as well as to the broadening of the social base from which subjects might speak. They were unable to grasp the work's radical departure from received narrative models of prose fiction and viewed it merely as the latest, in this case flawed, addition to a more or less stable literary form. They considered its narrative implausible and its construction fundamentally irrational, principally because a woman—the title character—confesses to her husband her love for another man. Traditional literary criticism has analyzed the novel as either psychological realism or historical fiction, but not until recently have a current of different critical voices—most notably feminist and to a lesser extent Marxist—lent us the tools to rediscover the work's dialogic and subjective ironies, ironies that generations of criticism have annulled in the construction of a unilinear literary history. *La Princesse de Clèves* has become canonized, often referred to as the first novel in French literature—whatever that might mean—but the fact that it was written by a woman generally plays no part in this observation. In addition, no contemporary and not even the author herself considered the work anything but an eccentric curiosity. Mme. de Lafayette, in fact, strenuously argued that the work was *not* a novel, and by contemporary standards she was right. The process of canonization has removed the critical edge from Mme. de Lafayette's radical departure from existing traditions, consequently silencing the dissonant voice it sounded. In the remainder of this essay I want to show how the decentering constructionism operating in *La Princesse de Clèves*—a quality distinguishing the work in 1678 but largely effaced by centuries of canonization—can once again come to the forefront in this highly ambivalent novel. By placing it in conjunction with a recent film as well as by considering it in its own historical context, I hope to show how it exemplifies what Matei Calinescu has identified as ideally postmodern, namely "an ironic concept of both the cultural tradition and innovation."[5]

Discovering why, however, the princess's idiosyncratic behavior—behavior which to modern readers seems more or less unproblematic—struck contemporaries as the epitome of *invraisemblance* and as a radical departure for fiction will require a brief excavation of the uses to which prose fiction was put in the seventeenth century as well as an analysis of models of verisimilitude. It will become clear that *La Princesse de Clèves* helped initiate a dialogic pluralism within the tradition of historical fiction in France that contested the claims to universality earlier aristocratic fiction had made.

In 1559, Pierre Boiastuau published his *Histoires tragiques,* a collection of short tales with little in common save the depiction of gruesome punishments meted out to those who engage in social misalliance. Boiastuau was one of the pioneers of tragic fiction in France, inaugurating a literary genre whose unusual goal was to shock and appall its readers. From 1559 until at least the 1620s, tragic fiction depicted the bizarre and sickening punishments awaiting those who failed to recognize legitimate authority; one of the most frequent crimes these tales portrayed was the socially incompatible marriage. Mismatched lovers accidentally ate their paramours' hearts, unwillingly executed their spouses, and sometimes inadvertently murdered their children. In virtually all cases, however, one is dissuaded from sympathizing with them precisely because they failed to respect the rigid class distinctions differentiating the true and noble aristocracy from basely born pretenders. It is difficult to diverge from the unequivocal interpretation narrators attempt to establish for their tales: quite often, they preface their stories with brief moral and political statements that establish the allegorical paradigms designed to inform readers' interpretations.

Of course, there is no compelling reason to allow one's mode of reading to be informed exclusively by generic considerations or by a text's specific interpretive directives. Ross Chambers has reminded us that the ideology informing a given text's self-definition needs to be read as part of the text and that "one should free oneself to recontextualize it (that is, interpret it) along with the rest of the text."[6] Nevertheless, significant historical events—including the growing centralization of the French monarchy, the move to legalize the bequeathing of nobility acquired from offices paid for with cash, and the efforts made by Richelieu and Louis XIV to crush the power and pride of France's aristocracy—contributed to the development of narrative forms in France underwritten by a master discourse of aristocratic superiority and designed to efface political and social opposition.

These narrative forms—of which the best known examples are pastoral fiction, most notably Honoré d'Urfé's *L'Astrée,* and the gargantuan historical romances of the 1640s through the 1660s—were written almost exclusively by and for members of the aristocracy. Often revolving around allegorical keys that masked the real-life identities of their characters, these novels required that readers possess a valorized cultural capital involving specific historical and cultural knowledge generally unavailable to the majority of the people. Later seventeenth-century fiction often alienated in practice those readers that earlier works strive to turn away in theory: by the time of the monstrous historical romances it did not suffice merely to accept the moral that narrators proposed; without a solid foundation in the partisan version of French history peculiar to the aristocracy, these works remain largely inaccessible.

Mme. de Lafayette's *La Princesse de Clèves* follows in the tradition of seventeenth-century aristocratic fiction by scrupulously observing the historical details of the milieu it depicts. Set at the court of Henri II, the novel portrays the events surrounding a young girl's debut into society and the ineffective manner in which she deals with the semiotic and discursive practices of aristocratic society. That is, *La Princesse de Clèves* depicts Henri's court as a hermetically sealed community distinguished by the production and interpretation of ambigous signs. Characters negotiate their ways through this community by confronting its complex discourse and constructing narratives; they erect an epistemological framework that provides the contexts and limits of knowledge at the court and that assigns them places within that framework. Henri's courtiers construct a narrative understanding of their world and are in turn constructed by the places they hold in that world. Their stories, all conforming to the same general model of court life, are based on an expressive causality reflecting seventeenth-century standards of verisimilitude. Each tale that courtiers tell expresses the overarching narrative and ideological structure of their restricted circle.[7] With a principal character whose behavior violates all convention, however, the novel explores the limits of verisimilitude and expressive causality by portraying Mme. de Clève's struggle to decode behavior at the court and her attempt to apply the interpretive strategies she gleans from others. Because her predicament differs radically from received models, her attempt to imitate courtly discourse fails and, like Barbara Rose, she pays for her distinctive, individual voice with her life.

The background for all the action in *La Princesse de Clèves* is the complex court of Henri II in which the one thing that can be taken for granted is that virtually all people are involved in behavior they need to disguise. Courtiers have to become adept at interpreting the equivocal speech and actions of their associates. Since most actions are undertaken with a vested interest in mind, people at the court must discern the likely reason for which a given person would undertake a particular activity or utter a particular sentence. Although the range of possible reasons is large, it is finite: given that all courtiers "thought only of elevating themselves, of pleasing, serving or harming others" (*PC*, 252), one need only determine the permutations and combinations of a given court activity. Consequently, courtiers have a sense of what kinds of motives are likely to provoke the outward behavior they see and they can react appropriately. There thus exists a narrative verisimilitude at the court that helps people read others.

Courtiers' reactions to events at the court consequently bear a striking resemblance to readers' responses to a text. Given a particular set of denotative raw material—that is, a collection of signs—they need to decode this material in order to construct a meaning behind the facade, a meaning that may or may not reflect a courtly reality. In either case it helps them negotiate court semiotics. One's ability to read the signs of the court depends on one's past reading experience and the attentiveness with which one has listened to explanatory narratives. The neophyte princess, for example, makes a casual remark to her mother concerning the apparently close relationship between the queen and the constable, only to be cut short by her mother, Mme. de Chartres: "Your opinion is in direct contradiction with the truth" (*PC*, 264). A lengthy digression follows in which Mme. de Chartres reveals the history of the queen's hatred for the constable.

The digressions into events of the past in *La Princesse de Clèves*, although among the devices most frequently criticized in the articles of the monthly *Mercure Galant* and Jean-Antoine de Charnes's contemporary criticism of the novel,[8] establish norms of behavior. Contemporaries familiar with the historical world Mme. de Lafayette depicts viewed the digressions as inessential to the novel's action. Jean-Henri Valincour, in a critique published just after Mme.

de Lafayette's novel, finds the digressions distracting: "I have difficulty understanding the relationship that might exist between what
[Mme. de Chartres] tells her concerning Madame de Valentinois,
Madame d'Étampes, the death of the dauphin, and the story of
La Princesse de Clèves. Nevertheless it seems to me that in works
of this sort one should permit nothing that is not necessarily tied
to the subject."[9] Valincour bases his criticisms of the digressions on
the readerly urge to get on with the story. Since he can see no
relationship between the tales courtiers spin and the unraveling of
the apparent main plot interest—the love triangle in which the
princess finds herself—he considers them dispensable. This is a far
cry from readers' reactions to heroic fiction that just a generation
earlier had employed the same type of digressions as a means of
both making up for inadequacies in the third-person narrator's
omniscience and filling out the psychological construction of particular characters.

These so-called digressions, however, are absolutely indispens-
able for this novel if it is to be, as its author once described it, a
"perfect imitation of the world of the court and of the manner in
which people live there."[10] Like maxims that help set standards of
behavior at court,[11] the digressions show how specific individuals
distinguish appearances from reality. They function as explanatory
narratives with a bivalent elucidative function. On the one hand,
these narratives provide background information that may be essential for deciphering the current state of affairs. On the other hand,
they provide a model of interpretive practice based on received
models of knowledge that demonstrates the level of inferential
sophistication required in order to function smoothly at the court.
The explanatory narratives offer inexperienced court interpreters
examples to emulate by laying bare the courtly decoding practice.

The digressions in the narration of *La Princesse de Clèves* serve,
then, to establish in the diegetic register of the novel's internal narratives an object of imitation for the inexperienced. Those unfamiliar
with the rigors of interpreting equivocal actions or ambiguous appearances learn to read the text of the court by imitating the reading
processes exposed in the narrations of experienced courtiers. Thus,
diegesis in the internal narratives becomes an object or model for
mimesis. Analytical narrations that show how a given interpretation

of a courtly situation was arrived at serve as models to be imitated.
They help the uninitiated learn, but more crucially they legitimize a
specific model of interpretation, one based on the unilinear and continuous master narratives of hegemony, a condition Lyotard has
defined as typically modern.

The publication of *La Princesse de Clèves* triggered a heated
debate about the outrageous confession of love for another man
that the princess makes to her husband. Most readers found her
confession *invraisemblable,* but not because they found it inconceivable that a woman would make such a confession; rather, it was
because it did not conform to received narrative paradigms. Roger
de Rabutin identified the princess's confession as *extravagant,* a
word which in the seventeenth century refered not only to the
unreasonable or eccentric but also to texts outside canonical tradition.[12] Significantly, readers' responses to Mme. de Clèves's confession matched those of the novel's characters: even the princess
realizes how extraordinary her action is. After Mme. la Dauphine
tells her that an unidentified woman in love with M. de Nemours
confessed everything to her husband, Mme. de Clèves, who knows
that the story is true because she is the woman in question, answers: "That story strikes me as hardly believable . . . and I would
like to know who told it to you" (*PC,* 345). Mme. de Clèves's
remark underscores the crucial distinction courtiers make between
what is plausible or likely at the court and what actually occurs
there and it shows the extent to which generalized narrative principles inform the way courtiers conceive of their relationship to
their society. Courtiers turn all their experiences into narratives
and the princess herself, as Dalia Judovitz has observed, experiences her own life as "a story rather than an event."[13] This brief
episode in the novel hypostatizes the contemporary critical and
aesthetic debates that distinguished factual accuracy from verisimilitude as the literary mode that depicted to a specific group of
readers a parochial version of the way things ought to be. That is,
the range of actions in which people engage is relatively restricted
at the court, normally to those activities that might advance one
politically; no woman had ever confessed such a thing to her husband, and such a confession was not verisimilar in this circle because as a purely personal or private affair it would accomplish no

social or political function. The verisimilitude of internal court narratives—that is, as the courtiers themselves perceive and interpret them—depends on an expressive causality in which each narrative element or episode expresses, often in overdetermined form, the inner essence of the entire structure. Courtiers perceive a master narrative, an abstract code, that structures all their attempts to understand their world and they strive to structure all narrative episodes according to that master code.

The plots of aristocratic fiction were also similarly restricted, normally to what was deemed politically and morally useful. Since at least as far back as 1638, when the Académie Française politicized notions of verisimilitude in its harsh condemnation of Corneille's *Le Cid*, literary discourse had become but one manifestation of an overarching social, political, and economic discourse of upper-class hegemony; the aesthetic object became an expressive signifier designed to render directly aristocratic superiority and political absolutism, a denominative phenomenon that reached its epitome in fiction during the era of the historical romance. When Mme. de Clèves characterizes her own confession as unbelievable, she articulates the intimate connection between narrative signifier and signified—between, that is *histoire* and *récit*—in contemporary fiction: a work's narrative content and enunciating discourse must share a common code—verisimilitude—that restricts the interpretation of possible narrative episodes to received paradigms. Narrative episodes or events that fail to express the politics of verisimilitude—at the court, the attempt to ingratiate oneself to powerful individuals or at the level of the work's *récit*, the rendering of upper-class political hegemony—seem unrealistic because they conflict with the seventeenth-century master narrative that dictates a function or political use for all works of art. The discursive convergence of *histoire* and *récit* had been aristocratic fiction's cachet: marking no difference between the language of its characters and that of its narrators, earlier seventeenth-century fiction had erected a hegemonic interpretive framework that valorized the pretensions of France's nobility. Restrictions on language and subject matter in fiction—verisimilitude—were motivated not by aesthetic concerns properly speaking but by ideological ones. Plausibility was governed by political utility.

The princess, however, never fully appreciates the social function that narrative can have, conceiving of it only as a means to represent the world about her. For example, when her mother advises her to feign illness in order to evade the social obligation of attending one of the court functions, the princess dresses the part of the ailing young woman but she is unable to display a convincing countenance. Mme. la Dauphine, one of the more experienced courtiers, spots the irregularity and immediately perceives that Mme. de Clèves pretended to be sick only because she feared letting another man know she was interested in him. The princess's failed attempt to reproduce the appearances that might lend an air of plausibility to her claim of illness characterizes her problematic relationship to the court's discursive practice. She imitates the enunciating register of this discourse but falls short of replicating its effect; experienced courtiers consequently perceive a gap separating what she says from what she does.

The princess's failure to negotiate the political dimension of narrative stems ultimately from the hegemonic force of the master narratives that form both her education and her restricted access to court history. Mme. de Chartres, the princess's mother, is the primary source of the girl's historical and social knowledge; the education she provides her daughter derives exclusively from received narrative paradigms of verisimilitude as they are deployed at the court (and, coincidentally, in seventeenth-century fiction). Mme. de Chartres' education of her daughter is fraught, however, with two fatal flaws: on the one hand, she warns her daughter of the crucial need to distinguish appearances from reality at the court without giving her the means to make such distinctions.[14] On the other hand, she strives to inculcate in her daughter principles of austere virtue that are no longer valued at the court. Intent in her family pride on bringing up her daughter "as someone whom no one could touch" (PC, 260), Mme. de Chartres makes her daughter vow to tell her everything men say to her and she offers in exchange to interpret the events of the court for her (PC, 253).

To the princess, Mme. de Chartres appears to have mastered courtly interpretation. She seems always to know precisely who is doing what and she can always penetrate the opaque veil of appearances to get to the reality they hide. Mme. de Clèves is frustrated, however, because her mother never tells all that she knows: "I am upset, madame, tht you have not informed me of all the current goings-on and that you have not taught me the many intrigues and relationships at the court" (*PC*, 264). Mme. de Clèves perceives her mother's master of courtly equivocation and furthermore she suspects her mother of withholding from her vital information.[15] Mme. de Clèves thus construes her mother not only as the repository of secure and unequivocal interpretation but as the cache of historical sources that endow court narratives with meaning and bestow on them a situational significance. She invests her mother with the power to articulate the expressive causality of the court and, of her own life. Because of her upbringing and her interaction at the court she accepts the proposition her mother's advice implies: that a single, comprehensive, and stable interpretation can present readers of the court with its unequivocal reality.

Although Judovitz, Hirsch, and others have noticed Mme. de Chartres' narrative influence on her daughter and Mme. de Clèves's tendency to experience her own life as a narrative, no readers of *La Princesse de Clèves* seem to have taken into account the fact that Mme. de Chartres has access to her daughter's life only through the latter's narrative construction of it. As noted above, Mme. de Chartres insists that her daughter confide in her all of the *gallanteries* men speak to her. More crucial still, Mme. de Chartres is totally removed from the court: in only one episode—cited above, in which she helps her daughter feign illness—does she participate in court events. She consequently relies nearly exclusively on her daughter's narration of court events and her ensuing interpretation of Mme. de Clèves's behavior draws not on the particulars of her situation but on traditional court verisimilitude. That is, although Mme. de Chartres has painstakingly educated her daughter to be unlike any other woman at the court, conventional wisdom concerning plausible activity at the court informs each of her readings of Mme. de Clèves's thoughts and deeds. Mme. de Chartres thus allows the master narrative of the court, which dictates that all people there get involved in *cabales* and adulterous affairs, to influence the story she constructs of Mme. de Clèves's life and consequently the advice she gives her. However exceptional, even unique, the princess may be, because she strives to imitate her mother's mastery of the court, a mastery based on conventionalized narrative, she is ineluctably drawn into the very situation her mother strenuously attempted to keep her away from. In short, by the time Mme. de Clèves's narrative passes into her mother's hands and back to her, it has been stripped of its particular significance and standardized to conform to the canon of court verisimilitude.

Mme. de Chartres' interpretive superiority and the power it gives her over her daughter are consequently largely responsible for the princess's unusual behavior at the court and, ultimately, for her love for Nemours. It is the mother who first articulates her daughter's passion for Nemours, which consequently incites Mme. de Clèves to produce more material for interpretation: she was "determined to tell Mme. de Chartres all the things she had not yet told her." After her mother's death, when the princess finds herself "disconsolate to be abandoned to herself," she lacks an adequate interlocutor to whom she can narrate her experiences and from whom she can learn their generalized significance. Her mother suspends the story of her life with the princess "hanging on the edge of a precipice" (PC, 277) and this is where she remains for the rest of the novel. Mme. de Chartres' last words to her daughter ("Remember, if you can, all that I have just told you" [PC, 278]) inscribe her continued influence on her and speak to her from beyond the grave as the princess strives to remain virtuous and unique as well as to seek out another person who seems to have mastered the court's narrative and its interpretation.

M. de Nemours calls forth from the princess the resistant and exceptional virtue her mother constructed for her as well as the discursive mastery of the court she continually strives to achieve. On the other hand, her affiliation with him is unique at the court in that she seems to be the only woman not to have had an affair with him. Mme. de Clèves's resistance to Nemours consequently continues to constitute her as exceptional and unique. Over and over again the princess sees various examples in her life of how unlike other women she is; she notices it, and others do too.[16] It is because of her wish or need to be unique that the princess cannot allow herself to become involved with Nemours, even after her husband's death: Mme. de Clèves fears being reduced over time to the lot of other women—that is, to sameness.

On the other hand, Mme. de Clèves is fascinated with Nemours's apparent mastery of all situations: "she saw him always surpassing others and making himself master of the conversation wherever he was, both because of his personal charm and because of his quick wit; consequently, he quickly made a great impression in her heart" (PC, 263).[17] In addition to being at all times master of the situation, M. de Nemours has the gift of projecting appearances that mask reality in order to keep himself from being read. When the court is discussing the recent predictions an astrologer has made concerning various members of the kings' entourage, for example, Nemours whispers to Mme. de Clèves a gallantry that reveals his love for her. Mme. la Dauphine spies a secret conversation going on and she asks M. de Nemours what he said; he replies with a banal generalization. "If he had had less presence of mind he would have been flustered at her question" (PC, 297), and he pulls off a response that both satisfies the queen and leaves Mme. de Clèves with no doubt that he is in love with her. Able to hide his true feelings and reactions when it would be dangerous to reveal them, Nemours possesses such great self-control that he can dominate most situations at the court.[18] The princess is irresistibly drawn to Nemours both because of his masterful ability to project plausible yet deceiving appearances and because he knows how to "make himself master of the conversation wherever he was"; that she is drawn to him and yet continually resists him validates her as uniquely virtuous and allows her to continue to be a character in her mother's master narrative.

Mme. de Clèves remains, however, "on the edge of the precipice": if she cannot resolve no longer to see Nemours or to have an affair with him, neither can she enjoy the *tranquilité* derived from loving her husband and being loved by him, the state of bliss her mother narrated to her. She never displays to her husband the passion he desired in her and, as the princess tells Nemours after her husband's death, her aloofness from M. de Clèves kept him in love with her: "But can men preserve passion in a life-long commitment? M. de Clèves was perhaps the only man in the world capable of sustaining love in marriage. My destiny is not to profit from such happiness. It might be that his passion only continued because he could not produce any in me" (PC, 387). Mme de Clèves kept her husband in love with her by never loving him in return. Nemours's passion was unbridled for similar reasons. In a somewhat perverse but perfectly comprehensible way, given her mother's tales of men's infidelity, Mme. de Clèves preserves men's love for her and consequently her control over them by withholding from them what they desire most.

Mme. de Chartres provided her daughter with a narrative image of the court ostensibly structured to protect the girl from danger, but since the mother had access to her daughter's life only through the latter's discursive representation of it, the interpretations she returned were steeped in local verisimilitude. Mme. de Chartres carefully depicted for her daughter court intrigue, interpersonal relationships, and even her daughter's emotional responses—but her unexpected death prevented her from reaching the end of the story. Consequently, since she fails to apprehend her mother's version of the master narrative's end, Mme. de Clèves prolongs the narrative indefinitely and she does so by perpetuating men's desire for her. Since by her own admission she cannot reach the *dénouement* of her mother's tale, the "woman's happiness of loving her husband and being loved by him" (*PC*, 248), Mme. de Clèves holds the two men in her life in thrall by projecting to each the image the other desires: to Nemours she is the dutiful and unreachable wife and to her husband she is the passionate lover capable of the most violent emotions, only not for him. Their sempiternal desire for her keeps M. de Clèves and M. de Nemours enthralled. Each expects from this exceptional woman behavior that conventional court verisimilitude would dictate. Their pleasure, however, is thrwarted because Mme. de Clèves cannot allow the narrative to wind down to one of two possible climaxes of equal courtly verisimilitude: living happily ever after with her husband or having an affair with Nemours.

Mme. de Clèves is in effect, then, quite a tease, but only because her mother articulated her relationship to the court and its history according to the hegemony of male desire. She can speak only through court discourse and Mme. de Clèves inflicts violence on that discourse and ultimately escapes the narrativization of her life by disfiguring local verisimilitude and confessing her desire to her husband. Her husband listens but refuses to believe that his wife's confession is not, as any seasoned courtier would expect, merely an appearance masking a more fundamental reality (*PC*, 336). Consequently, although she expresses herself as clearly as she is able, the princess's articulation of her desire is recast by her husband as merely another courtly ruse.

Craig Owens has argued that postmodernism is situated "at the legislative frontier between what can be represented and what cannot . . . —not in order to transcend representation, but in order to expose that system of power that authorizes certain representations while blocking, prohibiting or invalidating others."[19] The princess's confession, incites a crisis in the court's representational system that can in this context be labeled postmodern. At first it appears that her confession effectively reveals the masculine hegemony of court discourse because it exposes a lack constituted by the prohibition against articulating feminine desire. Careful consideration reveals, however, that it is not so much prohibited to articulate feminine desire as it is impossible: the court's discursive structure and its resident verisimilitude have no provisions for such voicing. Mme. de Clèves's "extravagant" confession falls outside the canon of court discourse and consequently calls for an interrogation of the temporal and referential functions of legitimizing historical narrative. The fact that M. de Clèves refuses to accept his wife's confession at face value demonstrates that this is one of the points at which court discourse breaks down. Because such a confession has no place in court discourse, neither he nor any other courtier can understand that it actually took place and that it signifies precisely what it says. Mme. de Clèves's confession so unsettles her husband that, unable to negotiate a courtly metaphor he has never before encountered, he dies shortly thereafter.

After her husband's death, Mme. de Clèves's chance of storybook happiness is forever foreclosed. She will never love her husband and be loved by him and she cannot be happy with Nemours because she cannot trust him not to have an affair and consequently fracture her unique identity. Forcefully ejected from the life her mother strived to manufacture for her, Mme. de Clèves retires to a convent and lives the rest of her life in seclusion. Here the narrativization of her life ends and she ceases to be a player in a drama over whose script she has no control. When Nemours comes to see her, the messenger to whom he speaks tells him that

"Mme. de Clèves had not only prohibited her from telling her anything on his part but even from telling her anything about their conversation" (*PC*, 394). Escaping at long last the narrativization of her life, which is where all her troubles began, the princess takes authorial responsibility and writes her own ending. The novel's last words, however, describe the somewhat ambiguous significance this well-ordered life conveys: "And her life, which was rather short, left inimitable examples of virtue" (*PC*, 395). Even Mme. de Clèves's death is inscribed in the narrative structure her mother had plotted. If she could not attain happiness, which was, after all, a secondary consideration in Mme. de Chartres's plan to make her daughter outshine all that was glamorous at the court, she was at least capable of remaining exceptional in her abiding yet ultimately pointless virtue.

Mme. de Clèves paradoxically deceived others by unconventionally avoiding duplicity and allowing her words and actions to express in unequivocal fashion precisely what she felt and thought. The novel's last sentence communicates not only her distinctiveness but the complete lack of expressive causality the narrativization of her life bears. That is, her "inimitable examples," of virtue or of any other trait, fail to close off the work precisely because they cannot be repeated. Inimitable examples serve no moral or political didactic function; they cannot restrict interpretation, as the morals of previous historical fiction had tried to do, to an unequivocal celebration of a specific ideology. Consequently, both virtue and the preeminence of verisimilitude remain marginal in this work. The novel closes with the depiction of an ambivalent virtue—ambivalent because it is unrepeatable and, moreover, because the princess attained it somewhat accidentally—and a dysfunctional interpretive practice—court verisimilitude—that can no longer adequately privilege a particular narrative point of view because it cannot negotiate the difference between reality and representation. In other words, the traditional distinction between truth and verisimilitude breaks down in this novel; fiction is consequently unable to prescribe a specific moral or political lesson because it cannot distinguish between the expressive causality that had been the hallmark of verisimilitude and the simple accidents of everyday life that compose reality. In the absence of a highly developed structuring apparatus of description able to show unequivocally that each episode of a work self-evidently expressed a specific and obvious ideological truth, the interpretation of fiction is thrown open to a broad spectrum of readers with differing allegiances and political affiliations.

The extreme self-consciousness that Mme. de Lafayette's novel displays toward its subject matter and the conventions of fiction, as well as its reification of those conventions as objects of analysis, might characterize the work as resolutely modern. Yet, the work's refutation of contemporary hermeneutical practices consists of far more than simply compensating for inadequacies in extant interpretive models the better to insert itself in the unilinear development of classical exegesis. *La Princesse de Clèves* contests the received models of narrative interpretation by hypostatizing, in the figure of Mme. de Chartres, an archaic mode of reading. Traditional exegesis conceived the interpretive process as a relatively simple act of decoding the material that constituted a text. However hermetic a text might appear, diligent analysis could ostensibly arrive at its final meaning by unpacking a work's rhetorical structure and laying bare the sense it contained. Such a model of interpretation served contemporary views of literature's didactic or politically useful function because it sought to control the meaning readers could extract from a text— a master code governed the interpretive process and literature afforded no surprises because it foreclosed competing or conflicting analyses. Philosophical or moral treatises as well as narrative or theatrical works afforded standardized views of contemporary social reality because only works based on conventionalized verisimilitude received a *privilège du roi*, the stamp of approval authorizing a work's publication.

Mme. de Chartres' narratives fail to negotiate their own temporality and remain unable to account for the complexities of the court in which they are told. Like the lawyer's tale in *The War of the Roses*, they stand for transhistorical truth and they obfuscate the acts of legitimation implicit in their didacticism. Mme. de Clèves, however, reifies a nascent contradiction in interpretive processes: that between the expressive causality of earlier fiction in which texts seemed to possess an inner essence reflected or expressed by each of their constituent elements and the motivated verisimilitude of budding fiction. In the latter form of fiction, aptly described by Gérard

Genette,[20] textual maxims theorize or justify characters' behavior. Motivated verisimilitude is not so much an intuitive collection of externalized moral and political principles that must be brought to bear on a work but a way of understanding sequences of events whose logic follows from psychological and physiological rubrics actuated by the unfolding of the plot. In *La Princesse de Clèves*, Mme. de Clèves lives her own life as the vicarious narrative expression of her mother's expectations. That is, she conforms to her mother's ostensibly omniscient knowledge of her feelings and actions; narrating to her mother the events of each passing day, she accepts her mother's interpretation of those events with the result that despite the particularities of her own situation she ineluctably conforms to what is expected of her. After her mother's death, however, Mme. de Clèves possesses no stable, unequivocal interpretation of her life and resorts to a prolonged seduction of her husband and M. de Nemours as a means of forever deferring the expected narrative climax. Her final withdrawal from the court seems less an unmitigated victory for the young woman than an inexorable ending to a tale that fails to resolve itself in a conclusive and satisfying *dénouement* and instead simply winds down and stops.

Mme. de Clèves does, finally, write her own story by leaving the court and consequently the pages of a textualized world whose limited narrative repertory dictates an extremely restricted set of possible narrative outcomes.[21] Her escape from the constraining parameters of courtly behavior represents an evasion from the expressive causality of aristocratic verisimilitude: the irreplicable nature of her behavior on which the work closes not only fails to conform to any of the models of conduct narrated in the court's explanatory narratives but it falls short of conveying any potential didactic message to the novel's readers precisely because of its uniqueness. Mme. de Clèves's actions thus lack verisimilitude with respect to both the internal narrative practices as they are observed at the court and the external, homogenizing conventions of contemporary fiction. In this respect, then, the princess's withdrawal from the court represents a victory, but it is a victory over the constraining conventions of narrative structure as the defining limit of epistemological and political practice. Her unprecedented escape from the court heralds a departure from the master narrative of aristocratic fiction and it ushers in a subtle resistance, the manifestations of which would grow stronger throughout the eighteenth century, to moral and political hegemony buttressed by the control of the production and interpretation of knowledge.

La Princesse de Clèves conforms, on the formal level of structural appearances, to the conventions of historical fiction as it was construed in the middle decades of the seventeenth century. However, Mme. de Lafayette's novel helped initiate resistance to the master code of hegemonic narrative by objectifying and criticizing contemporary interpretive practice. That is, although the novel demands that its readers be familiar with contemporary verisimilitude both in order to follow the explanatory narratives within the work's récit and to recognize the tradition into which the text inserts itself, it ultimately distances itself from that tradition by externalizing verisimilitude and transforming it from an interpretive model into a problematic and impeding discourse. It exhibits the restrictions that contemporary notions of verisimilar expressive causality placed on narrative by depicting the crucial scene of the princess's confession along with its interpretation in the form of the court's reactions. The reified analysis of Mme. de Clèves's actions becomes, like the actions themselves, an object of representation; the novel incorporates the discursive practices that normally function to elucidate behavior into its repertory of depicted objects.

In reifying the interpretive practices of her generation, Mme. de Lafayette dissociated histoire from récit and consequently initiated a critical examination of the master narrative codes that had informed aristocratic fiction. La Princesse de Clèves separates narrative from the affective response that seventeenth-century heroic and historical fiction had traditionally demanded from its readers. While on its surface the novel resembles traditional aristocratic fiction,[22] this is primarily because one of its tactics is to incorporate the styles and narrative strategies from both contemporary fiction and historiography. By appropriating features from its forebears, La Princesse de Clèves not only objectifies and reifies previous discursive strategies designed to promote a universal conception of reason, moral virtue, and truth, but it exposes the institutional and hegemonic nature of those strategies. Mme. de Lafayette's novel repudiates the aesthetic categories of the day but, as is the case with many modernist works of art or literature, this did not prevent it from being canonized in its own right. Having criticized the *grands récits* of contemporary literary practices, it wound up domesticated by the historicizing *grands récits* of criticism.

However, it is precisely because *La Princesse de Clèves* is often referred to as "the first modern novel" and has been incorporated into the canon of French literature that its oppositional and even radical features are frequently overlooked. Because it is generally placed either at the beginning or at the end of linear histories of the French novel, it is used to constitute a precarious boundary separating archaic and modern modes of fiction. Modernist accounts of the development of French prose fiction conscript the work to serve as a benchmark in their unilinear narratives, but construing the novel as a narrative element in a literary history endowed with its own expressive causality whose teleological purpose is to predict the development of realism strips the work of its own distinctive features. What distinguishes *La Princesse de Clèves* from other contemporary works of fiction whose innovations contested received conventions of verisimilitude is its oppositional stance to the politics and philosophy governing the production of narrative.[23] That is, in *La Princesse de Clèves* the traditional use of narrative as a standardizing didactic tool breaks down, causing a rupture in the historical continuity with the heroic fiction of the previous generation. Narratives that had served to legitimize readers possessed of the cultural capital necessary to interpret them as well as the blatantly partisan ideologies underpinning the works themselves broke out of the ruling-class solipsism that had given them their cachet. *La Princesse de Clèves* demystifies the ideological origins and purposes of its own use of historical narrative and consequently breaks the hold that aristocratic readers had had on fiction. Unlike de'Urfé's *L'Astrée* or any of the gargantuan heroic novels of the seventeenth century, *La Princesse de Clèves* does not require its readers to possess a key for its interpretation. Multiple and diverse subject positions from which readers might approach a work of fiction consequently open up, and if *La Princesse de Clèves* could not legitimize itself according to conventional aesthetic and ideological standards, it was able to reveal the limitations and dangers implicit in a literary form in which meaning was presumed to inhere in advance of interpretation.

La Princesse de Clèves thus introduces into the *récit* of an otherwise conventional form of fiction the possibility of incorrect or alternative interpretations. Its destabilization of traditional forms of narrative and historical knowledge reveals first and foremost that the conditions of that knowledge might no longer pertain in a world in which competing political alliances were multiplying. The novel thus construes contemporary epistemology itself as a narrative construction subject to the recontextualizations new narratives demand. The invalidation of reigning narrative constructions of knowledge that *La Princesse de Clèves* occasions does not, however, simply add one more chapter to the text of literary history as it was understood in the seventeenth century. Rather, by introducing new and problematic positions of knowledge to the subject sites constructed in contemporary fiction, it undermines the stability of those sites and calls for alternative narrative practices able to account for its own position.

The legitimizing, explanatory narratives in both *La Princesse de Clèves* and *The War of the Roses* provide linear social histories of the communities they depict. Both works mobilize ostensibly masterful interpreters, in the figures of Mme. de Chartres and DeVito's lawyer, who appropriate historical knowledge and who in their legitimizing capacities prescribe a specific use for that knowledge. Both works also depict neophytes—Mme. de Clèves and the silent young man who comes to DeVito's character seeking a divorce—apparently ignorant of the discursive structures demarcating subject positions, especially as those positions pertain to gender difference. However, the two works differ quite radically in the degree of irony they bestow on their respective explanatory narratives. The *War of the Roses* employs the narration of past events in order to obfuscate the mandating of specific, gender-encoded subject sites constructed in contemporary legal and patriarchal discourse; it makes history serve contemporary models of truth. The simple fact that the man seeking a divorce leaves the lawyer's office without a lawsuit and without ever having uttered a word underscores his implicit accession to the position the lawyer describes: although theoretically more powerful than women, economically and physically, men are actually subservient to their wives. The patriarchal voice of legal and social control, the film suggests, is silenced by dangerous and domineering females.

La Princesse de Clèves, however, exposes the appropriation of history for specific ideological purposes and reveals the *use* of that appropriation, rather than the demystification of origins history generally claims to offer. By giving the princess the last, inimitable word, the novel undoes the hegemony of the court's and especially Mme. de Chartres' explanatory narratives. It privileges the construction of new narrative paradigms that cannot be recontained and consequently mitigated by the existing canon of court narratives even though the new stories retain the look and feel of the old. *La Princesse de Clèves* undermines the unilinear tales of historical causality that its characters relate; by revealing how an apparently stable referential account of current affairs can become duplicitous, it foregoes any unequivocal relation of what happened in order to suggest what might be. Mme. de Lafayette's contemporaries may have been unprepared, both politically and artistically, to recognize the novel's significance but subsequent works drew on her models of narrative to advance alternative exemplary tales valorizing ideologically marginal figures. Truth and virtue descended from their privileged positions as hallmarks of aristocratic ascendancy and took their places as constructions of narrative. There is consequently no winning and there are no transcendent examples of virtue: what remains are sites of articulation in which opposition and difference can find room for expression.

Notes

1. See, for example, Nancy K. Miller, "Emphasis Added: Plots and Plausibilities in Women's Fiction," *PMLA* 26 no. 1 (Jan. 1981): 36–48; Sylvère Lotringer, "La Structuration romanesque," *Critique* 26 (1970) 498–529; and Marianne Hirsch, "A Mother's Discourse: Incorporation and Repetition in *La Princesse de Clèves,*" *Yale French Studies,* no. 62, 47–87.

2. Linda Hutcheon argues that "the postmodern . . . effects two simultaneous moves. It reinstalls historical contexts as significant and even determining, but in so doing, it problematizes the entire notion of historical knowledge" (*A Poetics of Postmodernism* [New York: Routledge, 1988], 89).

3. Coincidentally—this seems interesting as coincidence—this is how M. de Clèves meets his wife. "He was so taken with her beauty that he could not hide his reaction; Mlle. de Chartres could not keep herself from blushing upon seeing the trouble that she caused him" (Mme. de Lafayette, *La Princesse de Clèves* [Paris: Garnier,

1970], 249, subsequently referred to as *PC*. All translations from this and other French sources are my own).

4. I use the concept of "master narrative" in the sense that Jean-François Lyotard and Fredric Jameson, among others, have deployed. Jameson argues that the process of interpretation frequently demands that readers recast the elements of a text and that they can make sense of a text "within the unity of a single great collective story; only if, in however disguised and symbolic a form, they are seen as sharing a single fundamental theme, . . . only if they are grasped as vital episodes in a single vast unfinished plot" (*The Political Unconscious* [Ithaca, N.Y.: Cornell Univ. Press, 1982], 19–20). Lyotard refers to a collection of "grands récits" in which difference in the form of social collectives is effaced in favor of the construction of "a mass composed of individual atoms thrust together in an absurd Brownian motion" (*La Condition postmoderne* [Paris: Minuit, 1979], 31).

5. Matei Calinescu, "Postmodernism, the Mimetic and Theatrical Fallacies," in *Exploring Post-modernism*, eds. Calinescu and Douwe Fokkema (Amsterdam: Benjamins, 1987), 12.

6. Ross Chambers, *Story and Situation: Narrative Seduction and the Power of Fiction* (Minneapolis: Univ. of Minnesota Press, 1984), 27.

7. On expressive causality in the Leibnizian and Hegelian traditions, see Louis Althusser, "Marx's Immense Theoretical Revolution," in Althusser and Etienne Balibar, *Reading Capital,* trans. Ben Brewster (New York: New Left Books, 1979), 186–88.

8. Jean-Antoine de Charnes, *Conversations sur la critique de La Princesse de Clèves* (Paris: Barbin, 1679).

9. Jean-Henri du Trousset de Valincour, *Lettres à Madame la Marquise***sur le sujet de La Princesse de Clèves* ed. Albert Cazes (Paris: Blossard, 1925), 98.

10. Letter of 13 Apr. 1678, in *Correspondance de Madame de Lafayette,* ed. Andre Beaunier (Paris: Gallimard, 1942), 2: 63.

11. John D. Lyons claims that fifty-two utterances in *La Princesse de Clèves* can be considered maxims pertaining specifically to courtly behavior; he calls the maxims in the narration "A repertory of models of human conduct." He argues that Mme. de Lafayette creates a dynamic of exceptional behavior and that the energy of the narrative comes from the failure of what is experienced to coincide with what is said about experience ("Narrative, Interpretation and Paradox: *La Princesse de Clèves,*" *Romantic Review* 72 [Nov. 1981], 4.

12. Roger de Rabutin, comte de Bussy, was imprisoned in the Bastille for his *Histoire amoureuse des Gaules,* a collection of slanderous portraits of contemporary courtiers. He remarked that the author of *La Princesse de Clèves* deliberately tried to flaunt convention: "Mme. de Clèves's confession to her husband is outrageous (*extravagant*) and could only happen in a true story. But when someone is making up a story, it is ridiculous to give the heroine such a bizarre idea. The author, in so doing, was trying more not to resemble other novels than to follow common sense" (letter of 26 June 1678, cited by Geneviève Mouligneau, *Madame de Lafayette romancière?* [Brussels: Éditions de l'université, 1980], 47).

13. Dalia Judovitz, "The Aesthetics of Implausibility: *La Princesse de Clèves,*" *MLN* 99 no. 5 (Dec. 1984): 1051.

14. Most notably in the often cited phrase, "If you judge by appearances in this place . . . you will often be mistaken; what seems to be is almost never the truth" (*PC,* 265).

15. After Mme. de Chartres tells the long story of the stormy relationship between the queen and M. le connétable, the following mother/daughter exchange occurs:

> "I don't know, my daughter . . . that you won't find that I have told you more things than you wanted to know."
>
> "I am far from making such a complaint, madame," Mme. de Clèves answered, "and, without wanting to bother you further, I would like to ask you about some other circumstances of which I know nothing." (*PC,* 269)

16. The following exchanges exemplify the princess's uniqueness at the court: "'The fault is yours,' answered Mme. la Dauphine, 'for having given him the letter, and you the only woman in the world who tells her husband everything that she knows"' (*PC,* 327); "Mme. de Chartres argued for some time against her daughter's opinion because she found it so unique" (*PC,* 273); "'Ah! monsieur,' [Mme. de Clèves] answered, 'There is no adventure in the world like mine; there is no other woman capable of the same thing. Chance could not have invented it; no one has ever imagined such a thing and such a thought has never entered into any mind but mine"' (*PC,* 349).

17. The following description of the princess's behavior underscores Nemours's interpretive mastery: "However much she tried to avoid his gaze and to speak to him less than to anyone else, certain things escaped from her that let this prince know that he was not indifferent to her. A less insightful man might not even have noticed" (*PC,* 298).

18. Alain Niderst argues that the ability to hide one's true feelings leads to the power to control others: "Dissimulation is consequently always admirable. It signifies the mastery of self. It permits mastery over others. It allows one to escape any sort of dependency" (*La Princesse de Clèves: le roman paradoxal* [Paris: Larousse, 1973], 58).

19. Craig Owens, "The Discourse of Others: Feminists and Postmodernism," in *The Anti-Aesthetic,* ed. Hal Foster (Port Townsend, Wash.: Bay Press, 1983), 59.

20. Gérard Genette, "Vraisemblance et motivation," *Figures 2* (Paris: Seuil, 1966), 71–99.

21. Both Sylvère Lotringer, in "La Structuration romanesque," and Nancy K. Miller in "Emphasis Added," argue that Mme. de Clèves's flight from the court is a move to preserve the erotics of her current situation.

22. Pierre Bayle argued that *La Princesse de Clèves* was just like other heroic fiction and he found that Mme. de Clèves resembled other heroines, all of whom were generally described as inimitable or unique; he objected that she, like them, was too individualistic to be believable. Maintaining that no woman like Mme. de Clèves

existed in France, he made a provocative promise: "If there were such a woman, I promise you that I would go find her, even if I had to go four hundred leagues on foot" (*Objection,* cited by Maurice Laugaa, *Lectures de Madame de Lafayette* [Paris: Colin, 1971], 114).

23. Furetière's *Roman bourgeois* (1666), Saint-Réal's *Dom Carlos* (1672), and Courtilz de Sandras's *Mémoires de M.L.C.D. R.* (1687) might be the immediate forebears and successor of the kind of oppositional fiction I argue Mme. de Lafayette was responsible for producing.

8

The Paranormal Roxana

Veronica Kelly

Daniel Defoe's name does not appear in the annals of postmodern writers. On the contrary, the names of Defoe and his character Robinson Crusoe have become synonymous with the rise of the modern novel as the ideological apparatus of possessive individualism, mercantile opportunism, and colonial expansion. This early-capitalist Defoe emerges as literature's accountant, the numerate editor who prepares confessions of debt and credit before they go on to the higher authority (to men of means or, if they're not available, to God) for final judgment. This is the story of Moll Flanders. By confirming and extending Defoe's identity as *homo economicus*, literary history has maximized his receptivity to this political critique.[1] What we, as textual scholars, have been able to ascribe with confidence to "Defoe" resounds with an accountant's budgetary obsessions. They are, pretty uniformly, tales of dangerous exchange, guilty recounting, and personal redemption. In these "new realist" narratives associated with Defoe, the power of figurative language is apparently greatly attenuated—diminished, perhaps, into a quirky fascination with apparitions. The impulse to keep accounts seems so strong in this author that we can't even be sure that the economic terminology is metaphoric. Bodies and souls are valued, negotiated, bartered, lost, and reclaimed alongside cargoes and bills of exchange. It is as if the question of what can and can't be said is just cut out of the business of counting and communication, rendering language wholly transitive. In this

tightly regulated commerce, we can find the hope that nothing will
be lost fostered by the assurance that the real is simply what, having
been clearly labeled, circulates most efficiently as true.[2]

Understood as occurring under this economic rule, acts of resistance or transgression in Defoe—Moll's disguises, for example—
must serve merely to secure the bottom line. As readers alert to the
presence of political stakes, we realize that all the sins confessed by
Robinson Crusoe and Moll Flanders reinforce the moral imperative
of those "autobiographies": keep good records and you will be
saved. With this realization we cricle again around that familiar—
and depressing—power/knowledge cul-de-sac, where all possible
others are merely the doubles of a power that has hailed them and
which they, by resisting, strengthen. To critics uneasy in this impasse, postmodernism suggests that we—like the anachronistic
Defoe who narrates the supernatural—might begin to see ghosts
and to distinguish these hauntings from our more conservative and
orderly illusions, of which the "historically" determined, early-
capitalist Defoe forms a part.[3] An author collated from a particularly
vast diaspora of anonymous and pseudonymous occasional writing,
"Defoe" is very much an invented tradition, an author consolidated
by the modern in order to attest to its consolidation as the modern.[4]
To read "Defoe" purely as an index to the history of ideology and its
mechanisms is to forget this, and to perpetuate the belief that,
through a careful accounting, the modern can pay its debts and
move on. Such a belief lets the modern imagine itself again as the
next future and appear again under the stylishly revised nomencla-
ture of the new. To the extent that our readings of Defoe are faithful
to this progress—narrative and its cognitive tenets, we can finally
only reaffirm "Defoe's" imperative: keep good records and you will
be saved. This essay hopes that something as scandalous as a
postmodern Defoe can disperse this imaginary Defoe, the other who
is just one. To this end, it turns to *Roxana*.[5]

In *Roxana*, the gritty, empirical world of survival, what we
have come to call the "real" world because in it language operates as
transaction, is perplexed by the spectral shape of Protestant allegories. Alongside the story of Roxana's extraordinary financial success
runs a shadowy scaffolding of otherworldly vision and morbid
guilt. In her more dramatic experiences of the supernatural, Roxana

sees her jeweller-"husband" translated into a bloody death's head hours before he is murdered, and she wishes for a storm at sea soon before one blows up and nearly drowns the ship. She is visited by messengers "as silent as Death" (218). These gloomy episodes have not played much part in our understanding of the novel, except as they psychologize Roxana and yield her up to our judgment, perhaps because they have no effects on the plot and so seem like token gestures of Protestant asceticism, out of place in a narrative that accumulates and then luxuriates in the time of its own telling. Though affectively powerful, the paranormal phenomena in *Roxana* have no impact at all on her "history," which remains a tale of successful business and investment. As Roxana's narrative progresses, her empirical and affective fates diverge more violently and more quickly. She grows wealthier and guiltier until the novel rather than its heroine suddenly comes to what critics have agreed is a bad end: the story concludes with Roxana still haunted but still ascending, unpunished by the closure of discovery.

Disturbed by the implications of this double narrative, the novel tries to recover its missed moral high ground in a "Preface" that separates the sin from the success, arguing that Roxana "makes frequent Acknowledgements, That the Pleasure of her Wickedness was not worth the Repentance" and thus her memoirs may be read by the "Virtuous Reader . . . both with Profit and Delight" (36). With this claim, the "Preface" rewrites Roxana's story in an attempt to transfer the investment advantage from Roxana to the reader. Roxana's always rather passionless and economically motivated affairs are redrawn in overblown and licentious terms as the "Pleasure of her Wickedness." The voluptous diction implies that Roxana's "pleasures" were sexual after all, thereby distinguishing them from the pristine and intellectual "Delight" that will be experienced by "Virtuous" readers. In making this distinction, the "Preface" does not attempt to exorcise Roxana's regrettable "pleasure" but puts it to work: the distinction would not only render "Delight" morally compatible with profit, but it would make profit moral as well. Such a conversion erases the sensuality of profit (it is not pleasure but virtue) by isolating and disciplining illicit gain in the person of Roxana as penitent voluptuary. By insisting that Roxana's memoirs yield a measurable result (X is or is not worth Y), The "Preface" subjects the narrative's unanswerable differences, manifest most succinctly in Roxana's unanswerable "Why am I a whore now?", to a bottom line which asserts that pleasure and repentance are directly comparable in terms of calculated value. In claiming the ability to calculate the orders of value, The "Preface" would finally establish an economic paradigm that the main body of the novel apparently flubs.

The attempt to establish stable orders of value in the novel is unsettled by the possibility inherent in calculation itself of an ongoing and plastic parataxis. Only in ledgers such as the one Defoe organizes in The "Preface" do quantitative operations produce sums that sustain the fiction that numbers and their valuations can be purely referential, a transparent language that records the quantity and therefore the value of things. It is certainly to secure this fiction that Defoe insists in The "Preface" that *"this Story differs from most of the Modern Performances of this Kind . . . in this Great and Essential Article,* Namely, *That the Foundation of This is laid in Truth of* Fact; *and so the Work is not a Story but a History"* (35). This evocation of fact against fiction is a familiar trope of writing we associate with realist empiricism, but it is worth noting here that "Truth of Fact" differentiates "Story" from "History" not with accusations of inaccuracy but by putting a stop to the counting. For "Fact" to become "Truth" and "Truth" to become "History," the figures must undergo a final tally. This is where Roxana falters as a historian and why the novel requires the corrective of The "Preface." Though Roxana counts obsessively, she eludes a decisive bottom line capable of fixing reference and compelling her reformation, perhaps because—after her initial catastrophic bankruptcy—she is never technically in debt and so counts for the sheer pleasure of counting, of doing figures. Even when she and the Dutch merchant reveal their financial holdings to each other after their marriage, a scene that seems designed for final accounting, not only does Roxana divide and subdivide their assets according to their types, thus greatly protracting this counting narrative, but she prevents their final combination by preserving them in separate, incomparable columns, holding her own "ill-gotten Wealth" apart from his "honest Estate." The problem with pleasurable counting is that its recombinations give quantity a narrative opacity that keeps telling stories and sets the particularity of writing and figure against the tenet that a profit can be abstracted from the text in the form of a final, quantified value.

The novel *Roxana* stakes its claim to an emphatic modernity against its heroine's practice of narrative as pleasurable counting, and both Roxana's premonitions and her guilt can be made to serve that claim as forms of temporal discipline. Where Roxana's morbid visions and introspections fail to alter the course of her career as capitalist and kept whore, we can conclude that the novel is breaking with the metanarrative that spawned it: that the emerging regime of capital, which has drafted the object world, here vanquishes the orders of Providence, rather unconvincingly represented by otherworldly effects, in particular by specters of death. These specters and premonitions persist in the narrative because this defeat is also an inheritance and they work to ensure its continuity. Capital, in taking over from Providence, also takes from Providence its concept of millennial history, an apocalyptic modernity recognizable in the decisive "now" of Armageddon and the earthly paradise, and transfers it into a credit-driven, speculative economic discourse. The matter conveyed in this inheritance—its paradigm of a linear time and a final accounting—validates its progressive mode. This point is made explicitly in the "Preface," where the novel credits itself with the truth and morality of "History," and rationalizes its violence, by distancing itself from what it defines as the contingent (false) modernity of "Story." Unlike history, story keeps counting, continually bypassing the summative moment in which history arrests and delineates time. That Defoe's "Preface" transfers the power of "Truth" from the rambling, multivalent time of story to the orderly clean-room of history explains why Roxana's apparitions are harbingers of future events rather than *revenants* returning to resurrect old debts. Historical time aligns past and future through its editorial present, and Roxana's omens and premonitions propel her narrative toward the ever-imminent "Repentance" (36) that Defoe finally secures editorially, thus assuring his readers that this history can be profitable.

This assured profit indicates that Roxana's ghastly premonitions and guilt are merely temporal inversions of each other and that both, exactly where they pretend to alter linear time, serve instead to secure its logic. Roxana's premonitions do the work of history by clearly delineating the future, while her conscience imposes a "historicizing" penance on the past as something to be renounced. This neat inversion of omen and guilt represses the anomalous and unprofitable temporalities of story and figure. By conforming prospect to retrospect, this inversion can position Roxana in a controlled, stable space where she functions as an example; it doesn't matter what she exemplifies, just that her past, by abstraction from itself into typicality, can discipline time to the one-way traffic of objective history. The relation between exemplarity, history, and profit in this equation is closed. Roxana's exemplarity functions to define the novel as a "historical" space in which exemplarity underwrites reading as an investment in the past as history. And if any moral is encoded in Roxana's memoirs, it is that those who control their histories can make a bundle.[6] Roxana's exemplarity as penitent sinner thus assures the novel's readers that they will reap a profit from the past. The "Preface" and the autobiographer Roxana are complicit in this economy: the relation between the "Preface" and *Roxana* is the same as that between the autobiographer Roxana and her former self, in particular as it comes to be embodied by her daughter Susan, whose return is so untimely.

But while the novel's controlling economic metanarrative imposes a temporal order on the supernatural as guilt and premonition, these aspects of the narrative remain excessive in their spectacular ineffectiveness and amplifications. As one of Roxana's effusions illustrates, pleasurable counting and spectacular guilt play "against" each other in a mutual and ongoing escalation.

> Not all the Affluence of a plentiful Fortune; not a hundred Thousand Pounds Estate; (for between us we had little less) not Honour and Titles, Attendants and Equipages; *in a word*, not all the things we call Pleasure, cou'd give me any relish, or sweeten the Taste of things to me; *at least*, not so much, but I grew sad, heavy, pensive, and melancholly; slept little, and eat little; dream'd continually of the most frightful and terrible things imaginable; Nothing but Apparitions of Devils and Monsters; falling into Gulphs, and off from steep and high Precipices, *and the like*; so that in the Morning, when I shou'd rise, and be refresh'd with the Blessings of Rest, I was *Hagridden* with Frights, and terrible things, form'd

> meerly in the Imagination; and was either tir'd, and wanted
> Sleep, or over-run with Vapours, and not fit for conversing with
> my Family or any-one else. (310)

This passage is an instance, if an extreme one, of the continuous
repartee that Roxana maintains between her wealth and her guilt by
using each one to increase the other. The bathetic sleeplessness with
which the passage ends only heightens the play of speculative
rhetoric at work in it: Roxana's recurrent nightmares produce some
domestic discomforts but fail completely to compel her reformation.
She doesn't mend her ways and, in an almost comic allusion to the
recourse that Catholicism has to consign its penitent voluptuaries
to poverty and convents, Roxana emerges from these nightmares thankful that she isn't a Catholic and liable to confession:
"for . . . what Pennance wou'd any *Father-Confessor* have obliged me
to perform? especially if he had been honest and true to his Office"
(311). Roxana's imagined escape from Catholicism's elaborate and
infamous economy of sin and penance, a random comparison in
place apparently only to mark her historical authenticity, actually
displaces her supposed culpability onto the "greater" evil represented by the Whore of Babylon and always available in anti-
Catholic sentiment. With this displacement, Roxana defers the
demands of her own guilt and allows the inflationary play between
her wealth and her guilt to continue. This mention of Catholicism
threatens to taint all penitential economies, especially those that offer ritual endings: to clear itself, Protestant remorse must continue.
Because Roxana will not be brought to account by "any *Father-Confessor*," she circumvents once again the retributive logic of before
and after, whose photographs even today characterize the busi-
nesses of reform.

Roxana circumvents the closure of repentance by continually
upping the ante, and in this escalation her ongoing psychomachia
shares the rhythms of other verbal contests, including pastoral poetic games. Though the "Preface" would have us believe otherwise,
Roxana's mental anguish apparently cannot offset the pleasure of
the game in which she plays her gains against her fears. She reaches
such speculative heights in this internal dialogue that she finally
forces a break in her "History." The break comes in the coda that

Roxana appends to her history's first conclusion, to the initial "End of my Story" that settles her in Holland "in the height of my Glory and Prosperity" (307). Though this seems to be her destination, Roxana refuses it as conclusion by again increasing the stakes, now hovering at all or nothing: "And let no-body conclude from the strange Success I met with in all my wicked Doings, and the vast Estate which I had rais'd by it, that therefore I either was happy or easie: No, no, there was a Dart struck into the Liver, there was a secret Hell within, even all the while, when our Joy was at its highest" (305). Forced beyond its rightful conclusion by Roxana's unremitting escalation of the differential between her hoard and her horrors, the history narrative loops back to "another Scene," seeking effective discipline in the logic of generation as it emerges with a vengeance in the "the Story of my two Daughters" (311). The story of Susan, the daughter who represents the terrible recriminations that a child can bring against its parent, appears capable, if anything is, of subjecting Roxana to the strict time of history. In her stubborn pursuit of Roxana, Susan often seems no more than a personification of an oppressive and bourgeois patriarchy that controls women through the family. In this ideology, Susan becomes powerful only because she represents the punitive force of the "natural" law of mother-love that Roxana has broken. But this, I will argue in conclusion, is only part of Susan's story. Apparently a tool in the novel's final attempt to discipline its narrative to the theoretical paradigm of history, Susan instead recovers the past as the gamble taken by and in the present. Her return breaks the rule of history through an assault on the novel's (and Roxana's) investment in disguise. Such an assault challenges historical temporality because it is through and against the idea of disguise that history legitimates certain lines of progression; because disguise can be unmasked, the true and the false can be distinguished, and history has its inaugural foundation in fact.

Characterized as its master, Roxana herself is the primary locus of disguise in the novel. Sometimes obliged and sometimes happy to leave her past behind, Roxana accumulates an extensive "secret History." As The "Preface" indicates, the novel establishes its modernity, its ability to capitalize the present, on its ownership of this "secret History" and its ability to alienate Roxana from herself with it. Briefly put, the novel is modern because Roxana is false. In her role as historian, Roxana thus dis-covers her former, false selves for the "virtuous" reader's view. Positioning its female narrator within this linear perspective, the novel claims her as both its collaborator and its scapegoat; Roxana cuts short her digressions into political and economic theory with her well-known "My Business is History," yet it is finally her own "history" that she desperately flees. Abused and abandoned by a patriarchal legal system early in the novel, Roxana must command its temporal structures without inhabiting its public spaces, residing instead in the economic demi-monde of her woman's body: in legal and contractual loopholes, in paradoxically revealing pseudo-disguises such as her skimpy Turkish costume and her plain Quaker dress, in the hyphenated gender "man-woman," and in a persistent namelessness. But it is a mistake to accept these manifestations of Roxana as disguises, a commonplace judgment that is fostered by the novel's stated moral tenets and that packages Roxana's transgressions in a form that encourages puritanical readers, then and now, to claim both the cleanliness and the distance of theory. Our suspicions of the dangers of this position must be aroused by the bad example of Roxana's father, the French immigrant become London capitalist, who distances himself from later French immigrants by discovering them to be economic adventurers disguised as political refugees. This is the historian as "naturalized foreigner," the jealous guardian of his present wealth, and of the wealth of the present, who embraces and exemplifies the exclusionary tactics of nationalism and capital in the name of authenticity. His appearance so very early in *Roxana* indicates that the evidence of difference abides in the accusation of disguise.

Whatever her financial success, Roxana is not a man of business and cannot exclude the other as easily as her father does.[7] Thus her entry into the logic of profit and loss demands that she internalize this paternal example, using the controlling retrospect of autobiography and guilt to condemn the always unnatural foreignness within herself under the rubric of duplicity and disguise. But Roxana's so-called disguises actually disguise nothing, as the famous "paint" scene emphasizes.

It would look a little too much like a Romance here, to repeat all the kind things he said to me, on that Occasion; but I can't omit one Passage; as he saw the Tears drop down my Cheek, he pulls out a fine Cambrick Hankerchief, and was going to wipe the Tears off, but check'd his Hand, as if he was afraid to deface something; I say, he check'd his Hand, and toss'd the Hankerchief to me, to do it myself; I took the Hint immediately, and with a kind of pleasant Disdain, *How, my Lord!* said I, *Have you kiss'd me so often, and don't you know whether I am Painted, or not? Pray let your Highness satisfie yourself, that you have no Cheats put upon you; for once let me be vain enough to say, I have not deceiv'd you with false Colours.* With this, I put a Handkerchief into his Hand, and taking his Hand into mine, I made him wipe my Face so hard, that he was unwilling to do it, for fear of hurting me. (108)

Selected by Roxana as an exemplary episode in her history with the prince, this scene provides us with a tableau in which we can read how history traps Roxana in disguise. The entrapment begins with literary conventions: Roxana, uncharacteristically aware of genre, rejects the conventions of romance, the temptation to repeat everything, in order to recount the "one Passage" that cannot be omitted. With this decision, Roxana reaches for respectability as a historian. The point of this "one Passage" is that Roxana wears a plain face. Through the association of cosmetics and eloquence as ornament, and through Roxana's rejection of romance and its elaborations, the passage asserts an analogy between Roxana's face as clean and her narrative as straightforward. According to this analogy, the proof that Roxana's face is not painted with "false Colours" transfers to her narrative: as the one leaves no trace on the handkerchief, neither does the other. With this assurance, we can read her story without worrying that the ornamental beauties of textuality linger in it to cheat us with illusory truths. But a difficulty arises here because what doesn't transfer from Roxana's face to the handkerchief does transfer from her face to the narrative, and this transfer occurs at Roxana's expense. The claim that Roxana's narrative is plain history, that it is unornamented and true, demands that Roxana be unmasked as false. Thus while the prince hesitates to scrub Roxana, "afraid to deface something," the analogy recoils on her to do exactly that. Unmarred by the handkerchief, she is instead erased. For though the point of the passage seems to be that Roxana is a natural beauty, it creates the opposite effect: we come away from it convinced not that Roxana is undisguised, but that her disguise is beyond detection, neither ornamental nor external but, paradoxically, a doubleness essential to her as woman. The price that Roxana pays to recount history's "one Passage" is self-erasure. Roxana's predicament—one of brazen invisibility—suggests that her so-called disguises are not disguises at all but the evidence of a difference that is stripped bare, of something that cannot speak its own name within the time of its history.

When Susan—her eldest daughter and namesake—reenters Roxana's life, it is to pursue her with the slow, relentless footsteps of monsters in old films and to find Roxana by tracking down her secret history. Our readings of the novel have tended, intentionally or not, to mimic these tactics, as if they provided a good interpretive model and as if that were all there was to Susan's case. Perplexed by the novel's badly constructed finish, we have tracked its secrets in order to unmask them and, fulfilling Roxana's fears, to renounce them. In this we have been "Virtuous" readers, convinced that the novel, like Roxana, has secrets that we must demystify, and that demystification will make reading useful and turn it to our advantage and profit. It doesn't matter whether these secrets are the heretofore unknown underpinnings of Defoe's moralism or those of his ideological agenda, the motivation and result are the same: keep good records and you will be saved. But we cannot assume that Susan is merely Roxana's antithesis and that she, too, is seeking the satisfaction of history in an established genealogy and a firm knowledge of the truth. Despite Roxana's panicked reaction, Susan is not concerned with breaking her mother's disguise but with overcoming it, and she does this by haunting Roxana, first through her search and then through her unsubstantiated "death." Left among the uncertain dead, Susan begins to operate, like Lyotard's "as if phenomenon," to chasten reference.[8] The force with which she haunts Roxana, emerging from the differential between Roxana's wealth and her guilt, warns us that we cannot revisit the past, to make an easy peace with it, without its returning to claim us for its parent, and to lay its death at our door. This is not history's time but postmodernism's. When Roxana sends Amy to find her children and to provide for them financially, she is trying to buy off her past, to settle her debts with them and with her conscience. But Susan is not satisfied with money or with being merely instrumental to history: she comes back, as a ghost does, to be acknowledged and she is willing to lose all the new wealth that Amy offers her in order to be "owned" by her mother. Because such a thing was, and still is, impossible in the primogeniture of history, only Susan's ghost can speak of all that Roxana's pleasurable counting will have done for her name's sake.

Notes

1. Important touchstones in the evolution of this style of reading Defoe are Karl Marx, *Capital: A Critique of Political Economy*, trans. Ben Fowkes (London: Penguin, 1976), 169–172; and Ian Watt, *The Rise of the Novel* (Berkeley: Univ. of California Press, 1964).

2. Maximillian Novak documents Defoe's belief that national wealth results from the "CIRCULATION of Trade" in *Economics and the Fiction of Daniel Defoe* (Berkeley: Univ. of California Press, 1962), esp. 1–31.

3. In "The Rhetoric of Temporality," Paul de Man both acknowledges the work of G. A. Starr and J. Paul Hunter on Defoe's "puritanical" element and integrates it into his own discussion of Defoe's importance to Rousseau's allegory in *La Nouvelle Héloïse*. See "The Rhetoric of Temporality," in *Blindness and Insight* (Minneapolis: Univ. of Minnesota Press, 1983): 187–229.

4. See *The Invention of Tradition*, ed. Eric Hobsbawm and Terence Ranger (Cambridge: Cambridge Univ. Press, 1983).

5. For convenient access, all references to *Roxana* are to the Penguin paperback edition of the novel [*Roxana*, ed. David Blewett (New York: Penguin, 1985)]. Page numbers are cited parenthetically in my text.

6. In *The Complete English Tradesman* (1725), Defoe emphasizes that the tradesman builds his business on his reputation (*Selected Writings of Daniel Defoe*, ed. James Boulton [Cambridge: Cambridge Univ. Press, 1975], 225–239).

7. It is notable in this context that none of the other men in Roxana's memoirs suffers hysterical guilt. The jeweler Roxana lives with as if married suffers no guilt at all about their private arrangement, seeing it as fair, contractual, and legal. The prince and the Dutch merchant, when they become convinced that they are sinning with Roxana, immediately renounce or leave her.

8. See Jean-François Lyotard, *The Differend: Phrases in Dispute*, trans. George Van Den Abbeele (Minneapolis: Univ. of Minnesota Press, 1988), esp. 118–35.

Part Four

The Other Other Victorians

Telling Accounts

De Quincey at the Booksellers

Stacy Carson Hubbard

[T]he dread book of account which the Scriptures speak of, is, in fact, the mind itself of each individual. . . . there is no such thing as forgetting possible to the mind . . . whether veiled or unveiled, the inscription remains forever.
—Confessions of an English Opium Eater

Therefore the present, which only man possesses, offers less capacity for his footing than the slenderest film that ever spider twisted from her womb.
—Suspiria de Profundis

Postmodernism engages the uncanniness of history, experiencing the past, as Bill Readings and Bennet Schaber have put it, as "an imbrication or invasion," a troubling of the present;[1] it suggests the disordering of temporal certainties and the historical subject's unease with historical narratives. In *Confessions of an English Opium Eater* and its sequel, *Suspiria de Profundis*, Thomas de Quincey, that uneasiest of autobiographers, narrates the uncanniness of the self writing and written in time, its slender film of presence purchased through the risky effacements and resurrections of figuration. De Quincey's confessions set out to chart the "primary convulsions" responsible for producing the addicted dream-writer; however, it is the secondary turns (or tropes) of analogy that are revealed as productive of both text and author and that can be seen to drive the narrative's movements within and across a temporal landscape. Hence it is through the autobiography's many figures of resemblance, regression, and return that we can begin to trace De Quincey's relationship to a postmodern practice of reading and writing.

In the *Confessions*, De Quincey names among the primary torments of opium dreams the awful swelling and distortion of time and space, but De Quincey's writings are themselves structured by uncanny temporal and spatial amplifications, wherein images and ideas reverberate endlessly.[2] This essay follows some of these reverberations, or involutions of time and memory, by taking up the themes of debt and translation as they converge in *Suspiria de Profundis*. Both debt and translation produce temporal disorderings, the former in its guarantee of a return of past deeds in the form of an accounting, the latter in that interlining of original and echo in which the life of the text is seen to consist in its afterlife.[3] Jacques Derrida, in "Des Tours de Babel," asserts that the incommensurability of one language to another and of all language to meaning gives rise to the necessary "twists and turns" not only of translation but of figuration as well. Derrida characterizes translation's failed attempts at the restitution of meaning as "insolvent debt[s] within a genealogical scene,"[4] language suggestive of De Quincey's peculiar interlacing of familial and literary histories. De Quincey casts the translator's task as a response to the deaths and disappearances of a sister and her surrogates. Because his confessions turn thus upon the animating force of deanimated feminine figures, a special kind of recurring debt enters the narrative: the debt masculine narrative owes to feminine silence. The turn or revolution, the aerial leap and the launch, are De Quincey's figures for both translation and analogy, and they are, moreover, the very stuff of the *Suspiria's* sublime visions. Translation in its multiple meanings of spatial relocation, linguistic transfer, and temporal displacement structures De Quincey's perpetual quest for the origins of the writing self set in motion by autobiography.[5]

While doubts about origins and originality, the specter of repetition, and a guilty indebtedness drive those discourses of the new that comprise the modern tradition, postmodernism, in its very name, recognizes that every act of authorization may be a translation, hence an incurring of debt. Understood, in one of its aspects, as a tension between the impulse toward self-authorization and the knowledge of indebtedness, postmodernism can be thought as the return (as opposed to the repetition) of the Romantic notion of the sublime. The concern with the construction and violation of boundaries, the flooding of individual consciousness by history, the establishment of the mind's superiority or originality,[6] and the strange commingling of pleasure and terror in the contemplation of incommunicable or unrepresentable ideas that characterizes the Romantic sublime invites its being read together with the idea of postmodernity.[7] Both terms are inhabited by the recurring question of recurrence. It would, however, be a mistake to see postmodernism as a mere parallel to the discourse of the sublime, or as its simple repetition within an altered historical context. Rather, postmodernism may be understood as a *translation* of the sublime, in Benjamin's sense of that transaction: translation as significance superadded, which makes of its original a different thing even as it allows the incursions of the original's foreignness to reconfigure its own tongue.[8] It is such an indebtedness as only a free, never a faithful, translation can hope to repay.

In the *Suspiria*, De Quincey gives an account of a childhood debt at the bookseller's. This scene sits at the center of the text like a spider, drawing into its web the autobiography's preoccupations with memory, guilt, translation, and originality. The story of the debt is introduced in order to illustrate the revitalization of the memory of the dead—or, more precisely, the revitalization of grief, that emotion which marks loss and itself keeps memory alive—through association. Grief, De Quincey tells us, passes through three distinct phases: the most immediate of these has a "stunning and confounding" effect; the succeeding phase appears as an oscillation between violent tumult and languishing repose; and the final stage, emerging just as sorrow seems on the point of extinction, rekindles grief through its association with guilt and limitless anxiety. Thus grief (and memory) are sustained by anxiety, kept alive and on the move, as restless as sunbeams, infants, cataracts, or the "eternal wheelings" of water birds.[9] Just as these must continue to play, "incalculable" in the variety of their "caprices," only suspending play "as a variety of play" (154), so must De Quincey keep in motion his own great grief as a player on the stage of autobiography. De Quincey's comments on the three phases of grief set the stage for the elaborately burlesque account of proliferating anxiety arising from the bookseller's debt, an anxiety which serves to keep alive the child De Quincey's grief for his dead sister, Elizabeth. Grief is kept aloft and in motion, and, like the water birds, partakes of the "immortality" of "inexhaustible variety" (154) through participation in De Quincey's seriocomic fantasy of abundance. The role grief plays as a spur to memory mimics that which opium plays in providing access to the world of dreams and imagination in the *Confessions*, and, like opium, grief ostensibly works to ground the autobiography by giving it an origin.[10] However, as we shall see, the very necessity of grief's movement undermine's its own fidelity to an original cause; its continual oscillations come to resemble De Quincey's extempore translations of the daily newspapers into Greek, in which robust invention concocted Greek equivalents where memory could find none.[11] So, too, grief may need to reinvent its source.

De Quincey credits the onset of anxiety with keeping alive not only his grief but his understanding as well, by keeping him in a state of feverish irritation not unlike that later induced by opium. De Quincey comes under the tutelage of terror as a result of what he terms his "earliest trespass," the incurrence of a three-guinea debt for books (155). At the age of seven, De Quincey is initiated into the study of Latin, an initiation coinciding with his admittance into the world of money, and, significantly, with his withdrawal from a languishing desire to join Elizabeth in the grave. Although entrusted with a large weekly allowance, he soon finds that his insatiable desire for books outruns his resources, and he is responsible for a "mysterious" and "guilty" debt (155). Why this indebtedness gives rise to such extravagant visions of horrific consequence is perhaps to be discovered in the confluence of grief and understanding, of loss and gain, that occurs here. A complex series of associations is established in De Quincey's account: between dead sisters and "dead" languages; between monetary debts and more "mysterious" ones; between the growth or proliferation of understanding, anxiety, grief, and the written word. Indebtedness, for De Quincey, signals the presence of the past; it is the price of remembering.

Indeed, indebtedness, with its attendant horrors, falls to De Quincey as a direct result of his exceptional memory. Entrusted with the purchase of books for his guardian, De Quincey soon proves himself to be incapable of "such a thing as 'forgetting' in the case of a book," and, as a result, the "trouble of writing [orders] was dismissed" (156). Hence, the bookseller, knowing the boy to be acting as "factor-general" for the older man, has no reason to question his incurrence of a three-guinea debt. The debt is *covered* by association with the guardian's debts and, consequently, it "flow[s] homewards" to him, it becomes "lost in the waters of some more important river" (156). But the bookseller has yet another reason for placing paternal confidence in De Quincey, and this also as a result of De Quincey's gift for remembering "in the case of a book." Early on in his Latin studies, before he has yet acquired either love for or proficiency in the language, De Quincey visits the bookseller, who takes down a Latin Bible and assigns the boy a chapter to translate. Though his Latin is faulty, De Quincey recognizes the chapter as that of St. Paul "on the grave and resurrection" (157). De Quincey knows this chapter well and is able to "read it off with . . . fluency and effect," thus gaining the affections of the bookseller and "launch[ing]" himself on the "bosom of Latin literature" (157–58). Suddenly, he is struck with the "correspondence of the two concurrent streams—Latin and English" and the way is open to brilliant mastery of the ancient tongue. What is it precisely that succeeds in "knock[ing] away the 'shores' " (157), to use De Quincey's expression, with such violence? Memory permits him to gloss, or cover, the Latin with the English, which he knows (indeed, which has been impressed upon him) because it is the very text of the funeral service read for his sister, Elizabeth. In accounting for his memory of this service, De Quincey explains his remarkable powers of recall. "Rarely do things perish from my memory that are worth remembering. . . . I mention this in no spirit of boasting. Far from it, for, on the contrary, among my mortifications have been compliments to my memory, when, in fact, any compliment that I had merited was due to the higher faculty of an electric aptitude for seizing analogies and by means of those aerial pontoons passing over like lightning from one topic to another" (142–43).

The initial deflationary gesture of this passage—its disclaimer of boasting, the mortification at compliments—yields to the inflationary claim to a "higher faculty," an aptitude for analogy whose transformative power outstrips and renders unnecessary the merely retentive powers of memory, the sheer reptition of memory's mechanical process. With the autobiographer's promotion to analogic thinker—philosopher rather than memoirist—De Quincey hopes to slip the yoke of deadly repetition, to enfranchise both translation and autobiography. The dead hand hovering so conspicuously over the translator's task, threatening to claim all his words as its own, necessitates the cataclysmic "lightning" whose rupture enables free translation, the casting off of the reader's debt. It is appropriate that De Quincey's access to a new—rather, an old—language comes by way of its intersection with the figure of Elizabeth, for translation, as Benjamin tells us, touches its original "in a fleeting manner and at a single point," as "the tangent touches a circle";[12] or, to employ one of De Quincey's own figures for memory, as the child's stone "skim[s] the breast of a river" (167). Translation, like memory and grief, undulates. Derrida tells us that "the translator . . . appears to himself in a situation of debt," under the "injunction" of an "other," and needing to acquit himself "of something that implies . . . a fault, a fall, an error, and perhaps a crime."[13] Indeed, where the figure of Elizabeth touches the Latin text—translates it, analogically—the boy-reader finds himself touched by vague and irremediable obligations.

In this scene of translation, grief does indeed keep alive understanding by making possible those "aerial pontoons" that are analogy, or the "concurren[ce] of streams," by which De Quincey is able to pass over from the English to the Latin, from the memory of a dead sister to the acquisition of a dead language. Here memory, by covering one language with another, hence gaining the paternal favor of the bookseller, opens the way not only to mastery of a new language, but to indebtedness also: the older man trusts the boy, making possible transgression. "There was no river that would carry it off to sea," says De Quincey of his little debt (155); and, true enough, it is not the debt but De Quincey's anxiety that gets "carr[ied] off to sea," kept alive by association with yet another debt of far more monstrous proportions. Old debts, like old griefs and anxieties, keep on the move in De Quincey's writings, and this greater debt, into which anxiety over the first flows, focuses, appropriately enough, on the sea. The ceaseless movement of waters, De Quincey's image for the endless play of grief and anxiety, comes to form the substance of that anxiety: he contracts to purchase a potentially endless history of navigation "upon the inexhaustible sea" (159).[14] Here is a debt that will "knock away the 'shores' " with a vengeance, launching anxiety on a potentially endless voyage. The trespass is small, but the consequences are enormous—he has "purchased some numbers" of the navigational work "and obtained others on credit," thus, as he sees it, "silently contract[ing] an engagement to take all the rest, though they should stretch to the crack of doom" (159). The contracting of the small debt implies, in the boy's imagination, responsibility for a much larger debt. "[I]t was the principle," says De Quincey, "the having presumed to contract debts on my own account, that I feared to have exposed" (157). If he can be shown to have one small debt, he can be assumed to have any number of other debts, of any degree of magnitude. He may have contracted to buy the whole sea, or worse.

That this "earliest trespass" is in fact something more like a leak in the floodgate containing guilt is evidenced by the irrationally disproportionate anxiety it releases. Guilt, like grief and anxiety, partakes of the quality of infinity in the *Suspiria*; its vibrations, or implications, are endless. "[T]he primary convulsions of nature," says De Quincey, "come round again and again by reverberating shocks (154–55). Minds that are impassioned on a more colossal scale than ordinary, deeper in their vibrations, and more extensive in the scale of their vibrations . . . will tremble to greater depths from a fearful convulsion and will come round by a longer curve of undulations" (155 n.). This machinery of grief bears a striking resemblance to the operations of guilt and retribution as represented in the figure of the stationer's company, sitting in London like a murderous spider at the center of its web. De Quincey's "silent contract" has been heard at the center and he is liable to identification.

> I felt the fatal truth, that here was a ghostly cobweb radiating into all the provinces from the mighty metropolis. I secretly had trodden upon the outer circumference, had damaged or deranged

the fine threads or links; concealment or reparation there could
be none. Slowly, perhaps, but surely, the vibration would travel
back to London. The ancient spider that sat there at the center
would rush along the network through all longitudes and lati-
tudes until he found the responsible caitiff, author of so much
mischief. (159)

It is the volumes themselves that will, in fact, "rush along the
network" to find him—it is the "work" that can "disperse itself,"
"levy money," "put questions and get answers" (159). The book will
find out the "author of . . . mischief" and "expose" him, in a gesture
which collapses reader and author, the text read and the text written. It is the visible evidence of "past offenses" that De Quincey
most fears, and that he figures as the depositing of great heaps of
navigational volumes—fifteen, twenty, thirty thousand—on his
front lawn. The offenses are endless in quantity, the work having
acquired "supplements to supplements," and "lying in . . . [a]
conspicuous . . . situation" (160). We may recognize this scene as an
instance of the mathematical sublime, or what Thomas Weiskel has
called "the reader's sublime," realized in the mountainous concrete-
ness of an almost-natural spectacle. With his anxiety published thus,
De Quincey's fantasy of proliferating guilt begins to look suspi-
ciously like the autobiography itself—an endlessly supplemented
work confessing its author's transgressions, consuming his life's energies, wresting control away from him, and exposing him in ways
both pleasurable and horrifying. The reader, threatened by the magnitude of reading material, in danger of losing himself in the language of others, recuperates the self thus threatened by writing the
mountain that he cannot read. Yet the balance achieved through this
reversal, the redistribution of loss and gain that Weiskel calls the
sublime moment's "economic event,"[15] does not do away with debt.
The reader become writer writes in order to confess, and these writings too may "stretch to the crack of doom." The *Confessions*, De
Quincey's published commentary on the *Confessions*, its revisions,
appendix, and promised third part, and the perennially unfinished
Suspiria de Profundis, may be the real "books on the lawn." But what,
if anything, do they confess?

The books of the autobiography and the books that threaten to appear on the lawn both expose, or identify, the self (be it reader or author) as criminal. De Quincey makes explicit the importance of self-recognition as self-indictment when he parallels his situation with that of Oedipus. Like Oedipus, De Quincey is fated to enact prophesied crimes and to arrive at recognition of himself only through the retrospective matching of himself "with acts incestuous, murderous, parricidal in the past and with a mysterious fatality of woe lurking in the future" (156n). To identify oneself by reading oneself into the evidence of a crime is to be simultaneously both reader and "author of . . . mischief" (159), to attempt to control the unknown by giving it a name—one's own. De Quincey says regarding the stationers. "I had often observed them in popular works threatening unknown men with unknown chastisements for offenses equally unknown, nay, to myself absolutely inconceivable. Could I be the mysterious criminal so long pointed out, as it were, in prophecy?" (159).

This process of reading in, or writing over, recalls De Quincey's initiation into Latin, wherein recognition made possible reading and both were linked to the memory of the dead sister. Similarly, De Quincey's recognition of his own criminality is experienced as the rereading of a tale from the *Arabian Nights* that he was once in the habit of reading to his sister. The story is obviously an Oedipal one: a young porter woos the beautiful wife of a magician, fleeing at the magician's return and accidentally leaving his ropes behind; the magician attempts to return the ropes to the young man, who denies that they are his. De Quincey credits this tale with giving rise to his own fantasy of books—visible evidence of guilt—arriving on the lawn. He imagines that "in the rear of [these fifteen thousand volumes] there might also be ropes" (161). The books, like the ropes, bind one to something and to own them is to be bound by them. De Quincey tells us that he was particularly fond of ventriloquizing, for his sister's amusement, the young man's reply to the magician: "'O Mr. Magician, these ropes cannot be mine! They are far too good . . . I never had money enough to buy so beautiful a set of ropes' " (160–61). In recalling this story, De Quincey imagines the young man as himself, foretold in prophecy, "contemplated in types a thousand years before" (161). Like Oedipus, he recognizes himself as he who must fulfill prophecy by owning a deed, by recognizing his own story as already told. He is himself made redundant by the story, which is "literally reproduced in [him]self," forcing him to "repeat within [his] own inner experience the shadowy panic of the young Bagdad intruder" (161). Like the *Arabian Nights* themselves and like the books accumulating on the lawn, the records of his crimes proliferate—they can be read everywhere. De Quincey's voice-over of the porter's reply is his response to the fabulous proliferation of criminal debts: he knows himself to be the culprit, but he cannot possibly own the crime, for he cannot possibly pay its price. Yet, paradoxically, the proliferation itself serves to ward off punishment (just as the generation of stories in the *Arabian Nights* forestalls death), since the stationers cannot reasonably demand payment until all the volumes have been delivered. The appearance of Elizabeth at the scene of multiplying debts and texts points to her function as a figure for origins, and originary guilt, yet the nature of the debt owed to her remains obscure. De Quincey's "gallant spinn[ing]" (159) of autobiography may be said both to attempt reimbursement of the sister—grief is kept alive as a way of keeping *her* alive in memory—and to forestall payment in kind—the death of the autobiographer (and of autobiography). The record, or confession of crimes, which can be said to establish identity, serves also to defer punishment.

De Quincey's horror at the prospect of thousands upon thousands of books coming home to him is a horror of discovery, of having uncovered the infinite implications underlying a single transgressive act. Just as the English text of St. Paul was capable of being written over the Latin text, hence, paradoxically, making the Latin readable for the first time, so these few volumes purchased overlay an endless succession of other volumes. This writing over, which suppresses texts and at the same time makes possible their recovery, is, of course, a palimpsest, that stage upon which texts undulate in a seemingly endless process of loss and recovery, and which De Quincey likens to the operations of memory. In his discussion of the palimpsest in the *Suspiria*, De Quincey imagines this excavation of texts as a process of "back[ing] upon each phoenix in the long *regressus* and forc[ing] him to expose his ancestral phoenix,

sleeping in the ashes below his own ashes" (168); that is, he figures
the project as forced exposure of those dead from whom one has
taken life or those effacements that have cleared the road for new
texts. This description directly echoes De Quincey's earlier description of the imagined scene of the books' delivery. "Looking
out, I should perceive a procession of carts and wagons, all ad-
vancing in measured movements; each in turn would present its
rear, deliver its cargo of volumes . . . and *wheel off* to the rear, by
way of *clearing the road for its successors*" (160, emphasis mine). The
Suspiria abounds in palimpsestic images of marking and obliteration; to take just one example, the extravagance of the navigational
record that De Quincey feels bound to purchase is said to rival the
extravagance of the paths scored on the sea, "their
tracts . . . blend[ing] into one indistinguishable blot" (157) and
threatening to obliterate the sea itself.[16] This scoring and writing
provokes terror, because it lures one toward the infinite and blots
everything into indistinguishability by its very exuberance; what
begins as a distinguishing mark or track ends as obliteration.
However, a similar network of connecting or leading lines, imaged
as a giant spider's web or a magician's ropes, proves fearful for De
Quincey *because* of its very power to distinguish or identify. Because no vibration passes unnoticed along their sensitive net-
works, the ropes or webs will find one out and trap or bind one. To
be identified in this way is to be bound by identity, to be grounded
in that which is permanent and characteristic. And yet, De
Quincey's description of the palimpsest's successive covering and
uncovering of texts, the "alternate successions" by which it is
"sense for your own generation, [and] nonsense for the next" (166–
67), recalling his earlier description of the permutations of grief,
suggests that it is perhaps only movement itself that can truly be
called "primary."

A book . . . [is] sense for your own generation, nonsense for the
next . . . , revive[s] into sense for the next after that, but again
become[s] nonsense for the fourth, and so on by alternate successions, sinking into night or blazing into day like the Sicilian river
Arethusa and the English river Mole; or like the undulating
motions of a flattened stone which children cause to skim the

breast of a river, now diving below the water, now grazing its
surface, sinking heavily into darkness, rising buoyantly into light,
through a long vista of alternations. (166–67)[17]

What underlies the palimpsest in De Quincey's example—its
primary impression—is a Greek tragedy; that is, an old drama always in need of translation, not unlike the story of Elizabeth, who is
herself perpetually translated into other female figures, such as the
prostitute Ann and Wordsworth's dead daughter, throughout the
Confessions. As the Suspiria's eternally restless displacements of the
feminine attest, Elizabeth is the figure for a guilt without a name, an
account with no bottom line. She is the hinge upon which the mind
moves, as Kant tells us it must, in response to that spectacle of the
past that we call the sublime. Elizabeth as double takes on herself
the burden of stillness and silence, making possible the continued
movement and articulation of the figure of De Quincey within the
text. She must undergo erasure, that he may write over her not her
life but his own. Her death figures an origin for the wild proliferation of grief, anxiety, and guilt apparent in the tale of her and the
bookseller's return. Return, both wished for and dreaded, is what
promises to end proliferation and, incidentally, storytelling. The
young De Quincey longs for the sympathetic counsel of his sister
concerning his tormenting debt, "the knowledge that, having parted
with my secret, yet also I had not parted with it, since it was in the
power only of one that could much less betray me than I could
betray myself" (161). It is with her that the escalating threat of indebtedness and exposure would come to rest; she is the one he
could tell of his debt as if he were telling himself. The story would
go no further; the silent double would remain silent—but only at the
price, for De Quincey, of losing the exquisite, albeit painful, pleasures of self-betrayal.

It is both frightening to De Quincey that his sister might be
resurrected and reassuring to assuage his guilt with the thought that
she, like "the mysterious handwritings" on the palimpsest of the
brain, might "not [be] dead, but sleeping" (171), and might be
brought back to life by memory and by writing. De Quincey concludes the episode of the bookseller's debt with the recognition that
this debt stands in for another. "Forever I dallied with some obscure

notion, how my sister's love might be made in some dim way available for delivering me from misery, or else how the misery I had suffered and was suffering might be made, in some way equally dim, the ransom for winning back her love" (162).

Recovery of the lost sister would serve to halt the proliferation of anxiety, which is fueled by grief, but which itself seems a necessary payment for the recovery of Elizabeth, who is of course only recovered in the sense that she is remembered and recorded. The sister's absence and silence clear space for the proliferation of writing that De Quincey pays out—the books of confession and exposure, so long as they continue accumulating on the lawn, forestall and eventually come to take the place of retribution.

Guilt is the mark of an unknowable origin. The sister, who bears what De Quincey calls the one "insupportable burden," the burden of the "Incommunicable," figures what cannot be represented, and in so doing works to halt the escalation of abysmal vision. Guilt, in the *Suspiria,* is operative, rather than traceable—it is the price of authorship whose vague unease wanders in search of a cause. The revolutions of grief and the autobiographical subject whose movements they track, keep identity on the lam; the ropes, the threads, the vibrations, the "long curve[s] of undulation," like translation merely flirt with fidelity, touching down here and there on a word or a figure. Such is the striking passage in which De Quincey describes the mind's "mighty system of central forces" as continuous as "day and night ... whose moments, like restless spokes, are glimmering forever as they revolve" (173). De Quincey footnotes the word "glimmering."

> Here ... I restore to Mr. Wordsworth this fine image of ... the glimmering spokes.... I borrowed it for one moment in order to point my own sentence, which being done, the reader is witness that I now pay it back instantly by a note.... On the same principle I often borrow their seals from young ladies when closing my letters. Because there is sure to be some tender sentiment upon them about 'memory,' or 'hope,' or 'roses,' or 'reunion,' and my correspondent must be a sad brute who is not touched by the eloquence of the seal, even if his taste is so bad that he remains deaf to mine. (173)

With this note of payment, De Quincey inflates to deflate, paying back the father with a vengeance, and showing Wordsworth just how little his word is worth. The word of the literary father as mere sentimental seal serves to point out the son's eloquence, and the messages of the ladies' seals suggest that reunion, memory, and ladies themselves may be nothing more than the temporarily impressed emblems that hold a text together. Likewise, Elizabeth's location in the place of the Incommunicable—the silence with which she both threatens De Quincey's writing and confirms his own volubility—identifies her as an agent of sublime blockage, that which assaults the ego with its potential for dispersal but which, ultimately, holds the mind together. She functions as the uneasy resolution to that phenomenon Neil Hertz has called "the end of the line," where the spectacle of indistinguishability dictates a recuperative displacement, an "aggressive assertion of the subject's stability . . . bought at some other subject's expense."[18]

In conclusion, I want to glance at a story De Quincey recounts near the end of the *Suspiria*, one that may serve as a "sister-scene" to that of the books on the lawn. In this second scene, a lone female figure once again intervenes to halt uncontrollable proliferation. Attempting to account for the *Suspiria's* incompleteness, De Quincey claims that its concluding dream sequences were destroyed when he overturned a candle while reading, causing it to fall among the mountains of paper in his room; but for the timely intervention of "one sole person" with her wits about her, he would have burned up the entire house as well as all the records of his dreams (191–92). Here the figure of the unnamed woman appears in order to halt, not the proliferation of texts, but their destruction; she validates—or puts her seal upon—the autobiography by saving it. And yet we know this scene of the burning dreams to be a mere debtor's ruse, the excuse De Quincey gave his publisher for his failure to deliver the promised conclusion to the text. This story stands in for those unwritten. De Quincey's autobiographical writings, originally undertaken to remedy debt, bind him with new debts: where the reader pays *for* books, the writer must pay *with* books. The name with which De Quincey signed his serialized *Confessions* is, in fact, no name at all, merely the anonymous mark of the debtor: "X.Y.Z." The nameless author signs himself from a position at the end of language, thus acknowledging, even in his evasions, an indebtedness to all that has come before. De Quincey's terror of reading's remainder, the track that books leave behind, here turns its other face, appearing as the fearful fantasy of the track's erasure, when the reader's flood becomes the writer's fire. This reader reads by the light of his own burning books ("My attention was first drawn by a sudden light upon my book") yet even then arrives late to the apocalypse, for Wordsworth has surely preceded him here, with his dream of an Arab and his fragile books threatened by "the fleet waters of a drowning world."[19] Indeed, Wordsworth's waters, described as "a bed of glittering light" (129), seem to prefigure De Quincey's fire *and* his flood. And it is not this vision of endings alone that De Quincey owes to Wordsworth, for his sense of a beginning is borrowed as well: De Quincey's image for cataclysmic origins ("primary convulsions")—the wheeling waterbirds with which our discussion began—has its origin in a poem of Wordsworth's, as De Quincey acknowledges in a note.[20] It would seem that De Quincey's narrative is encircled by Wordsworth's wheeling figures. Where even apocalypse has a history, the already written and the yet to be written converge. It is the postmodern reader's sublime dilemma to be thus poised between historical narratives and apocalyptic dreams, to find oneself writing just a step ahead of (or is it behind?) the flood.

Notes

1. See their introduction to this volume.

2. *Thomas de Quincey: Confessions of an English Opium Eater and Other Writings,* ed. Eileen Ward (New York: New American Library, 1966), 90–91.

3. I paraphrase Walter Benjamin, "The Task of the Translator," *Illuminations,* ed. with intro. by Hannah Arendt, trans. Harry Zohn (New York: Schocken, 1969) 71–73, 82.

4. In Joseph F. Graham, ed., *Difference in Translation* (Ithaca, N.Y.: Cornell Univ. Press, 1985) 165, 176. Derrida's comments gloss those of Benjamin in "The Task of the Translator."

5. On the importance of anteriority and temporal inversion in De Quincey's treatment of language, see Mary Jacobus, "The Art of Managing Books: Romantic Prose and the Writing of the Past," in *Romanticism and Language,* ed. Arden Reed (Ithaca, N.Y.: Cornell Univ. Press, 1984) 215–46.

6. See Thomas Weiskel, *The Romantic Sublime: Studies in the Structure and Psychology of the Sublime* (Baltimore: Johns Hopkins Univ. Press, 1986), esp. 136–167.

7. Jean-Francois Lyotard suggests this link between postmodern art's attempts to put forward "the unpresentable in presentation itself" (81) and the "incommensurability of reality to concept" (79) in the Kantian sublime (*The Postmodern Condition: A Report on Knowledge,* trans. Geoff Bennington and Brian Massumi [Minneapolis: Univ. of Minnesota Press, 1984]).

8. Benjamin, "The Task of the Translator," 80–81.

9. *Suspiria de Profundis,* in Ward, 153–54. Unless otherwise indicated, subsequent page numbers within the text refer to this edition.

10. On this transfer of heroic qualities from opium onto grief, see William C. Spengemann, *The Forms of Autobiography: Episodes in the History of a Literary Genre* (New Haven: Yale Univ. Press, 1980), 91–109.

11. *Confessions,* 35.

12. Benjamin, "The Task of the Translator," 80.

13. Derrida, *Difference in Translation,* 175–76.

14. Elizabeth died of hydrocephalus, or "water on the brain." See *Suspiria,* 125–126n.

15. Weiskel, *The Romantic Sublime,* 25.

16. Another significant instance of this language appears in a meditation on the fate of the prostitute Ann—one of the autobiography's many analogues for Elizabeth—whose "ingenuous nature" De Quincey imagines to have been "blotted out and transfigured" by the "brutalities of ruffians" (*Confessions,* 56). See also the passages concerning the disfiguring of Elizabeth's face by surgeons after her death, and the equally horrible erasure of her countenance's familiar "traces" by heavenly transfiguration (134–35).

17. The *Confessions* contain many similar images of alternating light and darkness, including the following description of the way to Wordsworth's Grasmere home, which points to Wordsworthian autobiography as one of the subtexts the *Confessions* attempts to supplant by writing over: "[D]uring my first mournful abode in London, my consolation was (if such it could be thought) to gaze from Oxford Street up every avenue in succession which pierces through the heart of Mary-le-bone to the fields and the woods; for *that,* said I, traveling with my eyes up *the long vistas which lay part in light and part in shade* [emphasis mine], 'that is the road to the north, and, therefore to——, and if I had the wings of a dove, that way I would fly for comfort' " (*Confessions,* 57).

18. *The End of the Line: Essays on Psychoanalysis and the Sublime* (New York: Columbia Univ. Press, 1985), 223.

19. *The Prelude,* eds. Jonathan Wordsworth, M. H. Abrams, and Stephen Gill (New York: Norton, 1979), 5. 137.

20. *Suspiria,* 154.

Part Five

Modern and Contemporary

10

The Wrong "Saddest Story"

Reading the Appearance of Postmodernity in Ford's *Good Soldier*

ROBERT M. ROBERTSON

It has become customary to treat Ford Madox Ford's *The Good Soldier* as one of the great novels—perhaps *the* great novel—about a modern man's loss of the moral center from which right action should proceed, and then to read from this individual failure a general indictment of the whole lost generation that is modernity.[1] Certainly this reading of the personal and the political genuinely reflects Ford's intent, since sometimes openly and sometimes through such proxies as his amateur soldier and lifetime bureaucrat Tietjens (in *Parade's End*), the author himself would discover that everything comes down to a choice between behaving well and collapsing into a "wretched, irresolute Johnny," more than a decade after he had sat himself down to write his first novel on 17 December 1913.[2] The reading works, too, to explain the obsessive style of a book whose every sentence repeats its narrator's hopeless attempt to use what Denis Donoghue calls a "voice that has every power—except the power to change anything," as a weapon against the infidelity of women, the lies of friends, and almost everything else in a suddenly changing world.[3] And the humanist reading even brings out the uncanny power Ford's masterpiece still retains to predict the way that everyone would learn, after the Great War, to shape their anxieties around having nothing better than a private

171

and aesthetic counter to the disappearance of a world whose order-liness had made life meaningful for their parents. The problems only come when we try to stay in that same framework and describe the historical grounds of Ford's best novel. Apparently all this col-lapsing has something to do with the peculiar nature of the onset of the twentieth century, but it is hard to tell exactly what.

It is not that a reflection upon the failed attempt to aestheti-cally compensate for some cultural trauma occurring at the start of modernism—indeed, some cultural trauma that *is* the start of modernism—has proved altogether incapable of connecting these collapsing narrators and incoherent narratives to history in gen-eral. There is H. Robert Huntley's claim that this novel takes up "the central issue . . . of purpose, meaning, and pattern in an age of relative values," and though this only repeats pretty much what Ford's narrator had told us in the first place in order to lay the blame on the usual doormat of liberalism, there is at least a clear attempt to deal with the everyday lived experience of modernity.[4] There is, in different and more useful terms, Roger Sale's feminist insistence on "Ford's worst instincts" and profound misogyny as they are worked through John Dowell's attempts to blame some-one, anyone, anything, but preferably women for his own failures to meaningfully shape his relation to the new world that emerges once religion and class and pure aesthetics seem to start evaporat-ing.[5] Very generally, there are attempts like Paul Fussell's to crys-tallize Ford's lived experience of modernity into one sign of the general cultural losses that made "the Great War . . . perhaps the last to be conceived as taking place within a seamless, purposeful 'history' involving a coherent stream of time running from past through present to future."[6] These emphases upon one man's moral questionings, then, anchor a strong and elastic paradigm for interpretation that allows for politically very different readings fo-cused on the organizational problems of the text, its flawed at-tempt to work through the problematic landscape of the modern, and the stylistic attempt to regain a measure of control through the multiplication of objects in writing. But the paradigm built around picking out the individual subject's viewpoint leads the reader toward missing the very historical changes that are the essence of modernism; not surprisingly, the fact that the middle-class subject's viewpoint begins to fray badly in the Europe of 1913 and after is precisely what is most easily overlooked.

The problem for this essay, then, is that using a humanist paradigm of interpretation to produce Ford's congruent ideas and describe their initial reception also has the side effect of concealing what goes on historically. It particularly forces an apotropaic (in the sense advanced by Neil Hertz in his discussions of the similar events in and around Romanticism, where "apotropaic" refers to the symptomatology of male hysteria under political pressure) stance with regard to Ford's book and its buried history, leading the reader to insist upon critically isolating the blind spots in one man's story and then grieving for the loss of one man's ability to tell the tale that makes the world.[7] Such reading can only repeat that general modernist logic in which historical change becomes a castration. Accordingly, I want to argue here for ignoring that poignant figure at the heart of the text in favor of reading the historical processes that Dowell's produced voice and presence eclipse. I want to take *The Good Soldier* as a melancholy book that tries endlessly to resurrect a world that in some sense never was, an act of writing that can reveal the brand-new way of organizing human culture that emerges in *The Good Soldier* as the real threat. In other words what matters here, and what the Dowells of the world have little chance of figuring out, is the emergence of something beyond the moral configurations of modernism. The very historical processes we define as the postmodern erupt through precisely the long list of things that Dowell claims to know nothing about yet is haunted by. That emergence of a history without the old camouflage needs detailing. Once we get past his too-tight focus upon a secret that is at once sexual and moral, all the ugly little secrets about accounting and transportation and the remapping of the world come to matter most as the jumbled heart of this book. It is not a question of the death of the modern and attempts to resuscitate the corpse: it is a question of the birth of a postmodern, emerging as an uncanniness in Ford's literary masterpiece that can be broken down into a changed logic of circulations, a remapping of Victorian space, and a profound reordering of the human subject.

An attempt to leave the grounds of a modern moral landscape and look for the narrative logic of a history developing toward the postmodern might help work through the economic questions *The Good Soldier* keeps trying to sweep off the stage, only for money and class to keep coming back. After all, the book is built around the assumption that everybody who is anybody lives without the slightest financial worries in order to concentrate upon the important things in life, which is to say that its "realistic" treatment of modernity is built around the absence of money as something representing real labor. Even when Edward Ashburnham misplaces a large chunk of his inherited fortune, it is not long at all in a narrative time placed against the story time—the real time it takes to accumulate wealth; that is, the time of labor—before the Ashburnhams return from India and the happy husband can tell his wife, "there's nothing I like so much as to have a little to chuck away—and I can do it, thanks to you" (188). By the time Dowell takes over center stage at the end of the novel, everyone lives in a completely textualized world in which the old-fashioned way to make money is to talk about it. The narrator's only real problems with money, at the end of a developing process, are those of the potlatch ceremony: he cannot see how to give away enough of the stuff. For Ford, money is at most a hurdle to be gotten over, a problem on a moral obstacle course. It was, of course, first and foremost George Lukács who taught us how to read such characters, such plot developments, and above all such stylistic innovations as Ford made in the modern novel while keeping within the humanist framework. The essential thing is to see that *The Good Soldier* speaks for a whole class that attempts in such art to defend itself by retreating into a subjectivism and aestheticism. This defense goes so far as to seal itself off from a reality taken as completely other in ways that are the natural outcome of the inherent difference between the bourgeois and the workers' experience of the world. Dowell's failure to do more than mourn the loss of the self and the moral certainties that had been worked out in the older class structures then being translated (especially in the America Ford left behind), together with his insistence upon maundering about the world from the non-standpoint of a decentered Jamesianism in which the narrator's point of view is open to question, then amounts to little more than another example of the elegies a whole class was busily writing for itself, marking time until it learned how to handle the new situation. But doesn't

The Good Soldier suggest something more than an account of one class's receding dreams, dreams which would become more and more ironic as Ford himself drew closer and closer to having to beg his publishers for money around 1939?

The limitations of Lukácsian Marxism have repeatedly been mapped. They revolve around twin insistences upon evaluating everything in terms of the historical subject supposed someday to emerge through the veils of modernism and upon forcing everything that happens into the moral narrative of history rolling on toward its inevitable revolution.[8] Lukács can have only so much to say about the specific connections Ford draws between the greedy harpy at Monte Carlo who takes Edward Ashburnham's money and the Indian workers who give it back, for instance, because this sort of reading is trying to get past modernism and onto revolution as quickly as possible. What about—to put things on the most prosaic level—the fascination with counting in *The Good Soldier* that suggests how some other logic is emerging through the veneer of emotions, of tragedies? Certainly for Dowell, whose name suggests that he is a part in some analytical engine, the obsession with counting, recounting, and the coincidences of number (that seem immensely significant though their full significance never quite comes out into the open) is as important as anything else.

> The death of Mrs. Maidan occurred on the fourth of August 1904. And then nothing happened until the fourth of August 1913. There is the curious coincidence of dates, but I do not know whether that is one of the sinister, as if half jocular and altogether merciless proceedings on the part of a cruel Providence that we call a coincidence . . . It is however certain that the fourth of August always provided a significant date for her. To begin with she was born on the fourth of August. Then on that date, in the year 1899, she set out with her uncle for the trip round the world in company with a young man named Jimmy. But that was not merely a coincidence. Her kindly old uncle, with the supposedly damaged heart, was, in his delicate way, offering her, in this trip, a birthday present to celebrate her coming of age. Then, on the fourth of August 1900, she yielded to an action that certainly colored her whole life—as well as mine. She had no luck. She was probably offering herself a birthday present that morning . . .

> On the fourth of August 1901, she married me, and set sail
> for Europe in a great gale of wind—the gale that affected her
> heart. (*The Good Soldier*, 77–78)

Ford's cautionary moral lesson in such passages is fairly clear. A reader is meant to recognize Dowell's attempts to list everything in the world before he acts as one more way of ducking responsibility. The reader should perhaps even connect this individual failing to the general shortcomings of moderns, and then go on to *act* responsibly in the world. But the fact that Dowell leaves at least two significant dates out of his exhaustive list suggests that some historical machine may be operating to produce results beyond a humanist morality and psychology. One of those dates is merely repressed for a few pages. Certainly it was appropriate to Ford's careful construction of a methodical hysteric like Dowell to have the man hold off mentioning 4 August 1913, the date of his wife's suicide. Her death will remind him forcefully of his own shortsightedness; more importantly, it will bring up the fact that women—and, worse, men— are made of a flesh and blood that cannot finally be pinned down by the careful, narrative vivisection he has carried out at some length. As Freud repeatedly points out this is one of the worst recognitions tangled up in the castration complex.[9] This is an anxious man's response to a Medusa, and like all such responses it is a shorthand form for an extremely complex knot of problems that are as much social and historical as anything else—or it would be if Dowell were a real person. As it is, "his" delay in completing his ledger-book, like "his" insistence on blaming everything on women, symptomatically articulates how much this fragmentary text relies on an underlying and heavily Oedipalized narrative in which everything traces back to some (faked) sexual secret, and forward to the piling-up of individual deaths that eventually makes history.

Counting, then, becomes Dowell's ritualistic antidote to the lack he sees in people and for that matter in the nature of things. However it is not just the individual attempt to fill up a hole in the world with numbers, nor the way that an individual obsession dovetails with the logic of patriarchy, that makes *The Good Soldier* what it is. What counts more, here, is that the inventory of significant dates in August leaves out, indeed forecloses, the most important August of them all, the one that says the most about the scramble for new strategies of control and production in a radically new historical setting where individual lives would patently mean less and less. It was on 4 August 1914 that England declared war. The title was changed from *The Saddest Story* because of that day, which started the series of appalling battles in which Ford fought. He recycles it as the central metaphor of the tetralogy that begins with *Some Do Not* and ends with *The Last Post*. That omission of that date is no small omission, however unfair it is to demand a little clairvoyance from Dowell. But what does this "mistake" mean in Ford's writing, what does it mean in terms of history as Ford saw history? The author himself was never able to figure out the connections between what he describes as visual experience and the plain facts of the day, as he mentions in the 1914 essay "A Day of Battle." "As far as I am concerned, an immense barrier in my brain seems to lie between the profession of Arms and the mind that puts things into words. And I ask myself: why? and I ask myself: why?"[10] Others understood the changed conditions better. Writing at the same time, Wyndham Lewis was able to give a fairly shrewd interpretation of the historical transition that the war meant, beginning the second volume of *Blast* with a rigid attack on "every form that the Poetry of a former condition of life, no longer existing, has foisted upon us . . . (I mean to advance) the Poetry which is the as yet unexpressed spirit of the present time, and of new conditions and possibilities of life," in July 1915.[11] But Lewis had the advantage of an elitist and paranoiac viewpoint that served as a strong base for his attacks upon the modern, and could clearly see—even enjoy—the onrushing changes that were sweeping away the past. (Often enough, in fact, his work seems to have the weird ability to predict the future: as with Freud's famous psychotic Schreber, the fact that the lines between his own discourse and the social are so hard to draw gives his work an authority that derives from its very inability to offer more than a fairly inarticulate mirror of the modern.) Ford, always less sure and more human, was only ever able to manage the sort of allegory about profound change that gave rise to a poem about the "old houses of Flanders . . . (with) old eyes that have watched the ways of men for generations," and now "are no more," included later in that same volume of *Blast*.[12] Yet this, too, is an image of historical change, a poetic substitute for an explanation.

Ford, like his characters, could mirror what was beginning to go on; but without even a fixed paranoiac structure of the political to focus what he saw, he could not produce an analysis. It takes still more historical distance, a different set of blindnesses and insights, to respond to this historical impasse in knowledge without Ford's querulous aestheticism or Lewis's incisive fascism. Paul Fussell said as much when he wrote in *The Great War and Modern Memory* that, "it is only now, when those who remember the events are almost all dead, that the literary means for adequately remembering and interpreting are finally available," though we might want to strip away some of the sentimentality to understand this as a historical rather than a purely literary irony.[13] It takes, too, the full emergence of conditions in which Sartre can describe the serialization or "statisticizing" of human beings to enable *The Good Soldier,* at our distance, to speak for the general erasure of individuality in favor of the production of general types. It takes the emergence of conditions in which Canetti can speak of the "crowd-crystal," to understand that Dowell's problems come from the fact that around him and his small circle a restructured set of social relations begins to form in which everything he takes as most private will be endlessly duplicated. And it takes the developments after Taylorization leading to Foucault's identification of social-disciplinary apparatuses to sketch out the deep structures producing what Dowell himself calls "good people ... (who) will go rigidly through with the entire programme," as they cycle, human ciphers all, from health spa to health spa to health spa.

However, I would turn to Paul Virilio's recent books, particularly *Pure War* and *Speed and Politics,*[14] to get at the ways Ford's writing mirrors the rise of a militarized logistics as the dominant mode of organizing the social. For Virilio and, as we look back, for Ford, anything one thinks or believes after 1800 will have to fit somehow into the demands of forming men into large masses, drilling these masses more than adequately, and above all moving the resultant crowd about with rapid efficiency. Indeed, it becomes reasonable in many ways simply to follow Virilio and replace the ideal of "democracy" to which Ford keeps vaguely appealing with the new ideal of "dromocracy," since we find again and again that the quick, efficient movement of human masses matters more than anything else.

> Edward Ashburnham and his wife called me half the world over in order to sit in the back seat of a dog-cart whilst Edward drove the girl to the railway station from which she was to take her departure to India. They wanted, I suppose, to have a witness of the calmness of that function. The girl's luggage had been already packed and sent off before. Her berth on the steamer had been taken. They had timed it all so exactly that it went off like clockwork . . . It was a most amazing business, and I think that it would have been better in the eyes of God if they had all attempted to gouge out each other's eyes with carving knives. But they were "good people." (*The Good Soldier*, 248)

In this sort of world nothing more than efficiency is allowed to matter: not human identity in the old sense, not the older moral values, not the old institutions like the Church—nothing works for very long as a haven in a heartless world. (It may be worth noting, in passing, that for Virilio's analysis characters like Lenin take advantage of precisely the same new ability to marshal large groups that characterizes capitalism.) In particular the notion that individuals are charged with responsibility for their individual actions tends to disappear, since even the "good people" here work much more like Virilio's new fortresses "to contain . . . to dominate, even to facilitate," but never to stop the various movements of a world reduced to movements. Even confronted with the suicide of his best friend, Dowell's one thought is, "I didn't intend to hinder him . . . why should I hinder him?" (256).

This change toward the society of speed can be read everywhere in Ford's portrait of a man so wrapped up in the problems of rapid movement (crossing the Channel, making train connections in Belgium) and the minutiae of daily life spent on the move that though he thinks of himself as a species of pimp more than once, the more accurate term would be "quartermaster." Leonora herself, who comes closest to embodying the old moral virtues to a ruinous degree, "drove with efficiency and precision," explicitly draws upon military jargon to tell her future husband that "'I am still, as the

Germans say—at disposition' " (205). Then, too, Ford's language speaks for the new world of movement that cannot be stopped. Down to the level of what Andrew Ross calls "the new sentence . . . a flexible coordinate, at once a unit of measure, a relatively autonomous element of syllogistic (dis)continuity, and a wholly autonomous object of cognitive attention," this is an unaesthetic and even ugly language that acts like a shipping clerk, carrying out the demands to move things around that no longer come from some independent agent but seem to come from things themselves.[15] As Dowell uses them, words and syntaxes and citations of various genres do little more than mourn the failure of literary language to get any real purchase on a world that has "progressed" beyond the material circumstances that gave rise to the idea of literary language as a sovereign cure for the confusions of the real world.

This also suggests why *The Good Soldier* insistently equates stopping with pure fantasy, or turns a moment of quiet into an opportunity for Dowell to see into the emptiness of things, or directly associates rest with death. It is a matter of seeing through all the movement to the hollowness of commodity fetishization and circulation. In those moments of insight even Dowell's cherished dream of retiring with Nancy Rufford "to an island . . . and (to) teach that happiness can only be found in true love and the feudal system" becomes nothing more than an ironic comment upon the fact that the period in which people could slow down and think (a phantasmatic time, which had to be made up by all sorts of bourgeois romances) had already vanished forever. Certainly Ford himself tended to see such dreams as weak weapons. The moment of stopping to see reality was the occasion for anxiety, given a world his "Arms and the Man" describes as completely fascinating and completely unsecured. "[It was] . . . the most amazing fact of history . . . in the territory beneath the eye . . . a million men, moving one against the other, and impelled by an invisible moral force . . . It was an extraordinary feeling to have in such a wide landscape."[16] At first glance this is only an earlier version of Eliot's—really rather homey to us—Wasteland. It could in fact be read, as the whole of *The Good Soldier* could be read, as a discovery of one's pressing need to rely all the more upon some "invisible moral force," in a modernity that actively does away with coherence in every form. The difference is that Ford was less willing and able finally to say that all things rest in God, less sure that he would be able to aestheticize away these moments of "extraordinary feeling," indeed incapable of putting some defined figure behind history to back up his own viewpoint.

Again, however, something more than one man's anxious perception is at stake. In *The Good Soldier*, Dowell's attempts—and Ford's attempts, for that matter—to hang on to the older ways of explaining the world serve as distorting translations of historical developments. Jameson's recent essay, "Cognitive Mapping,"[17] sums up the sort of change Ford experienced by dividing capitalism into three distinct phases: first, a classical or market capitalism in which subjects contemplate the Cartesian coordinates of the world from a safe distance; second, a monopoly or imperial capitalism whose subjects must live through the "growing contradiction between the phenomenal description of the life of the individual and a more-properly structural model of the contradictions of that experience"; third—this late capitalism breaks into literary existence in the best modern novels—a world in which subjects are faced with a "new space involving the suppression of distance . . . and the relentless saturation of any remaining voids."[18] It is this last, postmodern space that Dowell envisions awaiting him, projecting a vision of the historical as a vision of last judgment.

> It is almost too terrible, the picture of that judgment, as it appears to me sometimes, at night. It is probably the suggestion of some picture that I have seen somewhere. But on an immense plain, suspended in mid-air, I seem to see three figures, two of them clasped close and one intolerably solitary. It is in black and white, my picture of that judgment, an etching perhaps; only I cannot tell an etching from a photographic reproduction. And the immense plain is the hand of God, stretching out for miles and miles, with immense spaces above and below it. (*The Good Soldier*, 70)

This comes very close to being the spitting image of Jameson's "saturated" world, the full space of a postmodern from which all the older orders of things, together with the empty space accompanying those orders, seems to be on the verge of disappearing. It will certainly become difficult for anyone living through 1913 and after who remains incapable of separating the real thing (sketched, here, as a variation on Arnold's famous "darkling plain") from his dreams, his dreams from "an etching," this older and still-tactile form of representation from a contemporary "photographic reproduction," even to set the simplest perceptual standards. Indeed, there is some question about such a subject's ability to survive at all in the new space, which for *The Good Soldier* can be defined as a world so thoroughly shaped and reshaped by mechanical reproduction that, as Edward Ashburnham himself says, it makes little difference whether one is "sniped at on the hills of Afghanistan" (171) or those of South Africa so long as one is sniped at somewhere in the Empire.

This may seem a bit abstract, or too much a matter of simply taking Dowell's nightmares as windows opening directly onto the pages of the kind of history that has only become fashionable rather later. However, modern art, and modernity, retain their peculiar pertinence and even their uncanny anticipatory power because of a unique historical situation that produces these effects. A book as rich in what it can say about modernity as *The Good Soldier* comes out of the period in western society when it became possible to see, clearly and almost undisguised, the economic logics that had been tunneling away inside capitalist society from the time of its inception. Indeed, keeping the big secret about the breaks and flows of the economy began to go against the grain of development toward a society—the postmodern society—in which everything would be put on general display. Ford, then, helps define modernism as an interregnum during which all sorts of deep cultural structures were beginning to come to the surface in the time it took for the old orders of repression and production to fall and the new orders of production (especially those connected with manufacturing the kind of repressive desublimation Baudrillard identifies with "the obscenity of the visible") to begin to appear.[19] Only during a period when all sorts of aberrations past and present and future were jumbled together as one cultural formation could Ford write this book, then inject into an emerging popular culture a vision of historical events that the theory of our own times has only gone on to formalize. Though obscured by a completely subjectivist (in Lukács's terms) method and received within a interpretive community learning to depoliticize everything during Ford's lifetime, the premonitions of a new world—or better, these recognitions of the deep structures already present around him—organized around a decoding/recoding and a confusion of times are frequent enough to amount to a political unconscious in Ford's masterpiece.

In a few peripheral anecdotes such marginal figures as Florence's Uncle John can even be allowed to show just what sort of world *The Good Soldier* encounters.

> Just before they set out from San Francisco old Mr. Hurlbird said he must take something with him to make little presents to the people he met on the voyage. And it struck him that the things to take for that purpose were oranges—because California is the orange country—and comfortable folding chairs. So he bought I don't know how many cases of oranges—the great cool California orange—and half a dozen chairs in a special case that he kept in his cabin. There must have been half a cargo of fruit . . . For, to every person on board the several steamers that they employed, to every person with whom he had so much as a nodding acquaintance, he gave an orange every morning. And they lasted him right round the girdle of this mightly globe of ours. (*The Good Soldier*, 18–19)

It is only necessary to let Uncle John's pilot project for the postmodern run a little further in order to see that inevitably the old order of things will have to disappear and the new space will have to become as filled with objects, mass-produced duplicates, as Dowell anxiously anticipates. It will not take God's vision to order that world from the outside, or even the secularized authority that emanates from the panoptical center of a tangible machine. The new world that appears in such images, as though of its own accord, will need only the solid support afforded by self-scrutinizing individuals sitting in those folding chairs and watching everyone else clutch those great, cool oranges: everyone good citizens of the Southern California that Thomas Pynchon has so closely identified with postmodernity.

In the new world individuals change into subjects, and it is finally through the changes in human nature Dowell sees everywhere except in himself that this writing can be pinned down to the page of history, and dated. This anxious narrator, who is supposed to speak and to know at the center of the text but who appears even to himself to be losing his grip appears at the end of the line of development that starts with the rise of the novel as part of the ensemble of machineries producing the individual, works through the invention of a Romantic subjectivity that confronts the world as other, reaches the culmination of its aesthetic isolation with James's theory of "point of view" narration, and begins its long fall back into the self-reflection marking much of the fiction produced in the 1960s and 1970s. *The Good Soldier* illustrates, then, the moment in the history of the subject when events outside books are about to produce something other than the individual as the primary metaphor for what people are. "I suppose that my inner soul—my dual personality—had realized long before that Florence was a personality of paper—that she represented a real human being with a heart, with feelings, with sympathies, and with emotions only as a bank note represents a certain quantity of gold" (*The Good Soldier*, 120–21). Of course, the results of the reading of the world behind such a passage are defensively projected elsewhere. One turns women into Woman, and that fetishization into a Medusa, in order to have something that will block out the vision of the historical processes that hollow out and rewrite the individual in a fashion that will lead directly to Foucault's infamous (and often misunderstood) comments about man's disappearing like a face sketched in sand at the edge of the historical beach. But at least Ford got the *image* of an intimate connection between the circulation of women and the circulation of money right. It would have taken a Marx to explain as well as identify this uncanny moment in history when the middle-class subject finds out about its own reordering in the wake of a capitalism that is going off the gold standard, beginning rapidly to shift toward a paper economy, and even sketching the first elements of the credit system organizing the postmodern. (Indeed it still takes a subject positioned a little oddly, such as a Gayatri Spivak, to explain the ways subjectivity has openly become a matter of relative value in a completely "free-floating" or decentered system).[20] Ford could only create characters like Dowell, representing some sort of "advance" over Tristram Shandy in purely literary terms and representing distantly a cultural crisis just starting to unfold. This now dates *The Good Soldier* along with much of the rest of modern art. But it may take the later perspective (provided by an economic system that has run a little farther) to turn the personal crisis of an anxious narrator speaking for a whole lost generation into the moment when the subject's long-standing dependence upon the happy alliance between capitalism and patriarchy came into the open.

Still, Dowell's world, Ford's world, is different from ours—and however familiar modernity seems, however clearly modernism has come to mark the time we learned things about human nature that are not forgettable, however uncannily the early part of the century brought out the logics of the social that continue into today, that difference has to be respected. The postmodern works by taking up and eating difference and elides the way that *The Good Soldier* tries to keep the "secret theatre of history," that William Gass located in Ford's writing, as secret as possible.[21] Certainly Ford kept work and workers out of the narrative—who picked those great, cool oranges? lowered the boats? rowed Mr. Hurlbird from island to island so that he could play the beneficent, dotty grandpa?—though they can appear as one of the images making up what might be called the "political preconscious" of Ford's best novel. Similarly, *The Good Soldier* can present only the picture of male hysteria under political pressure, and the first task for a feminist analysis would be to write in the story behind Dowell's fear of women and fear of all things feminine. But our own media are much more likely to bring everything out into the open after the fashion of those recent Gallo commercials showing workers in beautiful slow motion and tying their work back into a history of laboring in the vineyard. Our own times are much more likely to assert that a feminist reading, and the active pursuit of goals once only for a radical fringe, have already been made part of the mainstream agenda. Perhaps the real irony here, the historical irony, is that opening the doors of Ford's little theater and disseminating everything he concealed has turned out to be the very strategy that makes the postmodern.

Notes

1. See for example Mark Schorer's introductory remark, "finally, *The Good Soldier* describes a world that is without moral point, a narrator who suffers from the

madness of moral inertia," in Ford Madox Ford, *The Good Soldier: A Tale of Passion* (New York: Vintage, 1983), xiii. Subsequent quotations of Ford's novel are from this volume. Also see Samuel Hynes, "The Epistemology of *The Good Soldier*," in Richard A. Cassell, ed., *Ford Madox Ford: Modern Judgments* (London: Macmillan, 1972), 77–105.

2. Ford Madox Ford, *Parade's End* (New York: Knopf, 1950), 614.

3. Denis Donoghue, "Listening to the Saddest Story," in Sondra J. Stang, ed., *The Presence of Ford Madox Ford: A Memorial Volume of Papers, Letters and Essays* (Philadelphia: Univ. of Pennsylvania Press, 1983), 44–54.

4. H. Robert Huntley, *The Alien Protagonist of Ford Madox Ford* (Chapel Hill: Univ. of North Carolina Press, 1970), 7.

5. Roger Sale, "Ford's Coming of Age: *The Good Soldier* and *Parade's End*," in Stang, *The Presence of Ford Madox Ford*, 55–76.

6. Paul Fussell, *The Great War and Modern Memory* (New York: Oxford Univ. Press, 1975), 21.

7. See Neil Hertz, "Medusa's Head: Male Anxiety Under Political Pressure," *Representations* 4 (Fall 1983): 27–54, and "The Notion of Blockage in the Literature of the Sublime," in Geoffrey Hartmann, ed., *Psychoanalysis and the Question of the Text* (Baltimore: Johns Hopkins Univ. Press, 1978), 62–85.

8. Fredric Jameson provides an excellent and sympathetic critique of Lukácsian Marxism in his "The Case for Georg Lukács," *Salmagundi* 13 (Summer 1970): 3–35. His later *The Political Unconscious: Narrative As a Socially Symbolic Act* (Ithaca, N.Y.: Cornell Univ. Press, 1981) may in fact be read as an extended attempt to come to terms with Lukács's definitions of the social, the historical, the aesthetic, and the subjective.

9. An excellent discussion of the way castration, and death, and accession to the social are knotted together in psychoanalysis is in Juliet Mitchell, "The Castration Complex," in *Psychoanalysis and Feminism* (New York: Vintage, 1975), 74–91.

10. Ford Madox Ford, "A Day of Battle," reprinted in Stang, *The Presence of Ford Madox Ford*, 170.

11. Wyndham Lewis, "Editorial," in *Blast* no. 2 (July 1915), reissued as Wyndham Lewis, ed., *Blast* 2 (Santa Barbara: Black Sparrow, 1981), 5.

12. Ford Madox Hueffer, "The Old Houses of Flanders," reprinted in *Blast* 2, 37.

13. Paul Fussell, *The Great War and Modern Memory*, 334.

14. Virilio, Pure War (New York: Semiotext(e), 1987) and *Speed and Politics: An Essay on Dromology*, trans. Mark Polizzotti (New York: Semiotext(e), 1986).

15. Andrew Ross, "The New Sentence and the Commodity Form: Recent American Writing," in Cary Nelson and Lawrence Grossberg, eds., *Marxism and the Interpretation of Culture* (Urbana: Univ. of Illinois Press, 1988), 374. Although I do not entirely agree with Ross—his account of recent American writing describes writers like Adrienne Rich oddly—the essay seems to me one of the best attempts to deal with the stuff of literature, literary language.

16. Ford, "Arms and the Man," reprinted in Sondra J. Stang, ed., *A Ford Madox Ford Reader* (New York: Ecco, 1986), 457–59.

17. Fredric Jameson, "Cognitive Mapping," in Nelson and Grossberg, eds., *Marxism and the Interpretation of Culture*, 347–60, and see "Post-Modernism and Consumer Society," in Hal Foster, ed., *The Anti-Aesthetic: Essays on Postmodern Culture* (Port Townsend, Wash.: Bay Press, 1983), 111–25.

18. Jameson, "Cognitive Mapping," 348.

19. Jean Baudrillard, "The Ecstasy of Communication," in Foster, ed., *The Anti-Aesthetic*, 126–34.

20. See Gayatri Spivak, "Scattered Speculations on the Theory of Value," in her *In Other Worlds: Essays in Cultural Politics* (New York: Methuen, 1987), 154–77.

21. William Gass, "The Neglect of *The Fifth Queen*," in Stang, *The Presence of Ford Madox Ford*, 25–43.

11

The Ruins of Allegory and the Allegory of Ruins

GRANT I. HOLLY

> *Allegories are, in the realm of thoughts, what ruins are in the realm of things.*
>
> —Walter Benjamin

> *Imagine an explorer arrives in a little-known region where his interest is aroused by an expanse of ruins, with remains of walls, fragments of columns, and tablets with half-effaced and unreadable inscriptions.*
>
> —Sigmund Freud

Let us take the allegory of the cave from book seven of *The Republic* as a paradigm for problematic double coding that constitutes not only the significance of allegory but also its structure: not only the way it can mean many things, but also the way that we cannot tell what it means. In doing this, let us think of allegory as producing either the version of modernism in which a unified truth can be apprehended through a process of induction or its postmodern shadow, which awakens the suspicion that all facts are theory laden. On the one hand, the allegory of the cave is a didactic tale meant "to illustrate the degrees in which our nature may be enlightened or unenlightened," an illustrative process that Socrates ensures by developing his own interpretation: "Every feature in this parable, my dear Glaucon, is meant to fit our earlier analysis."[1] On the other hand, the central contention of the story undermines the possibility of its application. We could, of course, point to the well-known irony of the Platonic text's resorting at crucial moments to the very figurative forms it opposes ideologically. Or we could discuss the way the dialogues act out, emblematically, the subjects they discuss—producing in the process the subversive problem of the simulacrum. At this point, I would note that for the allegory to work the prisoners of the cave must be convinced of the reality of their world: of the illumination of firelight, of the substantiality of shadows. They must hear echo as voice. The problem is that while all of these things may be allegorical (in the limited sense of coded), conviction, in an important way, cannot be allegorical. The heart patient who dies imagining an intruder would not be more dead had the intruder been real. Once we have been convinced and discover we have been wrong, the possibility of enlightenment falls under suspicion. Since conviction does not indicate truth, enlightenment, now less than relative, comes to stand for the error we have not yet discovered. Escaping the cave means only that one can imagine oneself still "in the cave" relative to some more enlightened position, and so fall into the vortex of a spiraling skepticism.

Here we have the multiple problem posed by allegory in a single frame. What arises as a constructive mode, building its way to a transcendental signified, is revealed as containing the seeds, the semes (in the full homophony allowed), the necessity, the inevitability of its own deconstruction. Allegory is an allegory of the Tower of Babel and vice versa, for the act of construction in that story figures its own futility: in a problematic of distance, difference, deferral, time and being, construction merely memorializes and marmorializes the gulf that remains between desire and fulfillment; the quest for unity succumbs to the pluralities it tried to mask.

This paradoxical relationship between construction and deconstruction, so important to the work of Nietzsche, Heidegger, and Derrida, may have its most epigrammatic expression in Freud's *Beyond the Pleasure Principle*, when he arrives at the conclusion that *"the aim of all life is death."*[2] In this phrase we have the construction and the deconstruction of the Freudian hermeneutic and, more generally, the crises in the interpretation of representations that have erupted from time to time since Plato. Our life, it tells us, is an allegory—its elements not merely themselves but signs, emplotted to stand for something else. Such insight implies a promise. Life may be like fiction, but that is another way of saying that it has meaning and that meaning can be rendered apparent by decoding. The signified of Freud's allegory, however, here as in the concepts of repression and the unconscious, defies the logic of interpretation/ decoding that it promised. The problematic according to which poststructuralist theory has deconstructed the way fiction means prevails here as well. Death, from whatever aspect we regard it, is a figure for the decay of meaning. If we look at death from the outside, we see the decay of systems, the loss of organic form. True, organic degradation is itself an organic process, and the decay of systems produces systems; but the sheer force of proliferation overwhelms the idea of form with a chaos of orders, an aleatory metonymic chain that leads endlessly away from the recognizable totality of identity.

If we try to contemplate death from the inside, consciousness meets what it cannot know. Thought is forced into metaphor. In the poignant gesture of metaphor, which touches the mystery of death in its own inadequacy, in its repetition of a loss beyond naming, death can be thought only as something or *as like* something that is not death. In this paradox lies the problematic element that so troubled readers of Milton's personification of death in *Paradise Lost*.[3] Milton explores the limits and significance of oxymoron as a figure that produces itself under erasure to give a face, thoughts, the force of life to the opposite of all those things. Such a paradox might be mitigated by belief in the reality of spiritual beings, but the discomfort readers have expressed from the beginning suggests that, late in the seventeenth century, the juxtaposition of the spiritual and the existential already constituted merely another paradox. If we think of Milton's figure of Death as allegorical, then it is the perfect representation of Paul de Man's formulation of allegory's inability to represent: "The difficulty of allegory is . . . that this emphatic clarity of representation does not stand in the service of something that can be represented."[4] And yet there it is—a fact for which Coleridge's "willing suspension of disbelief" gives only a weak accounting; a fact that becomes increasingly salient as modern culture and subjectivity form in a mirror world of representations representing other representations. Indeed with Milton's personification of death we have, before Kant, a strange negative of the Kantian sublime. Kant would give as a scenario for the sublime the self, first threatened by the abyss vaster than its understanding then rescued by transcendent reason that surpasses the understanding and, we might say, colonizes the abyss, like a virus.[5] On the other hand, the impossible allegory of death, or allegory itself, viewed now as impossible but working nevertheless, colonizes the abyss like a retrovirus, a reason perpetually attacked by an unreason and producing a negative sublime from the perpetuation of this unreasonableness.

It is not accidental that our relation to death mirrors the structure of fundamental patterns of figuration: metonymy and metaphor. Death in Freud's formulation is the personification of the figurative itself, a characterization of the loss at the heart of art, of the repeated displacements of representation. It is perhaps in this formulation more than any other that the sublime of allegory in its deconstructive mode is bodied forth. This mode of allegory produces its sublime, not from the promise of a transcendental signified, but from the fear that any production, from a poem to a life, might without one's knowing it, even against one's intentions (since the allegorical injects the ordinary with the irreal), turn out allegorical: the common place or the casual, the undersigned or product of mere happenstance, might turn out to have all the fantastic pomp of the entirely formal, or the formal and painstakingly designed might turn out to have an unexpected and very different design. In any case, a scenario is produced in which the self sees itself recast as a mere signifier, a mere textual element in a drama produced by its own otherness. The sublime form of allegory is brought into play when we read Freud against himself and find his theories wandering from the objective paths of the scientific and returning repeatedly, like Freud himself in "The Uncanny," where his walk through a strange city leads him repeatedly back to the red light district, to the details of his own autobiography.

In the eighteenth century, we might say, allegory is in ruins— allegory, that is, as the stable repository of multiple significances. This destruction, however, releases the signifying power of allegory. What emerges is a new kind of allegory. Now it is no longer the text that works allegorically, but commentary as well (from the works of

Martinus Scriblerus to Nabokov's *Pale Fire*), and, of course, the commentary on the commentary, until all is joined in a generalized
textuality, a representational sublime.

Ironically, Coleridge frequently discovers this new sense of the
sublime of allegory—ironically because Coleridge is frequently cited
as inaugurating the modern disdain for allegory.[6] He records his
attempts at automatic writing, a modernist dream of pure discourse,
true only to itself, the foundation of an organic art. To his dismay,
however, indeed to his terror, the purity of the project is repeatedly
contaminated by an uncontrollable flow of associations. The significance of this concatenation of surfaces beneath which consciousness
can never go strikes Coleridge like the sounding of the bell in
Nietzsche's *Genealogy of Morals*—the recognition of a perpetual
misrecognition. As Nietzsche puts it, "We are unknown to ourselves."[7] Indeed, in a kind of allegorical intertextuality, Freud is invoked when we talk about the allegory of the cave. The figure of the
cave, the figurative cave, returns in his text: the cave of dream, the
caves of repression and the unconscious, the scene of analysis as
cave; and Freud himself plays the part of the escaped prisoner who
returns with the truth and receives for his pains the violent response
of those who would not be free—this by his own account, frequently
given. Like Socrates, Freud tells his story and interprets it. He does
this in the context of therapeutic goals, a unified vision, a total and
organic explanation—all elements of the modern sensibility. Exhibit-
ing the modern bias, Freud rarely uses the term allegory, developing
instead the organic and unified concept of symbol. But Freud's text
produces the same allegorical problem as Plato's. In Freud's 1915
paper on "Repression," it becomes clear that repression is not
merely a lock and key.[8] It is, rather, a storyteller, a master of disguises; in accordance with the logic of the unconsious, it is perpetually the other. Analysis is potentially interminable. For Freud to
resemble Socrates, after all, is to resemble a character in another text,
to be like a likeness.

The cave and the tower. Elements of another allegory? I argue
that they go together—as elements of a primal scene, as images of
birth and rebirth, as a demonstration of the relationship of the
paleolithic cave and the neolithic pyramid/ziggurat worked out by
anthropologists. But the ground of this connection is the element of

ruins. As I read it, the allegory of the cave leaves allegory in ruins, as the plurality of tongues ruins the Tower of Babel. We can establish a chiasmatic relationship between this version of these two stories, and say that the cave itself is the prototype of the ruin, and the telling of the story of the Tower of Babel is problematized by the event it recounts. The parallel drawn in Benjamin's remarkable insight between allegory and ruins can, then, be strengthened into an identity. Allegory and ruins replicate one another. They are part of the same realm. To be aware of ruins as ruins is to live allegorically. This axiom applies not only to the phenomenology of individual perception but also to historical and cultural developments. If there is not a particular historical moment when western culture is transfixed by remnants of the past, there is, nevertheless, historically, a repeated congeries of events that produce a postmodernity—a sense of an alien future littered with the remnants of an unremembered past.

Let us look again at the scenario of Plato's allegory. The prisoner who has seen the light of day returns to the "cavernous chamber," where the others are still chained by neck and leg watching the procession of "artificial objects, including figures of men and animals in wood or stone or other materials."[9] The scene of the allegory is created by the sciences of the ruin; anthropology and archeology. They treat their object as a representation of a concept that is itself a representation, a pure discursivity, in the way in which the human, beyond any specific example, or the restoration of a ruined city, must remain theoretical. The prisoner returns in possession of the knowledge of representation (with that knowledge *and* possessed by it) to find a world that is nothing but representation: the chained prisoners are no more than shadows of men, as the shadows on the wall are only shadows of the representations of objects. By returning to this world of representations, he inaugurates the anthropological and archeological voyages that will become essential to modernism—voyages that will seek to define their object on the representational grid: the grid of perspective, the grid of cartography, the grid of taxonomy, the grid of chronology. As the allegory of the cave can become an endless allegory, the definitive project of modernism, defining one representation by another, leads to the delirium of the simulacrum. Since it is always possible that what we are convinced is enlightenment merely locates us in the cave relative to some other position, it is possible that our being merely simulates real being and that there is no absolute difference between the prisoner who has returned, the ones who remain in chains, the objects, or the shadows on the wall. Joined in a general likeness, all can be allegories of one another. The procession of objects and people in the cave conforms to what Jean Baudrillard calls the precession of simulacra: "The whole system becomes weightless, it is no longer anything but a gigantic simulacrum—not unreal, but a simulacrum, never again exchanging for what is real, but exchanging in itself, in an uninterrupted circuit without reference or circumference."[10]

The archeological, anthropological, and biological projects of the eighteenth century conform to this circuit as well. In them we see the development of a scenario in which the encounter with the other provides the occasion to establish the identity of the observer. We can see this drama played out in the historical research of scholars, in a series of important archeological discoveries (notably Pompeii and Herculaneum), in the theorizing of the place of the human in the biological world, and in the accumulated encounters with other cultures, civilized and precivilized—at once producing and problematizing the notion of species (the issue that leads to the frenzied attempt to define the human in Swift's *Gulliver's Travels*). These encounters awaken Europe to the ideas of cultural loss and difference that would both open the way to the development of subjectivity through the imitation of imagined models of behavior and prepare an understanding for the concept of extinction. In these varied ways, the other becomes the model for understanding the self, and we have the scenario within which modern subjectivity is formed. The process follows the structure of Velásquez's *Las Meninas*, according to Foucault's analysis: an apparently strong subject position is actually produced from without, becoming an artifact of a representational system, a character in a discursive formation.[11]

Here we see the early stages, of what Baudrillard calls "museumification," of a world in which "we all become living specimens under the spectral light of ethnology . . . a world completely catalogued and analyzed and then *artificially revived as though real*."[12] Baudrillard describes three orders of the simulacrum that correspond to "the mutations of the law of value" since the Renaissance:

—*Counterfeit* is the dominant scheme of the classical period, from the Renaissance to the industrial revolution;
—*Production* is the dominant scheme of the industrial era;
—*Simulation* is the reigning scheme of the current phase that is controlled by the code.[13]

I would argue that these distinct chronological categories evidence a contemporary nostalgia for the very form of analysis that the theory they serve declares extinct. This is because these forms of the simulacrum can be collapsed, because the modern, emerging in the Renaissance, is accompanied by the parodic double we call the postmodern.[14] The modes of historical and scientific analysis, the eruption of representational technology that constitutes the Renaissance, in turn produced the conditions within which humanity and the emerging category of the "real" *could be thought* of as mere likenesses of the epistemological framework that made them apparent and to which they owed their existence. I emphasize *could be thought,* because this point of view constitutes the postmodern that emerges simultaneously with the modern, but as its shadow. That the human and the world come into view by virtue of the representational techniques of narrative, cartography, and perspective, implies to the modern sensibility a relentless progress toward the mastery of things. To the sensibility of the postmodern it suggests the vertiginous possibility that knowledge merely reflects ways of knowing, that consciousness is projected onto the subject from the mirror's surface, that once we have produced representational technologies they produce us, making us artifacts of our own artifacts. This division between the modern and the postmodern points of view follows the line of demarcation that separates those categories so important to eighteenth-century aesthetics, the beautiful and the sublime. Insofar as the techniques and technologies of representation produce a mastery of the material that affirms the place of the observer, they are part of the sensibility of modernism and the aesthetic of the beautiful. When the boundary between the observer and the world, with a host of related distinctions—subject and object, representation and the represented, etc.—breaks down, there follows a perverse version of Kant's mathematical sublime. In the dynamic of Kant's mathematical sublime, reason is a stable element,

first degrading the self by imaging a series that outstrips the capacities of the understanding, then producing a self-esteem, heightened
by reason's own power.[15] In the breakdown of the barrier between
the observer and the world, however, reason can reason itself to be a
representation imposed from without in a series of representations
that not only defies understanding but undermines reason.

The "replicants" of *Blade Runner*[16] are prefigured by the "automata" Hobbes invokes at the outset of *Leviathan.*

> Nature, the art whereby God hath made and governs the world,
> is by the *art* of man, as in so many other things, so in this also
> imitated, that it can make an artificial animal. For seeing life is
> but a motion of limbs, the beginning whereof is in some princi-
> pal part within; why may we not say, that all *automata* (engines
> that move themselves by springs and wheels as doth a watch)
> have an artificial life? For what is the heart, but a spring; and the
> nerves, but so many strings, and the joints, but so many wheels
> giving motion to the whole body, such as was intended by the
> artificer? Art goes yet further, imitating that rational and most
> excellent work of nature, *man.* For by art is created that great
> *Leviathan* called a *Commonwealth,* or *State,* in Latin *Civitas,* which
> is but an artificial man.[17]

The fierce materialism that governs Hobbes's argument em-
powers the modern, instrumentalist view, and brings with it the
prospect of mastery and control—as a product of its mastery of a
technology, here the technology of the mechanism. That mastery
and control separate the maker from the thing made, affirming the
place of the observer. For the postmodern sensibility, however, technology, or "artifice," is overdetermined, and a chiasmus reverses the
poles of the argument: if the *automaton* is an artificial replicant of an
animal, and the state is the artificial replicant of "man," then what is
to say that an animal is not the replicant of an automaton, or that it
is not the state—in Althusser's terms "ideology"—that calls "man,"
as a historically and culturally specific subject formation, into being.[18] In this reversal the term "artificial" either drops out of the
equation or becomes omnipresent. No longer distinguishing the
maker from the thing made, it ushers in the sublime intuition that
our understanding of ourselves and the world is a segment in a

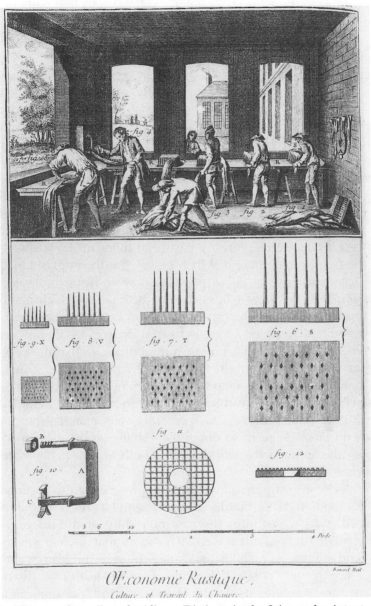

1. Hemp makers, *Encyclopédie, ou Dictionnaire des Sciences des Arts et des Métiers*. Courtesy of the Audio-Visual Department, Hobart and William Smith Colleges.

continuing series of representations, self-reproducing, without origin or end.

The modern, instrumental projects of the Enlightenment have their postmodern underside. The *Encylopédie* anticipates Borges, the laureate of the encyclopedic. Its vastness and inclusiveness announce representation's challenge to "the real." Its graphics, meant to be merely illustrative, take on a life of their own, as if the map were to become a landscape, the diagram an organic system (illustrations 1 and 2 from the *Encyclopédie*). We wonder at the lives of the figures that work in the imagined factory. The workers making hemp or candles, for example, are uncanny personifications, seeming now to be mere paradigms—automata illustrating typical behavior—and now to be the representation of actual beings. Are we to read these plates as a time-lapse representation of an industrial process, or does each capture a particular moment? Inevitably some of the figures look more real than others, but the implications here are also uncanny: as if the population were being infiltrated by manikins, or we were witnessing the process by which manikins became men. The illustrations in the *Encyclopédie,* itself the commodified result of a vast industrial project, are dominated by the theme of the manufacture of commodities, so that not only the image of the human but the idea of the human becomes a function of manufacture and commodification.[19] Similarly, as I have argued elsewhere, the Scriblerean satires of Swift and Pope, mounted, at least in part, as a counterattack on Hobbesian materialism, double back on themselves. In so doing they obliterate the distinction between the text and the world, joining both in an equally material, ahuman, textuality.[20]

Seeking to suppress this uncanny presence of the postmodern in the modern, Baudrillard's schematic emphasizes it all the more. Indeed, what constitutes the postmodernity of the discourse of Baudrillard (of Foucault as well), what gives that discourse its macabre and sublime aura, is that stalking within it—undead, we might say—are the very classical elements of whose death their discourse portentously assures us. In the classical period, personification of abstract terms is a way of representing the power of the linguistic itself. Since these terms have no precise representational equivalent, their use reflects the power of the linguistic as a grid or mechanism capable of being used with precision. To animate these terms, to

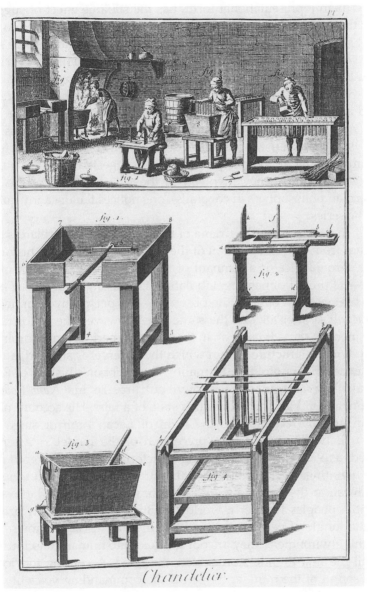

2. Candlemakers, *Encyclopédie, ou Dictionnaire des Sciences des Arts et des Métiers.* Courtesy of the Audio-Visual Department, Hobart and William Smith Colleges.

give them representational form, has the sublime effect of suggesting that the mechanism itself is animate, that what appeared to be a tool has a life of its own. Foucault's rhetoric exaggerates, to be sure, but continues this same process. "And how, after all (if not by a slow and laborious technique), are we to discover the complex relation of representations, identities, orders, words, natural beings, desires, and interests, once that vast grid has been dismantled."[21] Here writing about the end of the classical age, Foucault nevertheless employs a characteristic rhetorical device of that age. Without even examining the impossible point of view suggested by "after all," or the mysterious agency involved in the "dismantling" of the grid (German philosophers in coveralls), one notices the uncanny quality of the series.

In part, at least, the drama of Foucault's and Baudrillard's texts comes from the juxtaposition of the chronological and the historical. The chronological is a remnant of the classical age. It is part of the classical project of naming, tabulating, classifying. It implies a place for the observer outside the observed—the perspective implied by Foucault's "after all." At the same time, however, the historical, in the modern sense it takes on in that classical period, is anachronistic: a systematic structure within which the observer is situated, a mere character in an unfolding textuality. Thus Gibbon's history of Rome is also an account of his own culture. In his *New Science*, Giambattista Vico thematizes this state of affairs. His account of the first humans recapitulates the form of Lacan's mirror stage and what Baudrillard calls the "precession of the model."[22] After the flood, as Vico tells it—paralleling a pictorial history that goes from the paintings of Claude and Salvator Rosa, to the capriccios of Piranesi, to the sublime scenes of apocalypse of John Martin—the gentile peoples wander a world in which the ruins of civilization and a jungle of vegetation blend together inextricably. Grown feral in this environment, they are not shocked into human consciousness until the first thunderstorms after the flood. According to Vico, in the sound of the thunder they hear the commanding voice of what they imagine to be a gigantic version of themselves. This produces self-awareness. The self, in other words, is produced by an imagined likeness of the self. This reversal of the relation between fact and artifact continues in Vico's version of history. The first humans, invented by an imagined likeness of themselves, invent language, marriage, religion, and burial of the dead. The evolution of these institutions, not the behavior of men and women, produces human history. This version of the postmodern sublime resides in the perception that the history of the human could be written only as the history of representation. Making the human the artifact of its own artifacts corresponds to the danger of potential loss of self in Burke, and Kant's sense of the sublime that sends reason beyond the limits of the understanding.

Paul De Man calls prosopopoeia, the giving of a face to things dead, or absent, or nonexistent, "the master trope of poetic discourse."[23] In Vico's theory we see it as the master trope of culture as well. Culture is conceived of as a textuality and the human as a personification of aspects of the textuality. Vico's theory was not well known in the eighteenth century, but it corresponds to patterns of cultural displacement that characterize that time. The great archeological expeditions, starting with the Earl of Arundel in the seventeenth century and moving through those of the Society of Dilettanti and Lord Elgin, the discovery of Pompeii and Herculaneum, reconstitute Europe in accordance with a theory of the fragment. The fragment produces its context. Sculpture, in theories of aesthetics, of acting and action, of comportment and behavior, from Shaftesbury to Chesterfield and Winckelmann, produces the image of the human. The importance of the simulacrum is frequently evident in eighteenth-century art. After Ronald Paulson, one thinks of the depiction of Cheere's sculpture yard in Hogarth's *The Analysis of Beauty*, Reynolds's painting of Commander Kepple in the manner of the Apollo Belvedere, or of Master Crewe in the manner of Henry the Eighth, perhaps after Holbein.[24] The question is, however, whether the simulacrum is subordinated to a narrative purpose as in a Hogarthian progress, as Paulson would argue, or is it preeminent? We might ask the same question of the satires of Swift and Pope. Does satire, in other words, produce its simulacra for a specific purpose? Can we decode this allegory? Or does simulation lead to a relentless doubling, a world of forking similitudes, of likeness for its own sake? What is the portrait of Lemuel Gulliver on the frontispiece of the *Travels* but the portrait of a skill, a technique of representation, the depiction of sheer likeness? Similarly

3. Sir Joshua Reynolds, *Master Crewe as Henry VIII*. Private collection.

we might say that the subject of Reynolds's portrait is not precisely Master Crewe, or Henry the Eighth, or an intermediate representation, but the whirlpool of likeness that circulates all three in perpetual exchange (illustration 3, Joshua Reynolds, *Master Crewe as Henry VIII*).

The question then is not limited to satire. Consider Pope's "To Mr. Addison, Occasioned by His Dialogue on Medals."[25] Its structure is based on polyptoton and paradox; it is a world in an act of rhetorical pulverization, "ruins ruined."[26] In such a world, the fragment (here the fragment fragmented), provides the basis for a reality that can only be theoretical and speculative, that owes its presence to absence: "perhaps by its own ruins saved from flame, / Some buried marble half preserves its name." Construction in such a world is always reconstruction . . . but of what? An imagined precedent. It is the image within the mirror that produces the object. Rome is styled "its own . . . sepulcher"—as if the death mask were to precede the living person. One thinks here of the story Lewis Carroll tells of the mapmaker whose struggle to create the perfect map of England is achieved only when he makes a map the same size as England. The difficulties in using this map are so great that he discards it, and, in a gesture that foreshadows Baudrillard, uses England itself as the map.

In the world of ruin and fragment, the simulacrum is preeminent. In "To Mr. Addison," "Ambition" is a good example of the way what Steven Knapp calls the "radical self-absorption" of the personification produces a feeling of the sublime by allowing the figure's status as a mere illustration or as the representation of an actual being to remain indeterminate.[27] "Ambition," faced with the inevitability of ruin, follows her opposite, "Resignation," and "contracts her vast design" retreating into the world of the simulacrum:

And all her Triumphs shrink into a Coin:
A narrow orb each crouded conquest keeps,
Beneath her Palm here sad Judea weeps,
Here scantier limits the proud Arch confine,
And scarce are seen the prostrate Nile or Rhine,
A small Euphrates thro' the piece is roll'd,
And little Eagles wave their wings in gold. ("To Mr. Addison," 23–30)

Indeed, the reality of England and her heroes depends on their entering the register of the simulacrum, appearing on medals and in this way being "emulous" of Greece and Rome. This end figures and prefigures the activities of living nations, "enrolls" them in reality of representation where "Art reflect[s] images to Art." "Realms" are "vanquished," not to supply the needs of the living, but for "recording gold." In its final lines, the poem itself shrinks into an inscription (to James Craggs, the younger); it moves even farther away from the existential contingencies of *parole* into the realm of *langue*—or what we might call the sculpted similitude, the personification of language.

The seduction of the simulacrum is evident in Zoffany's *Charles Towneley and His Friends,* discussed by Ronald Paulson (illustration 4, Zoffany, *Charles Towneley and His Friends*).[28] The very title of the painting foregrounds the issue of the simulacrum. Are the "friends" the men or the statues—the statuesque men (Paulson call attention to the way the men replicate the attitudes of the statues) or the lifelike statues? As Pope would have it in "To Mr. Addison," "Statues of men, scarce less alive than they." The question of likeness, here, is underscored with special intensity. Once again it is a question of the likeness of likeness, endless similitude, a point of view supported by the additional register of the triangle of texts. Towneley seems strangely removed from the scene, in the thrall of the book on his lap—a riddle, like the adjacent sphinx. Could the rest of the painting be a dream inspired by the book? It is, as Paulson points out, not an actual but an ideal configuration of works brought from other parts of the house, a picture of a scene that does not exist—prosopographia, a kind of personification. An *Anatomy* lies open on the floor, suggesting the taxonomic principles according to which likenesses can be constructed. In the center of the picture, where we might expect to find Towneley, we find instead P. F. Hugues known as D'Hancarville, the archeologist, cataloguer of Towneley's collection, whose gaze seems about to be drawn back to the place his finger marks in the book—as if marking the path objects travel to and from the text. In marking making catalogue a metaphor for the entire work, making the entire work a metaphor.

4. Johann Zoffany, *Charles Towneley in His Gallery.* Courtesy of Scala / Art Resource.

5. Sydney Harris, *Piranesi Mall*. Drawing by S. Harris © 1987. Courtesy of the New Yorker Magazine, Inc.

Charles Towneley Among His Friends can be viewed as a special kind of allegory, what De Man calls an allegory of reading, for the registers of significance do not point to a transcendental signified, but to one another—a circle of representations representing representation. This same circulation of signification can be mapped to culture in general during the period. Caught up in this concatenation of representations, Europe becomes the cave with its chambers, the museum, the garden, the grotto, through which are brought the procession of objects that model the development of Europe through formation of their own simulacra: the prison, the hospital, the school, the factory.

The precession of the model is clear in the etchings of Piranesi. His prisons are a striking example of postmodernity, prefiguring the planned confusion and frustrating inaccessibility that Jameson fastens onto in his analysis of the Bonaventura Hotel (illustrations 5 and 6, *Piranesi Mall* and *Prisons*).[29] In the prisons, the human figures are not merely victims of incarceration, they are victims of a representational technique that denies them escape: first, because it produces a structure subordinate, not to the laws of physics or even to the rules of perspective, but to the possibilities of the technique itself. We can, therefore, find no up or down, no in or out. The difference between sign, symbol, support or fissure, barrier or passageway cannot be precisely determined, because all primarily express not themselves but the technique that produces them. This technique, a kind of writing, not only produces images but erases them, and preserves the possibility or immanence of their destruction, their disappearance and decay, in their production. Like allegory in Benjamin's sense, Piranesi's prisons are provisional structures. Their provisionality is inescapable, for as Benjamin puts it, "any person, any object, any relationship, can mean absolutely anything else."[30] This is the second reason the prisoners cannot escape: they cannot be distinguished from the prison, from the technique that produces them. Typically, the sculpted figures cannot be distinguished from "actual humans" in Piranesi's work, because what is represented is a representational grammar, "Statues of Men, scarce less alive than they" (illustration 7, Piranesi, Fora). In Piranesi's *Portici tirati dintorno ad un Foro con palazzo regio,* the whole scene exists to illustrate the classical orders, kinds of porticos, and

6. G. B. Piranesi, *Carceri*, pl. viii. Courtesy of the Huntington Library and Art Gallery.

7. G. B. Piranesi, *Portici tirati dintorno ad un Foro con palazzo regio*. Private collection.

fora, but it takes on life, gaining power in creating the sense that the representation is responsible for the existence of the real. We cannot but notice in this regard the way the human figures, almost without exception, seem to be simultaneously representations of statues and animate beings—as if animate beings were merely statues and statues could come to life. We have here a paradigm that produces a world. In so doing it produces the uncanny sense that there is no world beyond the paradigm, as if the map precedes the territory, as if, as Baudrillard would have it, the real is the map.

Piranesi's fantasies, produced from his archeological evaluations of the ruins of Rome, foreground technique, thus foregrounding ruin as they aim at reconstruction (illustration 8, *Modo . . . nel fabbricare*). The information given in his depiction of the way the ancient Romans accomplished massive stone work is so curiously but powerfully represented that it undermines itself. The details no longer contribute to our understanding, they become a world unto themselves. In the inserts, top left and center, the emphasis on the building blocks tempts us to read them as massive monoliths, inexplicably arrayed on and dominating in their size and in their technical perfection a boulder-strewn landscape punctuated surrealistically by immense eye bolts. Although the etching is presented as a historical reconstruction meant to place our understanding of these feats of architecture in perspective, its radical reversal of perspective leaves us disoriented. What we face here in pictorial version anticipates Foucault's analysis of microhistorical practices. In both cases we find a representational sublime—a vision of the productive power of reproductive practices so potent that they appear to have transcended the need for an original and to have become self-perpetuating: producing, among other products, human agents that labor like slaves within them; or characters in a narrative, never fully aware of the multiple contexts of their existence, only occasionally glimpsing aspects of the vast and intricate network of practices in which they are caught up. The repeated motif of inserts peeling back to reveal or imply other surfaces (to be peeled back in turn?), with the obsessive attention to detail at the expense of an overall view, suggest an infinity of surface and detail such that the detail, the fragment, the merely material and ahuman, begins to take on the aspects of animation. Indeed, the ironwork clasps seem to embrace each other by the neck like birds in the upper left and center inserts and to approach each other like courting serpents in the lower left corner. This focus on the purely technical, giving the personality usually reserved for animate objects to mere instruments, implies that technology is the master of representation, not the servant of a human agent. It makes the human a product of its own productive mechanisms. In this light, the representation of the technical within the etching can be seen as the analogue of the processes of etching and book production, discursive practices produced by humans that nevertheless produce human subjectivity.

The theme of reality as a representation is enforced when we note that not only are the left and center inserts details of the insert on the upper right, but, in a dizzying reversal of perspective, so, too, is the dominant foreground of the etching. Nor can we take the depiction of the upper right to be the stable, lifelike context into

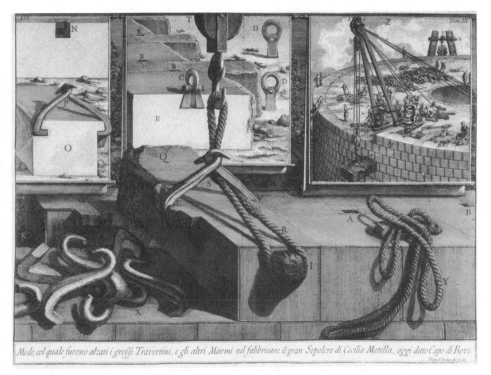

Modo, col quale furono alzati i grossi Travertini, e gli altri Marmi nel fabbricare il gran Sepolcro di Cecilia Metella, oggi detto Capo di Bove.

8. G. B. Piranesi, *Sepulcro di Cecilia Metella*. Courtesy of the Huntington Library and Art Gallery.

which the other elements fit and are justified like pieces in a puzzle, for the curling parchment underscores the precariousness of this reality by flaunting the fact that it is merely a representation.

The paradox of modernity is that its dreams of total understanding and the establishment of utopia manifest themselves in images of chaos and ruin. The explanation for this state of affairs, I have argued here, is that the technological power of the modern world overwhelms its human agents, making them feel like artifacts of vast representational systems into which their greatest insight is sublime: that they are caught up in an order they do not understand. Such an insight, an insight into blindness, to use De Man's phrase, is frequently conveyed in the form of allegory I have called postmodern. Unlike the scene of classic allegory, where the reader's

9. G. B. Piranesi, *Veduta, Castel Sant'Angelo.* Courtesy of the Huntington Library and Art Gallery.

separation from the text enables him or her to decode a meaning, the discoveries of the reader of postmodern allegory are allegorical only of the way he or she is caught up in a series of representations that refer to one another. From these there is no escape. The layered city of Rome becomes an image of such an allegory, and Piranesi's images of it, none better perhaps than that of the Castel Sant' Angelo, construct a bridge from the eighteenth to the twentieth century, leading us back to Freud in the process. In *The Interpretation of Dreams*, Freud recounts a series of dreams that have to do with his unfulfilled desire to go to Rome (illustration 9, Piranesi, *Castel Sant' Angelo*).[31] In the first, inspired by a well-known engraving of the Pont de St. Angelo (perhaps Piranesi's) that he had caught sight of during the previous day, he is in Rome but does not leave the train. In the second, he is led to the top of a hill and sees the city in the distance, shrouded in mist, like the promised land. In the third, he is in Rome but discovers this Rome is a pastiche of other landscapes. In the fourth, he is again in Rome, but this Rome is not Rome either. It is full of German street signs, suggesting, Freud says, that

Rome would be a better place to go than Prague, the destination of his real journey. Much can be said about these dreams and their relation to ruins and allegory, but I will be brief. That Freud should dream of Rome and never get there, figures, among other things, as a gloss on psychoanalysis itself as an interpretational system. Asking the way in his dream about Prague invokes Rome, he tells us, since all roads lead to Rome. What he does not remember here is his own description of the dream as "the royal road to the unconscious." Dreaming the impossibility of getting to Rome, then, dreams the impossibility of psychoanalysis, at least as a part of the modernist enterprise of finding a unified, organic solution. Freud himself sees these dreams as part of a recurring motif in his life of thinking of himself as Hannibal, the Semitic outsider, trying to move to the center, trying, in the context of his own time, to become catholic. What is at stake here is the strategy of interpretation: the symbolic, the motif, according to Benjamin, of absolutes, or the allegorical, the motif of the ruin.

Notes

1. Plato, *The Republic*, trans. Francis MacDonald Cornford (London: Oxford Univ. Press), 7. 513, 517. Further references to Plato use this text.

2. *Beyond the Pleasure Principle*, trans. and ed. James Strachey (New York: Norton, 1961), 32.

3. For another account of the significance of Milton's personification of death, see Steven Knapp, *Personification and the Sublime: Milton to Coleridge* (Cambridge, Mass.: Harvard Univ. Press, 1985), esp. 51–65.

4. De Man, "Pascal's Allegory of Persuasion," in *Allegory and Representation; Selected Papers from the English Institute, 1979–1980*, ed. with preface by Stephen J. Greenblatt (Baltimore: Johns Hopkins Univ. Press), 1.

5. See, for example, "*the sublime is that, the mere ability to think which shows a faculty of the mind surpassing every standard of sense*," and the sublime is that which "we cannot *know* but only *think*" in *The Critique of Judgment*, trans. J. H. Bernard (New York: Hafner, 1951), 89, 108.

6. See for example, "The Statesman's Manual," in *Lay Sermons, The Collected Works of Samuel Taylor Coleridge* 6, ed. R. J. White (Cambridge: Routledge and Kegan Paul, 1972), 30.

7. *Genealogy of Morals*, trans. Walter Kaufmann and R. J. Hollingdale (New York: Vintage, 1969), 16.

8. "Repression," in Freud, *Standard Edition*, vol. 14, trans. G. M. Baines (London: Hogarth Press, 1953) 141–58.

9. *Republic*, 7. 513–14.

10. Baudrillard, *Simulations*, trans. Paul Foss, Paul Patton, and Philip Beitchman (New York: Semiotext(e), 1983), 10–11.

11. Foucault, *The Order of Things: An Archaeology of the Human Sciences, a Translation of Les Mots et les Choses*, (New York: Vintage, 1973), 3–16.

12. *Simulations*, 16.

13. *Ibid.*, 83.

14. On the postmodern revival of allegory, see Craig Owens, "The Allegorical Impulse: Toward a Theory of Postmodernism," *October*, no. 12 (Spring 1980), 67–86, and no. 13 (Summer 1980), 59–80; repr. in *Art After Modernism: Rethinking Representation*, ed. Brian Wallis, (Boston: Godine, 1984), 203–35.

15. *Critique of Judgment*, 86–95; above, n.5.

16. *Blade Runner*, dir. Ridley Scott, 1982.

17. *Leviathan: or the Matter, Forme and Power of a Commonwealth Ecclesiastical and Civil*, ed. Michael Oakeshott, intro. Richard S. Peters (New York: Collier, 1962), 19.

18. Althusser, "Ideology, and Ideological State Apparatuses (Notes toward an Investigation," in *Lenin and Philosophy*, trans. Ben Brewster (New York: Monthly Review, 1971), 170–77.

19. On the *Encyclopédie* as a business project, see Robert Darnton, *The Business of Enlightenment: A Publishing History of the Encyclopédie 1775–1800* (Cambridge, Mass.: Harvard Univ. Press, 1979).

20. Grant I. Holly, "Travel and Translation: Textuality in *Gulliver's Travels*," *Criticism* 21, no. 2 (Spring 1979) 134–52, repr. *Modern Critical Interpretations: Jonathan Swift's Gulliver's Travels* (New York: Chelsea House, 1986), 147–62; and "ProsoPop(e)oeia," *New Orleans Review* 15, no. 4 (Winter 1988), 51–59.

21. *The Order of Things*, 303.

22. Vico, *The New Science*, trans. and ed. Thomas Goddard Bergin and Max Harold Fisch (Ithaca, N.Y.: Cornell Univ. Press, 1984); Jacques Lacan, "The Mirror Stage as Formative of the Function of the I as Revealed in Psychoanalytic Experience," trans. Alan Sheridan (New York: Norton, 1977), 1–7.

23. De Man, "Hypogram and Inscription," in *The Resistance to Theory* (Minneapolis: Univ. of Minnesota Press, 1983), 48.

24. Paulson, *Hogarth His Life, Art, and Times* 2 (New Haven: Yale Univ. Press, 1971), 168–72, and *Enblem and Expression: Meaning in English Art of the Eighteenth Century* (Cambridge, Mass.: Harvard Univ. Press, 1975), 86–98.

25. *The Poetry and Prose of Alexander Pope*, ed. Aubrey Williams (Boston: Houghton Mufflin, 1969), 117–19.

26. For a discussion of "the cognate accusatives that dream a dream, or see a sight, or tell a tale," see Joel Fineman, "The Structure of Allegorical Desire," *October*, no. 12 (Spring 1980), 46.

27. Knapp, *Personification and the Sublime*, 4.

28. Paulson, *Emblem and Expression*, 152–53.

29. Jameson, "Postmodernism: Or the Cultural Logic of Late Capitalism," *New Left Review* 146 (July/Aug. 1984): 80–84.

30. Benjamin, *The Origin of the German Tragic Drama*, trans. John Osborne (London: New Left Books, 1977), 175.

31. *The Interpretation of Dreams*, trans. and ed. James Strachey (New York: Avon, 1965), 226–30.

12

Postmodern Romance

Diane Elam

U mberto Eco's *The Name of the Rose* is undoubtedly the most economically successful piece of postmodern literature. And the *Postscript to the Name of the Rose* is Eco's attempt to explain that success. That the explanation of success might belong in a postscript shows the extent to which *The Name of the Rose* can be considered postmodern. This is no modernist project, the success of which might be predicted on the basis of the degree of prior conceptual elaboration of the grounds for the art object, on the strength of the manifesto that dictates the structure of the narrative that follows it. The legitimate grounds of postmodern art can be found only *after* the event, in a time the art work neither intersects nor produces. The postmodern art work does not inhabit the time of its own success. It is not complacently inaugural (like the Eiffel Tower), nor does it aim to produce the temporality in which it will have its effect (like Marx's *Capital*).[1] Postmodernism brings about a radically new relationship to time, which differs significantly from any modernist project. The distinguishing features of modernism's relationship to time—the condition of being either the inauguration or the determination of a historical project—are absent here. Instead, the bemused *belatedness* with which Eco confronts success, as not so much unexpected as it is radically unthinkable—a best-selling novel about medieval theology with only one sex scene—is the mark of how little *The Name of the Rose* is a modern novel.

Thus the postmodernism of *The Name of the Rose* consists neither in simply being published in the 1980s nor in using certain
formal techniques of an avant-garde, what might loosely be called
pastiche.[2] The postmodernity of *The Name of the Rose* lies in its
problematic temporality that the postscript articulates. The postscript, written after the novel, contains material—both "historical"
information about the Middle Ages and information about Eco's
process of writing—that precedes the novel; its narration both
causes and is caused by (the effect of) the narrative that is *The Name
of the Rose*.

In calling attention to this formal (anachronistic) property, I do
not want to suggest that all novels with postscripts are postmodern.
Novelists have long explained themselves in postscripts to their
work; just as postmodernism is not simply what follows modernism, it is also not just postscript. What is crucial about the troubled
temporality of *The Name of the Rose* is the extent to which, as a
historical novel, it can attempt to explain its *relationship to history*
only by means of a postscript, by means of an ironic temporality.

In making this association between postmodernism and irony,
I do not call up the ghost of New Criticism as my ally. I am not
arguing that Umberto Eco is really Cleanth Brooks in disguise; "The
Well-Wrought Rose" would not be an appropriate title for this essay.
If Brooks focuses on irony as a device or attitude that unified the
dissenting voices within a text, as a *perspective* from which one could
view all sides of the poem at once and synthesize partial and even
conflicting attitudes and interpretations, postmodernism is an
awareness of historical irony that cannot be mastered as a point of
view on history. Put simply, postmodernism is the recognition of the
specifically *temporal* irony within narrative.[3]

For Eco in the postscript the irony of the past is that there is a
problem in recognizing it as historical. "There is one matter that has
amused me greatly: every now and then a critic or a reader writes to
say that some character of mine declares things that are too modern,
and in every one of these instances, and only in these instances, I
was actually quoting fourteenth-century texts."[4] The past somehow
seems not other but altogether too familiar. In many respects, the
irony that what seems so familiar is really what is most historical

forms postaesthetics' inheritance from the modernist project. Modernism's treatment of the past may be understood by recalling the famous advertisement of the Philip Morris company's plug for MOMA, which juxtaposes primitivism in modern art with primitive art. The caption at the top of the page reads, "Which is primitive? Which is modern?" The point, of course, was that you would be hard pressed to tell the difference.[5] Primitivism is being made familiar; that kind of shock is quite modern. What is modern, what is primitive, is what is universal and hence *true*. Decontextualized and dehistoricized, the primitive and the modern become one and the same, both equally present. Eco's example from *The Name of the Rose* shows the extent to which the modernist project succeeded in making the past present, in making it familiar and "true" in a way curiously aligned with an ironic attitude as explained by Brooks. In contradistinction to the modernist project, postmodernism seeks to recognize the past as past, as historical other. At the same time, postmodernism can only supply such recognition through retrospective (or postscripted) irony, through an ironic temporality. It is no longer a universal truth that makes the modern and the primitive appear alike; rather it is ironical that we would confuse them. Unlike the modernist artist, the bemused postmodern author or critic is willing to point out that there *is* a difference, that the irony at play does not result in synthesis but in difference.

But what is the difference? How does the ironic evocation of the past insist upon an uncanny otherness to the historical? Or: what is the effect of the postmodern condition of ironic temporality? The crudest effect is that within his postscript Eco invites us simply to see the difference between the past and the present through his use of "historical" illustrations. Throughout he scatters photographs of medieval architectural elements and book illustrations. But rather than "identify" each photograph as an historical artifact (information reserved for a list of illustrations at the beginning of the postscript) Eco provides as caption a quotation from *The Name of the Rose*. For instance, on the page facing part of Eco's discussion of postmodernism, we find a photo identified by the illustrations list as a mosaic depicting "Empress Theodora and her court," from the "middle of the sixth century," to be found in "the Church of San Vitale, Ravenna." Yet, in the postscript, this photo is captioned with the following passage from *The Name of the Rose*. "At a merry signal from the abbot, the procession of virgins entered. It was a radiant line of richly dressed females, in whose midst I thought at first I could discern my mother; then I realized my error, because it was certainly the maiden terrible as an army with banners. Except that she wore a crown of white pearls on her head, a double strand, and two cascades of pearls fell on either side of her face" [Adso's dream in *The Name of the Rose*, 448] (*PS*, 69). Although we could argue that this is merely an instance of postmodernism as sales pitch, as self-promotion, such a position would not resolve the lingering question of the relationship between text and illustration. For the captain that Eco takes from *The Name of the Rose* does not simply explain the illustration, nor does the illustration go very far in "explaining" the novel. Although the picture may have been a source of Eco's novel-istic description, the novel does not attempt to discuss directly the Empress Theodora. Instead it asks us to believe that Adso's dream of women is a reenactment of the comedy *Coena Cypriani*. The disjunction between picture and text does not stop here, for neither illustration nor caption seems to have anything to do with the accompanying text of the postscript. In short, the past, in the form of medieval mosaic or historical novel, doesn't simply illustrate the present or vice versa. Authentication is not at issue. Rather, Eco's text forces us to think about the way the juxtaposition of word and image, of text and illustration, gives rise to a loss of meaning, to a moment of visual uncertainty.[6] In the postmodern condition of ironic temporality, the historical event as referent becomes problematic; any attempt to create a meaning for the past also precipitates a loss of meaning. Thus, the meaning that the modern detective William looks for with the aid of his spectacles cannot be discovered, just as the reader is not going to discover the truth about the Middle Ages within *The Name of the Rose* or about modernity within the *Postscript*.

This postmodern notion of ironic doubt rather than certainty about the past is perhaps nowhere more clearly illustrated than at the end of *The Name of the Rose*. After reading more than 600 pages of "manuscript," we are told by its "author," Adso of Melk, that "it is a hard thing for this old monk, on the threshold of death, not to know whether the letter he has written contains some hidden meaning, or more than one, or many, or none at all."[7] Adso, reflecting upon his narration of past events, cannot tell for sure what they mean, or if they mean at all. This predicament leads him to occupy the same position as the only woman in the novel; in Adso's words, "All I can do now is to be silent" (NR, 610). Silence and uncertainty—the ironic relationship to past events.

Eco's novel ends on a note of double uncertainty, for to cast doubt over the past is also to cast doubt over the future. The only certainty for Adso is the certainty of death, yet what that death means is no longer clear. The event itself is certain; its meaning is not. Although he once believed in the glory of divine revelation and elevation through death, Adso now sees the moment of death as a "sink[ing] into the divine shadow" that means silence, indifference, doubt. He even sees the future of his manuscript, lacking a divine purpose, as uncertain. Appropriately, then, the last words of the manuscript emphasize this point. "I leave this manuscript, I do not know for whom; I no longer know what it is about: stat rosa pristina nomine, nomina nuda tenemus" (NR, 611). Instead of finding the truth of or about the past, we find the name of the rose—a name we may or may not understand, as we may or may not (depending upon our familiarity with the untranslated Latin) understand the last sentence of the novel. Just what the rose might mean in the novel we can't decide. There are possible nominalist readings of the final sentence of the novel, but the sign (or name) of the rose is so rich in interpretive possibilities that it practically has no meaning at all. This is a point that Eco himself is not shy about making in his postscripted remarks. "The rose is a symbolic figure so rich in meanings that by now it hardly has any meaning left: Dante's mystic rose, and go lovely rose, the Wars of the Roses, rose thou art sick, too many rings around Rosie, a rose by any other name, a rose is a rose is a rose, the Rosicrucians" (PS, 3). This is no instance of the certainty of New Critical irony; we cannot resolve these different interpretations into any one synthetic reading that will render the truth of the text transparent. If there is anything that is certain, it is that we will find another text, concealing another text. Postmodernism, like the postscript, is not an attempt to make sense of the past, rather it is an attempt at revealing the troubled creation that is "a sense of history," a sense of history that extends beyond the mere allusions provided by literary history. And such revelation takes place in a way that departs from the historical avant-garde. Says Eco in the *Postscript*, "The past conditions us, harries us, blackmails us. The historical avant-garde . . . tries to settle scores with the past . . . The avant-garde destroys, defaces the past . . . But the moment comes when the avant-garde (the modern) can go no further, because it has produced a metalanguage that speaks of its impossible texts (conceptual art). The postmodern reply to the modern consists of recognizing that the past, since it cannot really be destroyed, because its destruction leads to silence, must be revisited: but with irony, not innocently" (*PS*, 65–66). Situating itself in contradistinction to the modern as avant-garde, postmodernism must respond to the pressure of the past. Postmodernism cannot simply ignore the past; it must reproduce "historical" manuscripts. However, in suggesting this response to the past by postmodernism, I do not argue that postmodernism produces either a metalanguage or a manifesto. Postmodernism is not futurism. Rather, in emphasizing the inescapable presence and future of the past, postmodernism stands in contradiction to projects such as those of the futurists. As Eco sees it, postmodernism cannot deny the historicity of the past. That would be to fall into the destructive formalism—the technical production of silence—that exemplifies the avant-garde. Postmodernism makes history *function;* it does not reveal the meaning of history. In the postmodern relationship between history and the art object both are dependent upon each another for their creation, but neither can straightforwardly explain the other. The text of the art object cannot explain the illustrations of history, and the historical pictures cannot gloss the text of art.

What is more, neither text nor object tells us when to be ironical. Unlike the manifestos of modernism, which emphasized understanding, and unlike Brooks, who believed in the importance and the possibility of spotting irony, postmodernism's ironic temporality calls into question the inevitability of such recognition and the necessity of understanding. "Thus, with the modern, anyone who does not understand the game can only reject it, but with the postmodern, it is possible not to understand the game and yet take it seriously. Which is, after all, the quality (the risk) of irony. There is always someone who takes ironic discourse seriously" (*PS*, 68).

Unlike Pound, who believes that the modernist project can be kept going with the imperative, "Be modern," or the futurists, who told us to "Be electric," Eco points out that you cannot just say, "Be ironical." There is always someone who will take the discourse seriously.[8] This is another way of saying that there is no pure certainty within the postmodern condition of ironic temporality. The subject is not reaffirmed as either universal or as presumed to know.

To this point, I have argued for the ways in which Eco articulates the postmodern condition as ironic temporality. However, Eco fails to deliver on a postmodernism that is rigorously attentive to the displacement of attitude by temporality. (This is no doubt some solace to those of us envious of his superstardom.) Eco's postmodernism does finally return to a matter of ironic attitude closer to romanticism and New Criticism than postmodernism, a failure inextricably linked to the position of woman in his text. We might say that the postscript ends by reinscribing the silent female as mark of the ironic attitude in much the same way as do the closing sequences of the atrocious film version of *The Name of the Rose*, when the silent woman, instead of burning for her crime, appears at the side of the road as Adso and William leave the monastery. The film may not have been all that unfaithful to Eco in its evocation of the romance trope of the ironic silence of woman.

In the *Postscript*, Eco defines postmodern irony in a way that brings us back to Brooks.

> I think of the postmodern attitude as that of a man who loves a very cultivated woman and knows he cannot say to her, "I love you madly," because he knows that she knows (and that she knows that he knows) that these words have already been written by Barbara Cartland. Still, there is a solution. He can say, "As Barbara Cartland would put it, I love you madly." At this point having avoided false innocence, having said clearly that it is no longer possible to speak innocently, he will nevertheless have said what he wanted to say to the woman: that he loves her, but he loves her in an age of lost innocence. If the woman goes along with this, she will have received a declaration of love all the same. Neither of the two speakers will feel innocent, both will have accepted the challenge of the past, of the already said, which cannot be eliminated; both will consciously and with pleasure

play the game of irony... But both will have succeeded, once again, in speaking of love. (*PS, 67*)

The wisdom of postmodernism—postmodernism's ability to revisit the past—is once again made possible through a loss of innocence and a fall into irony: Eco's after-the-fall tale of postmodernism is a fittingly ironic replay of the oldest romance of all—the tale of Adam and Eve.

Eco reduces irony to a matter of attitude because he cannot articulate the relationship between women and romance, between gender and genre, as they become the concerns of *both* "high" and "low" culture. Eco's postmodern romance narrates the story of a man in love with a *"very cultivated"* woman. We might wonder whether Eco's parable refers to everyman; quite certainly it does not refer to just any woman. Post–George Eliot and –Virginia Woolf, if women have a problem taking part in culture it is of no concern to Eco; within his version of postmodernism women can, in fact, become such formidable representatives of culture that men have trouble speaking to them ... or at least speaking to them of romance. And it is important that it is romance about which men have trouble speaking. Romance is not simply the genre of Eco's postmodern parable but (ironically) it is also the genre of Barbara Cartland. Significantly, it is this later type of romance that gives Eco, or Eco's male character, the most trouble. However much Eco tries to negate the fact (as he does in the opening remarks in *The Name of the Rose*), romance is still the genre *of* and *for* women in mass culture. Eco comes to terms with this female genre only by making it the site of an ironic attitude: it is not the stuff Eco's very cultured woman values; rather it is precisely what she *knows* about and *devalues*. Thus, woman must be detached from her genre by the division of high from low culture, and Eco turns to Jamesian prose to do justice to his predicament. Eco reduces the postmodern condition to the fact that silly romances by silly women only get in the way of real romances by men, as Eliot might put it. Presumably, *The Name of the Rose* is to be preferred to Barbara Cartland's romances. In setting this priority, Eco diverts the problem *of* woman into a problem *for* women. Eco's postmodernism proclaims that real romance is a matter of culture, a matter of transforming mere acquisition of knowledge into cultural meaning, a position that begins ironically to echo George Eliot's pronouncements on "fellow feeling."

The thematization of romance seems to be at the very heart of Eco's postmodernism. The only way we can succeed—recall that in Eco's parable both parties are suppose to have succeeded—"in speaking of love," in speaking across the cultural and historical barriers imposed by women and their popular romances, is to engage in the self-conscious and pleasurable (for Eco) play of ironic citation of romance. Yet to make this argument is to go along with Eco's assessment of the postmodern predicament, and believe (falsely) that both the man and the woman succeeded in speaking. This, I would suggest, would be to fall into an ironic attitude, as Eco describes it in his postmodern romance. Instead of following Eco quite so blindly (and forgetting about the consequences of an ironic temporality), we need to slow down and reassess the relationship between women, history, and romance as they are situated *in* and *by* postmodernism.

First, postmodernism and women. Eco's postscript articulates the postmodern romance, and likewise the romance of postmodernism, as a tale told by a man for men. Women, whether represented by the female character in *The Name of the Rose,* by the women in the photo of the mosaic, or by the very cultivated woman in the postscript, are not allowed a voice. Eco's situation of woman as the silent other who silences men leads to the conclusion that women cannot actively participate in the discourse of postmodernism. Postmodernism becomes one more seductive technique, a way for men to talk to, or at, women. Put another way, postmodernism's attitude, and not its ironic temporality, is "that of a man," a man's voice heard in high cultural romance, in the postscript to Eco's successful novel. For Eco, women participate in postmodernist discourse only through their silence; their voice is to be found only within the vulgar pages of Barbara Cartland's popular romances. If we are to believe Eco, women can either produce romance as popular culture (Cartland's novels, for instance), or they can become the narrated, very cultivated object of postmodern romance, which thematizes romance and representation as problems for men.[9]

In taking Eco to task, I am not isolating one example of postmodernism's "bad" attitude, with its significant ignorance of the force of gender. Craig Owens, seemingly sympathetic to the plight of the silent woman, says, "The absence of discussion of sexual difference in writings about postmodernism, as well as the fact that few women have engaged in the modernism/postmodernism debate, suggest that postmodernism may be another masculine invention engineered to exclude women."[10] Owens does not seem to recognize that it is not biological "sexual difference" that the postmodern debate ignores; Eco's texts are full of that. Rather, in each of these instances it is the force of gender *tout court* that is ignored. "Postmodern" fashion is still draped on women's bodies in *New York Times* advertisements. Although Eco's postmodernism, like Owen's, does not exclude women *per se*, it is an instance of men putting women in their place. If much primitivism managed the "shock" of the primitive, then Eco's and Owens's postmodernism manages the "shock" of women. In a way, both Cartland's romance and Eco's postmodernism actually serve *modernism* by representing history as accessible escape rather than as irrecuperable other. Cartland offers women history as an escape from their own lives; Eco offers readers history as an escape from women. If much of modernism refused to acknowledge the transgression of primitive art, Eco's postmodernism and Cartland's romance equally ignore the transgressiveness of the figure of woman within history.

To end here would be to give Eco the last word (the postscript) on postmodernism and concede that postmodernism is only a fashionable attitude, only modernism accessorized for a new season to wear. I would like to suggest instead that postmodernism and romance may offer something more disturbing than Eco is willing to consider—a less easy resolution of gender as history or history as gender. I want to move from an ironic attitude back to an ironic temporality.

To do this would be to rethink the way that history can represent or be represented. Postmodern romance can then become a citation of the past that allows the past to inhabit a position that can neither be controlled within a realist narrative of modern history nor produced, as it is for Eco, at the expense of the silencing (or burning) of women. Postmodern romance is potentially an uncanny way to evoke a past that is both displacing and displaced. The evocation of the past disrupts the modernist understanding that makes sense of the past as chronological sequence ("progress") because the past returns elsewhere than in the position modernist history has assigned it, as a matter of romance rather than realist historical accounting. We have seen this in Eco's struggle to account for the relationship between the medieval and the modern in *The Name of the Rose*. A stronger example would be Walter Scott's uncanny evocation of the romance of the Highland tribes in his Jacobite novels: *Waverley, Redgauntlet,* and *Rob Roy.* The battle of Culloden (1745) stands for modernist history as the site of its own "progressive" battle, its defeat of the Highland uprisings. Yet this site of modernist progress, this inscription at the center of modernist history itself, is also the site of a marginal erasure, of eradication, to which Scott returns in the pages of romance in order to illustrate the destructive force of modernist progress. If modernity tries to forget the burden of the past (in this instance, Highland tribal culture and its eradication under the hands of modernity), the postmodernity of Scott's romance makes it unforgettable, not merely a site for nostalgia. Romance escapes the condition of mere nostalgia precisely when it does not simply account for what has been lost (Eco tries to do this by burning the woman in his novel or silencing her in his postscript); rather, it acknowledges the lost past as a burden that continues to weigh upon the present, when the displaced past is encountered as displacing. The uncanny return of the past as romance reminds us that we can neither dispose of the past nor dismiss it because we don't understand it. The past is lost to the "now" of modernity. Postmodern romance can make the burden of the past felt as it returns not as itself but as uncanny displacement.

In referring to the way postmodern romance evokes the past, I am not simply trying to find another way to describe the transgressions performed in the name of the avant-garde. As Hal Foster explains, the avant-garde is a modernist project that "connotes revolutionary transgression of social and cultural lines."[11] He argues that postmodernism, on the other hand, is characterized by resistance that "suggests immanent struggle within or behind" social and cultural lines. Where the avant-garde transgresses, postmodernism resists.[12] Although I have described postmodernism as transgressing historical periodicity, postmodernism can more accurately be considered a *resistance* to historical periodicity, in that the work postmodernism performs does more than exceed a boundary or break a law; it has to do with an opposing force that interrogates what is at stake—politically and aesthetically—in having historical boundaries and aesthetic laws in the first place.[13] Not transgression for the sake of transgression (the avant-garde) but interrogation in the form of a resistance that would consider the historical circumstances, the context in which we are necessarily located, at the same time that it acknowledges the impossibility of totally defining those circumstances.[14]

Thus we could understand the failure of the avant-garde as its tendency to place romance as the genre that allows the modernist categories of historical reality and unreality to function unchallenged. This would make for romance like Cartland's; it would prove merely escapist. The hole it would open in the synchronic field of the real (escape from the modern world) would be sutured in the diachronic field of historical possibility as a potential reality. This same charge could also be leveled against Eco. His ironic postmodernization of issues of genre and history is vitiated by being mortgaged to a classical portrayal of gender. The problematic intersection of gender and genre threatens history. Eco's text may try to avoid this, but it continues to haunt the narrative. The nature of this threat is not simply inaccuracy, which would presuppose a proper way to write history, a way to be properly faithful to the original event. The tangled web of sources, the focus of the introductory pages of *The Name of the Rose*, places us at a great remove from any question of simple fidelity to an authoritative original. We are in a postmodern field, where history is always already something to be written. Rather, the threat that woman and the genre of romance pose—the threat with which Eco cannot come to terms—has to do with the very meaning of history: women can threaten our understanding of history by suggesting that history might mean something more than itself.

We can begin to think about how this may work by considering postmodern romance as transformative and progressively resistant when it enters the diachronic field of history as a *constitutive unreality,* realizing itself in the synchronic field of culture. Thus romance does not offer alternative realities; rather, it underscores the fictionality of the "real" and the unreality of culture. Culture becomes unreal like the romance myths that are an integral part of the narrative in Joseph Conrad's *Nostromo:* the cultural voice of the colonized is heard within the tropes of romance, while their oppressors speak realist history. Postmodern romance as synchronic genre, as ironic temporality, cannot simply be dismissed as unreal fantasy. As a result, it upsets the "reality" of culture. Romance does not find history to be innately realist; instead it transforms history by refusing to escape the unreality of the event (the structural unreality that is the silencing of minorities) by exchangine it for the potential of an otherness too alien to be "reality." History stops making sense. The aesthetics and the politics of postmodern romance are bound to the transgressive relationship it forges between a theory of history and a theory of culture.

If as Adorno suggests, Beckett's modernism obliterated the meaning that was culture,[15] postmodernism—as it has become a question for the thematization of romance—attempts to revisit culture by refusing to dismiss the challenge of the past, by refusing to represent it either objectively (realistically) or subjectively (as a matter of attitude). Instead, the ironic temporality characteristic of the postmodern condition means that we can never take hold of the "now" or "the present from which we can claim to have a right view over the successive periods of our history."[16] Postmodernism is not a "now" but a haunting, excessive return of past events. Even if we take it seriously.

Notes

1. The construction of the Eiffel Tower can be viewed as an event that marks a beginning of modernism. This marking does not pretend to a self-conscious critique of that event. Marx's *Capital* produces the time of capitalism by defining the time of capitalism as the ground of its analysis. Accordingly, the time of capitalism produced and defined by *Capital* is also the time in which a Marxist analysis of capital will have its usefulness.

2. Fredric Jameson argues that pastiche *is* a defining characteristic of postmodernism. He sees pastiche as a blank parody, that occurs when "the producers of culture have nowhere to turn but to the past" and when there is no "normalicity" to which parody refers. "The disappearance of the individual subject, along with its formal consequences, the increasing unavailability of the personal *style*, engender the well-nigh universal practice today of what may be called pastiche" ("Postmodernism, or The Cultural Logic of Late Capitalism," *New Left Review* [July/August 1984], 64–65). I would argue that pastiche is a formal property of the avant garde, not a defining characteristic of postmodernism.

3. Within the terms of postmodernism's ironic temporality, we are not surveying the ironical picture of world history from a single, synthesizing perspective, as Brooks's analysis would recommend. Ironic temporality does not confirm what one knows or sees; rather it casts *doubt* upon the possibility of understanding at all.

In this respect, my use of "irony" is closer to Paul de Man's than to Cleanth Brooks's. De Man contends that, "irony divides the flow of temporal experience into a past that is pure mystification and a future that remains harassed forever by a relapse within the inauthentic. It can know this inauthenticity but can never overcome it. It can only restate and repeat it on an increasingly conscious level, but it remains endlessly caught in the impossibility of making this knowledge applicable to the empirical world." ("The Rhetoric of Temporality," *Blindness and Insight: Essays in the Rhetoric of Contemporary Criticism*, 2d. ed. revised [Minneapolis: Univ. of Minnesota Press, 1983], 222). De Man adds that this is a "dangerously satisfying and highly vulnerable" conclusion, for it does not take into consideration the "predicament of the conscious subject." He seems to be suggesting that this incomplete formulation of irony can easily turn into just another version of the modernist myth of supreme self-consciousness—even if that consciousness is of inauthenticity.

4. Umberto Eco, *Postscript to The Name of the Rose*, trans. William Weaver (New York: Harcourt Brace Jovanovich, 1984), 76. All further references to *PS* parenthetically within the text.

5. See Hal Foster, "The 'Primitive Unconscious of Modern Art, or White Skin Black Masks," *Recodings: Art, Spectacle, Cultural Politics* (Port Townsend, Wash.: Bay Press, 1985). Foster also reproduces the Philip Morris ad to which I refer (189).

6. Roland Barthes raises a similar issue in The *Empire of Signs:* "The text does not 'gloss' the images, which do not 'illustrate' the text. For me, each has been no more than the onset of a kind of visual uncertainty, analogous perhaps to *that loss of meaning* Zen calls a *satori*" (*The Empire of Signs*, trans. Richard Howard [New York: Hill and Wang, 1982], xi).

7. Umberto Eco, *The Name of the Rose*, trans. William Weaver (New York: HBJ, 1983), 610. All further references to *NR* parenthetically within the text.

8. It is perhaps ironic that the book around which the mystery plot of *The Name of the Rose* turns is Aristotle's lost book on comedy.

9. Robert Caserio's excellent consideration of Eco's theory of language, "The Name of the Horse: *Hard Times*, Semiotics, and the Supernatural," *Novel* 20 (1986):, points to the homophobic aspects of Eco's novel. Although I agree with Caserio's

reading, I would argue that *The Name of the Rose* is more conflicted in that it plays through a narrative that is both homosocial and homophobic.

10. Craig Owens, "Feminists and Postmodernism," in *The Anit-Aesthetic*, ed. Hal Foster (Port Townsend, Wash.: Bay Press, 1983), 61.

11. Foster, *Recodings*, 149.

12. Whether postmodernism is really a form of resistance is the question that Fredric Jameson struggles with, as he reworks his essay on postmodernism. The running problem for Jameson is that postmodernism may only mirror and not critique the logic of late western capitalism. I am more convined than Jameson of postmodernism's resistance to capitalism. Jameson's argument appears in three essays, which read like two versions of a hit single alongside the extended-play release: "Postmodernism and Consumer Society," *Postmodernism and Its Discontents*, ed. E. Ann Kaplan (New York: Verso, 1988); "Postmodernism and Consumer Society," in *The Anti-Aesthetic*, "Postmodernism: Or the Cultural Logic of Late Capitalism," *New Left Review* 146 (July/Aug. 1984).

13. "Resistance," as I use it, would differ radically from Linda Hutcheon's notion of "critique from within," a phrase she is fond of employing in connection with postmodernism (*A Poetics of Postmodernism: History, Theory, Fiction* [New York: Routledge, 1988]).

14. On the impossibility of exhaustively defining context, see Jacques Derrida, "Signature Event Context," *Margins of Philosophy*, trans. Alan Bass (Chicago: Univ. of Chicago Press, 1982).

15. Adorno, "Trying to Understand *Endgame*," in *Notes to Literature*, trans. Shierry Weber Nicholsen (New York: Columbia Univ. Press, 1991), vol. 1, 241–275.

16. Jean-François Lyotard, "Re-writing Modernity," *SubStance* 54 (1987): 3.

Part Six

Postscripts, Ripostes, Afterwords

13

A Skeptical Feminist Postscript to the Postmodern

JUDITH BUTLER

Like other labels, "postmodern" was applied to me long before I came to study its linguistic uses in contemporary intellectual debate. I remain unclear about its meaning, about whether I *am* postmodern, or whether anyone knows. It seems to function as a sign under which debates occur, most of them large and sweeping. I cannot help wondering whether the term functions as a temptation to massive generalization, the kind that has become taboo since "totalization" became a bad thing. Of course, to call totalization bad is to totalize once again. It seems to me that I do not know how to read this sign of the postmodern as it operates in the cultural field, because it is not a text, and it is not a political "position." I know that I do not agree with Nancy Hartsock's condemnation of the postmodern,[1] for she appears to use the term to make large generalizations about works it appears she does not read. And I think that Seyla Benhabib has also used unfortunate passages in Lyotard to generalize to Lyotard himself, and then to postmodernism.[2] Once an "example" of postmodernism is invoked, a problem has already occurred, for can postmodernism offer examples of itself, as a universal offers a set of instantiating particulars, and wasn't that what Hegel did and why we thought that was a sleight of hand, and that totalization is a bad thing?

I want to raise the question whether "postmodern" can operate as that which one is either *for* or *against,* and as that which can enumerate and concretize itself in the form of examples. A few years

ago, after I was called a postmodernist, I wandered into a book store
to find out just how bad this new career was going to be. There I
read Charles Jenckes and became interested in the notion that a
single architectural structure would embody and enact the collapse
of temporal frames.[3] It seemed to me that this collapse of temporal
frames characterizes cultural life under transnational capitalism.
Ironically, it meant that no postmodern could come *after* the modern, for the historical narrative that could secure the place of the
"before" and the "after" had, through the collapse of temporal
frames, lost its ontological moorings. Does this mean a postmodern
position—whatever that is—cannot account for change? I think not:
it means, rather, that the unquestioned temporal preconditions for a
narrative history have to become objects of historical inquiry as
well. In a sense, to ask whether the "then" is securely over, and the
"now" fully free of the "then," is to historicize more radically.

Similarly, I hear the claim that within postmodern positions—
whoever has one—there are no foundations, and that without foundations feminist theory and politics cannot proceed. And so I hear
that feminism must have its foundation in the body, or in universal
norms, or in history or experience. If we take, say, history to be the
condition *without which* feminism cannot proceed because feminism
cannot be *political* without history as its foundation, then history
must remain what is unquestioned and taken for granted, a
foundationalist premise insulated from inquiry and contest. In a
sense, foundationalism constructs a *prohibition* against taking the
foundation as a sign, a site of contest, thematizable within the terms
of feminist debate. For if there is to be a debate, we must assume
history, so there can be no debate about history *as a premise* if the
debate is to be secured as feminist from the start. I sympathize with
this desire to ensure that *from the start* a debate will stay within the
terms of an already circumscribed feminism—and yet who will
enunciate this prohibition on further inquiry, and who can control
the future of feminism as a signifier? And is it not—frightening as it
may seem—*desirable* that feminism should not know its future, and
that is meaning be open to revision? For if feminism cannot be political without assuming history as its foundation, then the very
notion of history that is the foundation cannot be subjected to his-

torical inquiry. The "history" that functions as a foundationalist premise is thus radically dehistoricized, and the postmodernist who puts this foundation into question turns out to be more radically historicist than the foundationalist historian.

Here the premise of "history" functions as the theoretical point of departure, but also as that which comes *first*. After it theory tags along, reflecting, analyzing, hypothesizing. Yet it seems that the version of "history" installed in the slot of the foundationalist premise emerges only after other premises have been dismissed, and perhaps other versions of history. So there is, prior to any foundationalist premise, any "ground," a set of exclusions that prepare the ground, that construct the ground. They are then erased by the construction that they enable. This constitutive exclusion or erasure is, of course, not thematizable within the foundationalist frame, yet it seems that these exclusions that form the grounds of foundationalism return time and again to haunt and disrupt the proper workings of those grounds, so that competing foundationalisms emerge (sexuality, sex, gender, woman, women, care, maternity, lesbianism, relationality, biology, nature, universal norms), and a set of contests emerges about proper and improper foundations. Unwittingly, the debates enact each and every sign enclosed within the parenthesis as a *site of discursive contest*, a term that Denise Riley proposes to describe the category of "women."[4] If foundationalism inadvertently produces the contests by which it is destabilized, perhaps a *value* in this contestatory function of political debate emerges in the aftermath of secure foundations. It is not as if foundations are all useless and gone, but that they persist as sites of contests that cannot be quelled by becoming grounded in an alternative foundation. This nonclosure is not *nihilism* or the end of politics, but the possibility of an affirmation of that "failure" that opens up the future of a democratic struggle over political signifiers.

I used to worry about settling the foundation of identity: which category was the most important, which came second, which third, and how was I to explain the relations between them such that none of those hierarchical positions became destabilized? I risk an example here, but I insist that the example does not exemplify or totalize the field of the postmodern, for the example means to be

about the impossibility of that totalization. Yet, of course, I have no
ultimate control over what I write. Hence:

I sometimes swim at the Jewish Community Center in Baltimore, which appears to have only Jewish members in a traditional
Jewish neighborhood. When I was a child, I would accompany my
father to the Jewish Community Center in Cleveland, where I grew
up. It was always a scene of promised kinship and community and
inevitable estrangement. My efforts to return to that center in a city
where my family has never lived at first seemed to me to intensify
that sense of estrangement, for here I would never really belong.
The theme is a characteristically modern one: exile, loss, no return,
all that in the midst of the conventions of kinship and intimacy.
Every week or so I enter the women's locker room only to have
some anxious attendant run after me to yell that I have missed the
men's room, where she or he thinks I belong. When I undress, there
is, every other week or so, someone who inspects my flesh and
offers advice. Because the presumption is that we are all in some
sense "related," various individuals who have never before ad-
dressed me stop me in the shower and ask whether I am married
yet, why I do not shave my legs, whether I am observant. After a
barrage of such questions and an intensification of that old feeling of
exile, I walked one day into the pool to discover that there was a
"hydro-aerobics" or "hydrobics" class in progress, and things began
to look up. A group of older Jewish women, most of them with very
large thighs in a dancelike motion, were lifting their legs out of the
water and splashing them down again to a remake of Tommy James
and the Shondells' "Mony, Mony." As I looked closer, I saw that
some of the women keeping up with this simulacrum of Tommy
James had blue numbers on their arms from concentration camps—
which made me understand that these were compensatory thighs.
And here they were, entering the postmodern hybrid of "hydrobics"
to the "remake" of an "original" that belonged to an adolescent
culture they never had. Now, happily, it reappeared in their present.
They raised their huge thighs with obvious pleasure. I thought to
myself that perhaps this was the collapse of temporal frames as the
occasion for affirmation—and I dove in.

Notes

1. Nancy Hartsock, "Foucault on Power: A Theory for Women?" in *Feminism/Postmodernism*, ed. Linda Nicholson (London: Routledge, 1990), 157–76.

2. Seyla Benhabib, "Epistemologies of Postmodernism: A Rejoinder to Jean-François Lyotard", in *Feminism/Postmodernism*, 107–33.

3. Charles Jencks, *The Language of Postmodern Architecture* (New York: Rizzoli, 1984).

4. Denise Riley, *"Am I That Name?": Feminism and the Category of "Women" in History* (Minneapolis: Univ. of Minnesota Press, 1988).

14

Across the Ages

BRUCE ROBBINS

Postmodernism across the ages. If one has trouble digesting this calculated affront to literary periodization, one should be careful to decline it in the proper terms, and not for its offense to historical pieties that are properly treated with disrespect. It would not be helpful, for example, to defend periods as units in the departmental division of labor, where they function to isolate archaic fiefdoms against public scrutiny and fresh exchange. Nor is there reason to defend the supposed prelinguistic reality of period concepts. The ungainliness of the term "periodization" justifies itself, I think, by reminding us that periods are not natural divisions but manmade fictions. "The categories of periodization," Fredric Jameson writes, "troublesome indeed if we take them as exercises in linear diachrony where they seem to generate the usual unanswerable questions about the chronological establishment of this or that 'break,' this or that 'emergence'—are meaningful only on condition we understand that they draw on a linear fiction or diachonic construct solely for the purpose of constructing a synchronic model of coexistence, nonsynchronous development, temporal overlay, the simultaneous presence within a concrete textual structure of what Raymond Williams calls 'residual' and 'emergent' or anticipatory discourses."[1]

If the phrase "postmodernism across the ages" is resisted in the name of political urgencies, those urgencies should therefore not be confused with a notion of history as an unproblematic foundation, a single linear narrative of "succession or progress," to quote the editors, which any given literary interpretation must squeeze itself into or else be banished to the netherworld of ahistorical idealism. Any such history would have highly questionable politics. Since the "new social movements" of the 1960s, whose constituencies (women, people of color, gays and lesbians, and so on) helped carry both Marxism and poststructuralism to their current academic eminence, the notion of history as an evolutionary singleness with a single subject has been largely and correctly abandoned on the left, which now speaks in many voices of an irreducible plurality of interdependent political actors, hence of entwined, overlapping, and problematic histories. After the long vogue of Benjamin's "Theses on the Concept of History"[2] and the Marxist/feminist antinarrativism of *Screen*, the left should no longer need to be told that "history" is a "debatable" term, as the introduction to this collection puts it, a term "requiring thought."[3]

But if nothing so simple as an opposition between contemporary leftist theory and the impatience with linear history is being forcefully articulated in the title "postmodernism across the ages," then what is it about the eloquent title phrase that remains indigestible?[4] The wit, one sees, is in the play between postmodernism as a *period* (in the most common view it starts around 1945 and takes over from modernism) and postmodernism as a *way of thinking* valued precisely because, expanding aggressively "across the ages," it refuses the constraints of periodization. But this witty duplicity reflects a double indebtedness. On the one hand, no caveats can sufficiently dissociate the title's rhetoric from the triumphal vanguardism (latest equals best) that goes with confusing the period of the now with the editors' own version of the best that has been known and thought. Linearity exacts its due. On the other hand, the editors' manifest intention not to advertise postmodernism as an absolute novelty is insidiously realized in the form of an all-too-conventional servitude to the past. Here, as in many other discussions, the origins of postmodernism are traced in part to a reaction against the institutionalization of modernism. The arrangement of literature by period is of course one aspect of that institutionalization. But periodization is nowhere near as central to the institution of criticism as is the transhistorical reverence for the literature of the past and salvaging of that literature for the purposes of the present, accompanied by an explicit disregard for historical differences of value, ideology, and so on that the discipline has inherited from Arnold and Eliot. And just as the title "postmodernism across the ages" requires that we hold onto a residual "period" sense of postmodernism in order for its witty anitperiodizing point to emerge, so too, I think, the volume's concept of postmodernism (the concept of a refusal of concepts) requires that literary study cling to an institutional heritage, a disciplinary rationale based on reverence for the past, that it tries to renounce but finally can only embrace.

This disciplinary rationale is clearest in the discussion of Freud's *Nachträglichkeit*, or deferred action, as an alternative mode of temporality. When Bennet Schaber suggests that history-writing in this mode "makes possible a return of the past that would pressure its own narcissistic and masterful gesture," he exposes the model's repressed allegory: the return of the past as a return of the repressed. Or, as the introduction puts it: "One does not simply construct a past but repudiates a fragment of the present in order to clear a space for the reappearance of a repressed past." But nothing could be less self-evident than a strict analogy between the past, as preserved in the texts of the canon, and the psychoanalytic repressed. On the contrary, if the analogy applies, it would seem to apply better to all the texts, voices, and experiences that were not preserved, that were excluded from if not repressed by the cultural heritage, and that cannot therefore be assumed to remain somehow buried within it, waiting for a long-delayed appreciation. From this point of view the return-of-the-repressed allegory, which at first glance may seem plausible, is actually audacious. But it also has other implications that are worth spelling out. The past, waiting to be revealed, must always figure as an immensely and intrinsically valuable truth, just that truth required to destabilize or reorient an arrogant but intrinsically needy, innerly troubled present. The present, figured as the false totality of the ego, is "narcissistic" and "masterful"; the adjectives betray a contempt it is felt to deserve. The past, on the other hand, is its truth, and accordingly merits respect. The editors wax sardonic about temporality modeled on the ages of man, "the linear analogy of human development," but this reinscription of history as a single collective subject retrieving a repressed past is nothing if not a reinscription of that anthropomor-

phic model. And what a model! Foucault chided Freud for institu-
tionalizing the deeply conservative belief that our essential truth is
to be discovered in our parents. But even Freud balanced the claims
of the generations more evenhandedly. This allegorizing of the psychoanalytic metanarrative comes closer to Matthew Arnold, who
declared the present a wasteland, thus authorizing the humanities
to retrieve from the world of our fathers what could henceforth only
appear to be, by contrast, cultural riches.

This disciplinary logic, like Arnold's, feeds off a certain political oppositionality. But like Arnold's it also makes it nearly impossible for the critic to *focus* that oppositionality. Bill Readings defines
capitalism as the "accountable time" of commodities; he thus generates "unaccountable time" as its opposite, and can then go on to
identify the unaccountable and uncommodifiable as, to the surprise
of no literary critic, the literary. Does it need to be said that there is
nothing inherently capitalistic about the rationality of counting or
accountability? (Here, as so often, a poststructuralism that supposedly refuses all linearity in fact prefers Weber's linear narrative of
rationalization to Marx's nonlinear dialectic.) If one wishes to resist
capitalism, one must be more specific in one's targets: this is one
meaning of "history" that is not "metaphysical." From the left, a
monstrously abstract and darkly monolithic view of "society" such
as this one seems not historically rigorous but, rather, disciplinarily
convenient, as it has been convenient for the romantic "Culture and
Society" tradition. It segregates a realm of "culture," poetry, or
literariness—the realm of the singular, particular, irreducible, incommensurable, nonconceptual—which can then present itself, and the
discipline founded on it, as both autonomous and valuable. To identify the poetic with the postmodern, as the editors do, is to add the
interesting suggestion that this assertion of autonomy from history
is itself historical. But it is not to make that assertion any less nar-
rowly self-serving. "Postmodernity means the possibility of reading
the text as an event that will not be foreclosed, of reading the problematic temporality of the literary work as not an effect of anything
other to itself."[5] All such a position can muster, by way
of opposition to any particular event or tendency within history, is
the poetic itself—that is, as defined here, a history that transcends
history.

This logic does not serve even the discipline well. From the point of view of disciplinary rhetoric, periodization appears as a legitimating check on humanism's transhistorical practice of retrieving cultural monuments from the past—that is, as a way of setting standards for the results and thus raising or protecting the value of what is retrieved in extradisciplinary eyes. If literariness is taken to defy periodization, then there is no historical check on the results of interpretation, and the only content of any given act of interpretation can be literariness itself, a contentless and therefore universal content, a value beyond value, that must serve again and again as the point of every interpretive exercise. What is left to protect the discipline against skeptics who find the value of literariness inflated or accuse us of saying anything we want?

To pose this question is, of course, to assume a compromised, impure point of view within the discipline. As there is no room here to make the argument, I will simply assert that no one, leftists included, can responsibly do otherwise. The left has no pure, extrainstitutional place from which to criticize the institutional self-interest of others; all it can do is measure different versions of self-interest against each other to see which overlap more extensively with the general interest, open up more or less room for the interests of extrainstitutional others. This necessarily involves self-critique. In pointing out the parallel between "postmodernism across the ages" and the "Culture and Society" line, I was confessing that the cultural left has made its own compromises with institutional humanism. These compromises include a willingness to overvalue the aesthetic, on the one hand—Jameson's account of postmodernism has been accused of a Eurocentrism in which the aesthetic sensibility of "the West" provides the new, more covert totality that subjugates "the rest"—and, on the other hand, more manifestly, a willingness to treat "history" as if it were, indeed, unproblematic and foundational.[6] At a time when "theory" is sometimes said to be waning, it seems useful for the left to interrogate what looks like a backlash on behalf of historical specificity. We might ask whether "specificity" is not on occasion a rhetorical effect, like Barthes's *effet de réel*,[7] disguising behind the innocuous mask of modesty and scholarly precision both antitheoreticism and a will to political quiescence. And we might wonder whether periods don't serve on occasion as straw men that give us, as a securely trivial program of scholarly work, the task of unpacking them straw by straw.

It matters, however, which of these contiguous but also competing attitudes to the making of history find their way into our pedagogy. Contemporary versions of Marxism, like the version of postmodernism championed here, can factor the fact of writing history into the history written. Like the concept of *Nachträglichkeit*, they can acknowledge the noncoincidence of word and event: "the event occurs both too soon and too late. It occurs too soon to be understood, and it is understood too late to be recovered."[8] But this need not mean a permanent deferral of action, or as its consequence a categorical refusal of political accountability: "We don't think that any position, consciousness, or attitude can bring the postmodern to account. . . . If resistent to anything, postmodernism resists the assurance of a conscious stance or position of knowledge, critique, or historical survey."[9] As an alternative to this dissolution of agency into (the discipline devoted to) interpretation, there is reason to prefer Marshall Grossman's formula: "historically urgent action in the dark."[10] Forsaking any claim to clarity of interpretation in the moment of action, Grossman does not for that reason abandon the possibility of discriminating better from worse actions, or the peremptory urgency of taking some action.

In the mid 1930s, when the army and the working class were fighting in the streets of Vienna, Freud's response to the inconvenience—all citizens were asked to carry identification papers—was a quotation from Shakespeare, in English, which the visitor to Berggasse 19 can still see under glass: "a plague o' both their houses." We need not blame Freud for failing to understand the traumatic event that was happening while it was happening. But his conspicuous inability to do so does not define the Freud, or the postmodernism, we most need now.

How, then, does this collection respond to our timeliest demands? The introduction's self-consciously "polemical or provocative tone," which might seem out of place if the point were only to reconfirm business-as-usual for the humanities, can perhaps be explained by what is truly novel in this project to renew the fortunes of literary criticism. Its stylish gamble would appear to be the following: historical change, which relativizes all values, threatens to deplete the value of canonical texts; but this value can be restored if criticism will read back into those texts, as value, precisely the relativizing of value that had seemed to threaten them—in other words, if the results of any given act of historical interpretation are the transhistorical constant of literariness. In a sort of parodic *Aufhebung*, history is cancelled, preserved, and raised to a higher level.

But why should history be the chosen target if, as I've suggested, criticism's disciplinary logic has always tended to work against history as much as and perhaps more than with it? Perhaps, one can speculate, because of the recent historical trend toward "cultural studies," whose expansion of the field of interpretable objects is perceived by many (inaccurately, in my view) to mount a new kind of threat to the value of the canon. If cultural studies— heralded by some as the dialectical successor to "theory"—is indeed the incarnation of history that "postmodernism across the ages" aims to counter, the implied antagonist against which it is struggling to give its name to the changes of our epoch, then its defiant magnification of canonical literariness within a classically restricted field of texts would make a certain sense. It is too early to compare the *petite pedagogie* that results with a cultural studies pedagogy whose dimensions are still unknown. Certainly we have no assurance that cultural studies will handle the vexed question of the aesthetic any better, or any differently, than the discipline is wont to do. We can, however, wonder whether the cost of moving so effortlessly "across the ages" must be to remain so firmly planted within the perimeter of our own familiar field.

Notes

1. Fredric Jameson, "Nostalgia for the Present," *South Atlantic Quarterly* 88, no. 2 (Spring 1989): 517–37.

2. Walter Benjamin, "Theses on the Philosophy of History," in *Illuminations*, ed. Hannah Arendt, trans. Harry Zohn (New York: Schocken, 1969), 255–66.

3. Students in search of leftist thought that does something other than repudiate postmodernism in the name of a foundational, unproblematized history are urged to consult *Universal Abandon?: The Politics of Postmodernism*, ed. Andrew Ross (Minneapolis: Univ. of Minnesota Press, 1988).

4. Leftist "common sense" has gone far, perhaps too far, in a direction that I assume this volume would welcome. "The idea of progress, as it has been understood in Western culture for the last 200 years, turns out to be a belief in the superiority of the West to the East, the male to the female, the white race to all other races, and the superiority of man to nature. This is why I am no longer a progressive" (Juliet Schor, "Why I Am No Longer a Progressive," *Zeta Magazine* 2, no. 4 [April 1984], 56–59).

5. Bill Readings, "Milton at the Movies: An Afterword to *Paradise Lost*," in *Postmodernism Across the Ages: Essays for a Postmodernity That Wasn't Born Yesterday,* ed. Bill Readings and Bennet Schaber (Syracuse: Syracuse Univ. Press, 1993), 103.

6. On the Eurocentrism of leftist views of postmodernism, see for example Kum Kum Sangari, "The Politics of the Possible," *Cultural Critique* 7 (Fall 1987): 157–86.

7. Barthes, "L'effet de réel," in R. Barthes et al., *Littérature et réalité* (Paris: Seuil, 1982), 81–91.

8. "Introduction," in *Postmodernism Across the Ages,* ed. Readings and Schaber, 9.

9. Ibid., 8.

10. Grossman, "The Hyphen in the Mouth of Modernity," in *Postmodernism Across the Ages,* ed. Readings and Schaber, 84.

15

Beat Box

A Short Walk Around the Postmodern Block

STEPHEN MELVILLE

Sometimes a phrase, hardly unheard before, nonetheless shifts registers, turns a different face toward its reader, and becomes an obligation of a different kind.

The editors of this volume, building toward their full Lyotardian rhapsody, write of "the blocking together of incommensurable historical elements,"[1] and what shows itself to me is not a theoretical point made over and against the idea of *bricolage* but that "block" around which it abruptly feels as if I have been walking for some years now. In moving toward this block I pass over perhaps too quickly the editors' (and Lyotard's) use of a verb and not the noun before which I am arrested, and I take it perhaps too directly in the English in which it presents itself: so there will be a question in the end about the justice of my proceedings and about my obligations to this word in this text and in those it echoes or follows. It is, however, not mine to answer.

For the moment there is simply the block: a solid cube of a certain size, dark I think, perhaps set in an urban space (or perhaps that is just my imaginative effort to hold this block within the penumbra of the word that has brought it ot this presence). As an imaginative *donnée* it seems in some sense (Platonic?) torn between its dark solidity and its geometry, and it is mute.

246

But this block is not simply imaginative and so not simply available as the object of some possible phenomenology of the material imagination. It communicates immediately with particular blocks—Mallarmé's "calme bloc ici-bas chu d'un désastre obscur," for example; or, more curiously because less obviously a "block," the tombstone on which Marcher falls at the end of "The Beast in the Jungle"; and then there is, a there has been for some time now, Tony Smith's cube called "Die," a block around which something like a passage from a modernity to a postmodernity happens or has been said to happen.[2] The communication of these blocks, real and ideal, seems itself direct and immediate, the work of neither reflection nor resemblance—as if, it is tempting to say, they are blocked together, their copresence itself a version of what each of them offers to figure.

The claim to which I am tempted by this figure or blocking of figures is that this block is somehow native to our attempts at articulating what we want to call postmodernity.

That this might be so is not at first sight obvious. If we take our bearings from the general rhetoric of French theory, we are likely to recall the vehemence of the structuralist repudiation of depth, a repudiation that seems to be continued in much of the writing that is called poststructuralist (perhaps most tellingly in Lacan's repeated efforts to find models for the unconscious that show it to be inscribable on a surface). If poststructuralism breaks with anything here it is with the rigid implicit geometries of structuralist analysis, subverting its tables and grids by putting things in motion and, above all, flow—one thinks of Deleuze and Guattari on the cuts and flows of capitalism and desire[3] or of Lyotard on the great white libidinal skin or of the explicit fluidity of Derridean dissemination and the watery mirror of the *pharmakon*.[4] And if one moves away from French theory, there are still the blank palimpsests of David Salle's painting, or the applied ornaments of Michael Graves's buildings and the refusals of logics of volume and interiority in the architecture that gets called deconstructivist. Whether one looks for one's postmodernity to Marxian notions of commodification and the dominance of the ideological or Baudrillardian simulacra or even Lacan's logic of the purloined letter,[5] the postmodernity one finds seems above all a matter of surface—the language of depth consigned to the theoretical oblivion of interiority, subjectivity, and the grand narrative.

But then there is also in poststructuralism an extraordinary reorientation toward depth: there is Lyotard on blocking and matrix and all those forces that operate at right angles to the grid of Saussurean accounts of language;[6] there is the Deleuzian "body without organs"; there is the impulse to replace historical continuity with a language of strata and sedimentation; there is a recurrence of opacity; and there is the angled cryptic space of Derrida's *fors*:[7] all this then my cube, turning within (beneath?) the discourses out of which we build our postmodernity. It is a question how we are to think together the repudiation of depth and its transformed return.

One source of this return is perhaps Heidegger, whose writing always aims toward what persists somehow beneath the frozen articulation of the world. In the late Heidegger, Being turns within or beneath our discourses, sending or ordering them. But it is spherical. The cube belonged to Husserl and phenomenology—as indeed it belongs generally to modern philosophy in its confrontation with skepticism. Being was spherical because it repeated, its turning the work of history. Philosophic things were cubical because they hid themselves from perception, threatening to become utterly alien on the far side of us. The human equivalent of the philosophical cube is the android, threatening to become utterly alien on its inside. One of the reason's Tony Smith's work has been important is that in its scale and explicit hollowness it holds itself at the juncture of these two skepticisms, leaving its beholder in profound uncertainties about the terms in which relation to it might be resolved. One way to take this object's measure is perhaps to play it off, on the one side, against David Smith's work—*Zig IV*, perhaps, or *Blackburn: Song of an Irish Blacksmith*—and, on the other side, against Richard Serra's. And against this background what may emerge as interesting would be Anthony Caro's turn toward a certain art of metal phrasing ("The mutual inflection of one element by another, rather than the identity of each, is what is crucial"[8]). All this seems to be part of a complex play between sculpture and the arts of surface through which certain claims to postmodernity have been compellingly advanced.

The point here is, however, not to sketch a history of a figure; it is to understand more nearly how an object that seems above all available as a figure of timelessness and solidity can offer itself as a site for thinking temporality. It is clear enough that sculpture is, over and against painting, a temporal art in that to be fully seen it must be circled, its aspects taken necessarily in time. But this hardly brings us to thinking of the sculpture as in itself temporal or temporalizing; rather, it suggests that the dynamic of sculpture unfolds precisely between its atemporality and our perspectival finitude. Sculpture may impose time, force our acknowledgment of it, but in itself it appears profoundly indifferent to that constraint on our experience; its relation to time does not seem internal to it. We need to understand how a thought of the temporality of sculpture can, in the hands of Rosalind Krauss, become a thought of photography, how the practice of painting can, with Robert Smithson, become a practice of geologic sculpture.[9]

The drift of these thoughts is, it seems to me, never far from our imaginations of the unconscious, that dark atemporal and tangled mass around which our histories turn and pivot. And if we extend the meditation in this direction it quickly doubles over on itself: am I offering my block as the unconscious organizing a certain postmodernity? If so, how far am I taking up this mass in relation to Heidegger's Heraclitean sphere and its problematic of repetition and how far in relation to skeptical questions about aspects and interiority? When Heidegger's appeals to circularity become legible as concealings of a deeper logic of oscillation and discontinuity; when the cube begins to be the self-showing of its faces; when the two figures of sphere and block begin to interfere with or participate in one another—then perhaps we feel ourselves to occupy a space no longer easily grasped as modern.

Certainly one can at least suggest that Jean-François Lyotard's "matrix," described, in *Discours, Figure* as "having several places in one place, blocking together that which is not compossible . . . transgression of the constitutive intervals of discourse, transgression of the constitutive distances of representation,"[10] is a version of the block as theory. Another might be at work in, for example, Borch-Jacobsen's recent reading of the Freudian subject as inextricably and unanalyzably intimate with the others. "A subject will be born here, identifying itself with all positions, assassinating everyone and playing all the roles . . . Everything will have begun through the angle, the primordial angle—of an identification without model, an identification that is blind. . . . This dream (this throng) is ourselves, it is you and I, *ego*."[11]

This imagination surely captures something of the density and radical transitivity of the postmodern block in which things and subjects are embedded only as pure passage toward the other, radical heterogeneity. But it does so at a certain cost: the beat and pulse of Lyotard's matrix seems diminished here, volatilized into the pure myth or phantasm of the dream. Borch-Jacobsen surely means to think the depth at which we are primordially struck by others and imagines this depth as in some sense a surface—our being struck would be then a typographical fact. But such typing is a matter of a certain beat, a pulse of connection and disconnection; such transitivity is not continuous, neither open passage nor permanent resonance. Postmodernity does in this sense not simply dream its past but offers itself for the imprint of the block, submitting itself to that intermittence and scansion.

"Typography" is Lacoue-Labarthe's name for this, and his writing of it links it intimately to mimesis and to certain deep transformations in the logic of activity and passivity. "Mimesis is consequently grounded in this *original* dependency and subjection of the 'speaking-being.' It is, as we habitually and lazily say, a matter of 'influence.' But stated more rigorously, mimesis is the effect of *typography* and (if we may ventue this *Witz*) of the fundamental 'insemination' which at bottom defines the essence of the *paideia* (of formation or *Bildung*) and by which what we call the 'subject' is (not) engendered as being necessarily of the order of the figure or fictive in general."[12]

The subject thus radically impressed is only as and in its further imprinting, its alteration and alternation of itself in prolongation, mimesis being thought here not as imitation or metaphor but as something more like extension and metonymy—as if the work of

the block around which I continue to move were neither to express
nor fail to express, neither to represent nor to conceal, some interiority but more simply and more obscurely to show itself, to hold itself
in representation understood as "absolute vicariousness . . . endless
and groundless."[13]

This is the time of the block, and it is above all rhythmic. "We
are," Derrida writes, "constituted by this rhythm," in other words
"(de-)constituted by the marks of this 'caesuraed' stamp, by this
rhythmo-typy which is nothing other than the divided idiom in us
of desistance. A rhythm collects us and divides us in the prescrip-
tion of a character . . . We are 'rhythmed' in such a way that rhythm
no longer comes to us as a predicate [as it does, for example, in
Hegel's way of telling time and logic together]."[14]

Let us say that there is a block of time. Not a segment but a
mass. How to name what pulses rhythm this cube, what altering
and alternating currents nerve it? How to speak it not as if we were
outside beholding it but inside and rhythmed by it? This perhaps
brings us as close as we can get to what Walter Benjamin means to
point to in making the communication of constellations the center of
historical writing—but what will interest me here is the proximity to
Mallarmé's interlocking motifs of constellation, veil, and block in
which Benjamin is thus placed, and so the sense he asks to make of
"materialism."[15] Such a juxtaposition places us before the sheer difficulty (I mean real difficulty, but real and difficult because also transparent, and because transparent hard to cling to, like a window,
the face of a cliff—or of a cube) of writing material history (or of
writing/material/history as if these [now] nouns named the axes of
the block in which we are to find—not found, struck more than
forging—ourselves). The block in all its dark solidity is the object of
no phenomenology; it is not to be imagined but only written
(within).

If modernism means in part always an attempt to reduce and
purify our language, the language of the tribe, postmodernity might
name the impulse to exercise that language in all its impurity. But to
see this as a choice is to see it through the eyes it describes as
modern, assuming the integrity of the tribe and its possession of its
language as a form of self-possession. To call this tribe nomadic is

not to imagine it free of territorial constraint; it is to imagine it in itself as displacement, transition: "we," in its language, does not refer. It connects, cuts, extends. It dances. "Postmodernity" likewise does not refer; it rhythms, it scans. This does not deliver it from chronology, does not let it float free of the logic of periods—something has, after all, happened (is, after all, happening)—but reinscribes that logic within a grammar within which a period, whatever place it may have in our sentences, places our sentences within each other as well.

All this is no more remarkable than the transparency of words, the spaces between them, and the angles our marks cut in them: block of print, veil of writing.

This, then, an afterword but no last word, at the limit of the book, on the far side of this now traversed block of text, enclosing it not within itself but within its exposure. *Ça, boîte.*[16]

Notes

1. "Introduction," in *Postmodernism Across the Ages*, ed. Readings and Schaber, 9.

2. Tony Smith, "Die," 6 x 6 x 6 cube of Cor-Ten steel, 1962.

3. Gilles Deleuze and Félix Guattari, *Anti-Oedipus*, trans. R. Hurley et al. (New York: Viking, 1993).

4. Jean-François Lyotard, *Economie libidinale* (Paris: Minuit, 1974); Jacques Derrida, *La dissémination* (Paris: Seuil, 1972).

5. Jean Baudrillard, *Simulations* (New York: Semiotext<e>, 1983); Jacques Lacan, "Le séminare sur 'La Lettre volée, "'*Écrits I* (Paris: Seuil, 1981), 19–75.

6. Jean-François Lyotard, *Discours, Figure* (Paris: Klincksieck, 1971).

7. Jacques Derrida, "Fors," in K. Abraham and Maria Torok, *The Wolfman's Magic Word*, trans. Nicholas Rand (Minneapolis: Univ. of Minnesota Press, 1986), xi–il.

8. Michael Fried, "Art and Objecthood," in *Minimal Art: A Critical Anthology*, ed. Gregory Battcock (New York: Dutton, 1968), 137.

9. Rosalind Krauss, *The Originality of the Avant Garde and Other Modernist Myths* (Cambridge, Mass.: MIT Press, 1986).

10. Lyotard, *Discours, Figure*, 339.

11. Mikkel Borch-Jacobsen, *The Freudian Subject*, trans. Catherine Porter (Stanford: Stanford Univ. Press, 1988), 239.

12. Philippe Lacoue-Labarthe, *Typography: Mimesis, Philosophy, Politics*, ed. Christopher Fynsk (Cambridge, Mass.: Harvard Univ. Press, 1989), 127.

13. Ibid., 116.

14. Jacques Derrida, "Introduction: Desistance," in *Typography*, 31.

15. Walter Benjamin, "Theses on the Philosophy of History," in *Illuminations*, ed. Hannah Arendt, trans. Harry Zohn (New York: Schocken, 1969), 255–66.

16. Jacques Derrida, *La carte postale: de Socrate à Freud et au-delà* (Paris: Aubier-Flammarion, 1980), 433 (punctuation modified).

16

The Postmodernist and the Homosexual

Gregory W. Bredbeck

The homosexual and the postmodernist have been sleeping together a lot lately. And yet, as with much intercourse, the experience has been less than fully pleasurable. Homosexuality, as it is theorized within most discourses, is presented as a flourish, a bow, an ornament or after-the-fact bauble that simply decorates the package. The reason for this is, I think, the dominance of psychoanalysis within postmodernism and the subsequent belief that the discussion of sexuality in general is appropriate only within a *sexualized* discourse. The assumption seems to be that homosexuality and psychoanalysis are *natural* bedfellows, and hence homosexuality is inevitably subjected to the originary inscriptions of psychoanalysis itself. To see the ramifications of these inscriptions, we need only look at Freud's famous letter of 1935 to an American mother regarding her homosexual son.[1] "Homosexuality is assuredly no advantage, but it is nothing to be ashamed of, no vice, no degradation, it cannot be classified as an illness; we consider it to be a variation of the sexual function produced by a certain arrest of sexual development."[2] While the liberalism of the letter at first appears laudable, the rhetoric betrays it.[3] For within the acceptance is a notion of homosexuality as, again, a secondary construct—a "variation" of a theme, a troping or turning of the "natural" language of sexuality.

In the brief space of this postscript, I would like to suggest that both the homosexual and the postmodernist can find a far more pleasant intercourse if we view homosexuality not as a sexuality but an epistemological conditionality—that is, a set of conditions, propositions, discourses, and assumptions that delineate a field of significance. For homosexuality is not just constructed within the discourses of sexuality in our culture, but is also disseminated along and defined by an infinite number of axes. Homosexuality is tellingly analogous to Jonathan Culler's definition of "literature": "a species of writing, a mode of representation, that occupies a very problematic role."[4] Homosexuality *is* textuality in its most potent and postmodern form: "not a line of words releasing a single 'theological' meaning . . . but a multi-dimensional space in which a variety of writings, none of them original, blend and clash."[5] My stress on textuality rather than sexuality is willful, meant to open an interchange between homosexuality and postmodernism. Such a project is not unique. Vestiges of it appear throughout the field of queer theory, and can best be summarized by Thomas Yingling's claim that "the homosexual's subjectivity is always already poststructural, a personal narrative experienced as absence and denial."[6]

I propose to examine the much more radical flip side to this song: namely, that postmodernism is *always already* homosexual. I will do so not to question the validity of Yingling's claim but to define it as one distinct position within a dialectic—perhaps a multiplicity—that will demonstrate how an intercourse between the postmodernist and the homosexual can liberate the most potent tenets of each. To do so, I consider briefly a germinal tract of postmodernism, Jacques Derrida's "White Mythology: Metaphor in the Text of Philosophy," and its punningly disruptive conception of *plus de metaphor*.[7] Analyzing the function of metaphors in the discourse of Western philosophy, Derrida suggests that

> if one wished to conceive and to class all the metaphorical possibilities of philosophy, one metaphor, at least, always would remain excluded, outside the system: the metaphor, at the very least, without which the concept of metaphor could not be constructed, or, to syncopate an entire chain of reasoning, the metaphor of metaphor. This extra metaphor, remaining outside the field that it allows to be circumscribed, extracts or abstracts itself from this field, thus subtracting itself as a metaphor less. By virtue of what we might entitle, for economical reasons, tropic

supplementarity, since the extra turn of speech becomes the missing turn of speech, the taxonomy or history of philosophical
metaphors will never make a profit.[8]

Derrida's dense and rewarding argument does not benefit
from summary, but I would stress the difference between
"originary" and "derivative" metaphor; that is, in Derrida's formulation the derivative, Aristotelian metaphor—the *part of speech* or
figure—is always an anxious displacement of an originary metaphor
that must precede and give rise to the conditions of metaphoricity.
The delineation and definition of metaphor, therefore, is never an
"explication," but is rather a continued and complicated movement
away from and obfuscation of this originary conditionality. There is
always one metaphor less: the absent metaphor that "metaphor"
itself anxiously effaces.

The ascription of metaphor to a secondary status within philosophy immediately recalls the inscription of homosexuality as a
secondary action or deviance within psychoanalysis. Metaphor is
figured as misplaced words, homosexuality as misplaced penises. In
each case, the "natural" fecundity of a "center"—whether it be language or heterosexuality—is posited as an absolute standard against
which the "flourish" of a metaphor or a faggot is posited as a pale
anomaly. It is difficult to underestimate the effect of these precepts
on the praxes of the postmodernist and the homosexual. For the
postmodernist, the repression of contingency pinpointed by Derrida
is experienced in the "common sense" of liberal humanists: the
problem of theory is that the "real" business of literary history and
liberal education is left to lapse.[9] For the homosexual, the effects are
felt in the chillingly fascist edicts of people like William F. Buckley:
"if everyone were homosexual, there would not, tomorrow, be anyone at all."[10] In each case the goals of one system are hypostatized
under the ideological adjectives "natural," "fecund," "real," while
the status of the other system is derogated as "unnatural," "sterile,"
and "false."

Postmodernism is experienced within hegemonic discourses as
a derivative metaphor, but its very terms also provide the means of
recognizing this status as an effacement of originary metaphoricity.

For the postmodernist's response to such accusations is, correctly, to assert that they presuppose a manifest validity to a set of goals and presuppositions that postmodernism itself seeks to delimit and demystify. A similar dynamic can be seen in the case of homosexuality. In his important, tract, *Homosexual Desire*, radical French philosopher Guy Hocquenghem explores this possibility, especially as it focuses on the anus.[11] As he notes, "the anus does not enjoy the same ambivalence as the phallus, i.e., its duality as penis and Phallus. . . . Every man possesses a phallus which guarantees him a social role; every man has an anus which is truly his own, in the most secret depths of his own person. . . . All the libidinal energy directed towards the anus is diverted so that the social field may be organised along lines of sublimation and the private person."[12] The implications of Hocquenghem's position are manifest; for my purposes here I would like to assert several premises that follow from the argument:

1. The formation of the phallus is achieved through the repression of the anus.

2. The phallus, therefore, is not a *constitutive* concept, but a *reactionary* one.

3. The symbolization of the social order through the phallus is, therefore, also constitutive of a reactionary epistemology.

4. What is reacted against in each instance is not the anus *per se*, but the symbolic potentiality of contingency represented in a recognition of the anus as a possible alternative focus of symbolization.

In other words, if we grant the anus a symbolic potentiality, the phallus becomes a *choice* rather than an *inevitability*. The threat of recognizing the anus is obvious not just in theoretical discourses but also in quotidian ones: think of the relative frequency of the epithet "cocksucker" within our culture and the relative absence of the epithet "assfucker." Homosexuality, then, which is written within hegemonic discourses as an *ex post facto* fluke, is also a signal of an *a priori* contingency.

Therefore, while it is true, as Yingling says, that homosexuality in our culture is experienced in terms that imitate the postmodern, it is equally true that postmodernism within our academies is experienced in terms that imitate homosexuality. This latter part of the equation is, I think, the topic that has been ignored (repressed), and is the direction in which our theorizations must travel. Both the postmodernist and the homosexual stand to gain from exposing the antitheory bias as another form of fag-bashing. An entire book could easily be devoted to defining what I mean by this; but the constraints of this essay demand that I offer it as a polemic suggestion rather than a fully realized methodology. Moreover, I do not intend to draw any conclusions, for the very desire to conclude plays into the tropics of the phallus; as Hocquenghem reminds us, within normative discourses "all sexual acts have an 'aim' which gives them their meaning; they are organised into preliminary caresses which will eventually crystallize in the necessary ejaculation, the touchstone of pleasure."[13] I prefer to leave us, the postmodernist and the homosexual, in a state of *coitus interruptus*, with the memory and tease of a process and not the assurance and smugness of orgasm. I offer, instead, an equation: when I gaze at your theory, your text, I see myself. And when you gaze at my text, my "self," you see your theory. But let's keep in mind that a gaze is more than a fixative of the "other"; it is also a gesture, a flirt, a cruise, an invitation to intercourse as assured and potent as a tongue licking the lips or a hand cupping a crotch.

Notes

1. I return to the words of the father here to avoid offhandedly dismissing the considerable advances made by feminists working within the general tropics of psychoanalysis. See, for example, Nancy Chodorow, *The Reproduction of Mothering: Psychoanalysis and the Sociology of Gender* (Berkeley: Univ. of California Press, 1974); Jane Gallop, *The Daughter's Seduction: Feminism and Psychoanalysis* (Ithaca, N.Y.: Cornell Univ. Press, 1982); Juliet Mitchell, *Psychoanalysis and Feminism: Freud, Reich, Laing, and Women* (New York: Vintage, 1974); and Ellie Ragland-Sullivan, "Dora and the Name-of-the-Father," in *Discontented Discourses: Feminism, Textual Intervention, Psychoanalysis*, ed. Marleen S. Barr and Richard Feldstein, 208–40 (Urbana: Univ. of Illinois Press, 1989).

2. Sigmund Freud, *The Letters of Sigmund Freud 1873–1937*, ed. E. Freud (London: Hogarth, 1970), 419.

3. For a complementary analysis of this issue, as well as a broader discussion of the relationship between homosexuality and psychoanalysis, see John Fletcher, "Freud and His Uses: Psychoanalysis and Gay Theory," in *Coming On Strong: Gay*

Politics and Culture, ed. Simon Shepherd and Mick Wallis, 90–118 (London: Unwin Hyman, 1989).

4. Jonathan Culler, *The Pursuit of Signs: Semiotics, Literature, Deconstruction* (Ithaca, N.Y.: Cornell Univ. Press, 1981), 213.

5. Roland Barthes, *Image Music Text*, ed. and trans. Stephen Heath (New York: Hill and Wang, 1977), 146.

6. Thomas E. Yingling, *Hart Crane and the Homosexual Text: New Thresholds, New Anatomies* (Chicago: Univ. of Chicago Press, 1990), 36.

7. Translator Alan Bass supplies a worthy synopsis of the punningness and intertextuality of the phrase (Jacques Derrida, *Margins of Philosophy*, trans. Alan Bass [Chicago: Univ. of Chicago Press, 1982], 219, n. 20). The primary pun rests on the double signification of "more metaphor" and "no more metaphor" inherent in the phrase.

8. Derrida, *Margins*, 19–20.

9. Cf. Reinhard Kuhn, "The Return to Basics in Graduate Studies," *Modern Language Studies* 9 no. 1 (Winter 1978–79): 9.

10. Quoted in Leigh W. Rutledge, *Unnatural Quotations: A Compendium of Quotations By, For and About Gay People* (Boston: Alyson, 1988), 133.

11. The focus on the anus here may put off lesbians and feminists. I do not intend it as such, but male homosexuality is still so disenfranchised as to demand primary assertions of the experience of our own sexuality. My hope is that the strategy I am opening here might also be co-opted by other groups and with other organs. For one such effort that I find very convincing, see Spivak's "Unmaking and Making in *To The Lighthouse*" (Gayatri Chakravorty Spivak, *In Other Worlds: Essays in Cultural Politics* [London: Routledge, 1988], 30–45).

12. Guy Hocquenghem, *Homosexual Desire*, trans. Daniella Dangoor (London: Allison and Busby, 1978), 83.

13. Hocquenghem, *Homosexual Desire*, 81.

Index

Postmodernism Across the Ages
was composed in 10 1/2 on 13 Palatino on a Mergenthaler Linotron 202
by Partners Composition;
with display type in Avant Garde Gothic Medium
by Dix Type, Inc.;
printed by sheet-fed offset on 50-pound, acid-free Natural Smooth
and Smyth-sewn and bound over binder's boards in Holliston Roxite B
with dust jackets printed in 2 colors
by Braun-Brumfield, Inc.;
and published by
Syracuse University Press
Syracuse, New York